ETHNIC HERITAGE AND LANGUAGE SCHOOLS IN AMERICA

ETHNIC HERITAGE AND LANGUAGE SCHOOLS IN AMERICA

Developed by
Elena Bradunas

Compiled and Edited by
Brett Topping

The American Folklife Center

LIBRARY OF CONGRESS
Washington 1988

Studies in American Folklife, No. 4

Library of Congress Cataloging-in-Publication Data

Ethnic heritage and language schools in America.
  (Studies in American Folklife; no. 4)
  Bibliography: p.
  1. Ethnic schools—United States—Cross-cultural
studies. I. Bradunas, Elena. II. Topping, Brett,
1947-   . III. Series.
LC3802.E74   1987   371.97'00973   86-28679

For sale by the Superintendent of Documents,
U.S. Government Printing Office,
Washington, D.C. 20402

Contents

3

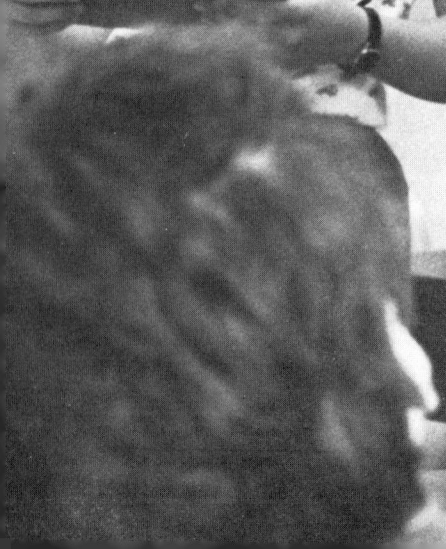

Preface

The reports in this volume developed out of the Ethnic Heritage and Language Schools Project undertaken by the American Folklife Center in the summer of 1982. That project in turn was inspired by the experience of the Center's 1977 Chicago Ethnic Arts Project. During the Chicago project we were struck by the number of activities organized for the youth of some of the city's ethnic communities. Community members expended much time and energy to involve young people in the cultural and social affairs of the group. Among the numerous youth programs and activities, we often heard references to schools—the Greek Sunday school, Hebrew school, Ukrainian Saturday school, and Polish classes. They are special educational programs which, as their names imply, take place outside of regular school hours. Because our fieldwork took place during the summer months, we were able to observe only one school event, a convocation ceremony of a Polish Saturday school. It suggested, and the interviews corroborated, that the schools represent a vehicle for the conscious transmission of culture from one generation to the next.

The concept of cultural transmission is a foundation of the folklorist's discipline, yet few studies document or analyze the actual processes by which traditions pass from one generation to the next. One reason is that a great deal of transmission occurs almost automatically, in subtle exchanges rarely isolated from the continuous flow of everyday life. Unless folklorists are constant participant-observers, they must depend on reminiscences to learn how a skill, craft, or tradition was passed down from an earlier generation.

Students in Taunton, Massachusetts, giving reports at the Portuguese School, which is sponsored by the Taunton Sports Club. (ES82-197202-1-1) Photo by Marsha Penti

The ethnic school, however, organizes cultural transmission around specific, regular, and formal activities. Although it is but one of many possible means by which young people learn about their parents' and communities' culture, it is probably the easiest to observe and document. One can observe the interaction and note the dynamics that govern it. It is a separate and distinct forum in which culture is transmitted in a conscious manner and where the teacher and student roles are clearly defined. As a conscious effort requiring coordination among a number of individuals, it is institutionalized within the community. But even as an institution, it is outside the formal, governmentally regulated educational system of our society as a whole. Usually it is a private, community-based venture, requiring a voluntary organizational effort and grassroots sustenance to keep it alive. Thus, from the standpoint of its community base and the cultural content of its curriculum, the ethnic school can be considered a "folk school."

Library research following the Chicago project led us to sociolinguist Joshua Fishman, who has written several articles about community-based ethnic heritage and language schools. Through years of research he has amassed an impressive listing of various ethnic education programs, which he estimated in the early 1980s to number about six thousand serving some six hundred thousand pupils. Fishman classifies the educational endeavors into three types: (1) all-day schools, (2) weekday after-hours schools, and (3) weekend schools. The all-day schools are generally private schools affiliated with religious institutions. They incorporate ethnic language and cultural instruction into the regular school day. Weekday after-hours schools are in session during one or more weekday afternoons or evenings, and weekend schools are held on Saturdays or Sundays. Attendance at either is in addition to attendance at regular public or private schools. (*See* Joshua A. Fishman, *Language Loyalty in the United States*, London, The Hague, Paris: Mouton & Co., 1966)

Realizing that the phenomenon of ethnic schools had a national scope, and that it lent itself to field study, the American Folklife Center launched the Ethnic Heritage and Language Schools Project in the spring of 1982 to sample the nature and texture of these "folk schools" on a national scale. Out of seventy respondents to our call for proposals, we selected twenty-one researchers to study an ethnic school located in their area. Some considerations in the selection process, in addition to the fieldworkers' educational background and fieldwork experience, were a desire to include the schools of a variety of ethnic groups, in all parts of the country, that met at different times (all-day schools, weekday after-hours classes, and weekend schools).

Unlike most other Center field projects, the fieldworkers on this survey did not work as a team. Each fieldworker conducted research independently, receiving instructions, information, and advice from project coordinator Elena Bradunas. To get a first-hand impression of how such schools functioned and how a fieldworker's visits might work, Bradunas visited a Lithuanian and an Ethiopian school in the Washington, D.C., area.

We asked fieldworkers to make several visits to the ethnic school over a three-month period and to interview individuals involved in the programs. Written communications to the fieldworkers outlined our initial observations about the phenomenon of ethnic schools and a list of hypotheses we wished to test.

One assumption was that the community-based schools are examples of conscious transmission of cultural knowledge. We also felt that by looking carefully at the reasons why such schools have been established, analyzing the curricula, and observing the school in process we could discern aspects of cultural heritage that a group cherishes and deems worthy of transmission to the next generation. In addition to discussing these assumptions with the fieldworkers, we provided some general interview guidelines to ensure the receipt of comparable information from each researcher on the history of the schools, their economic and administrative concerns, curricula, and relationship with parents, teachers, administrators, and students.

After the fieldwork phase ended, each researcher submitted a final report and accompanying documentary materials. The project collections are available at the Library of Congress for research. Appendix I lists an inventory of the project materials, including fieldnotes, sound recordings, photographs, and appropriate logs. Each fieldworker received a copy of everyone else's final report, so they could absorb each other's findings. After reading the reports, we met as a group for the first time in August 1982 at the Library of Congress. During the two-day meeting, we compared notes on particular schools and tried to establish general guidelines and themes for the presentation of our findings.

The data we gathered is rich in detail and somewhat overwhelming in scope. The fieldworkers' essays present all the particulars of each

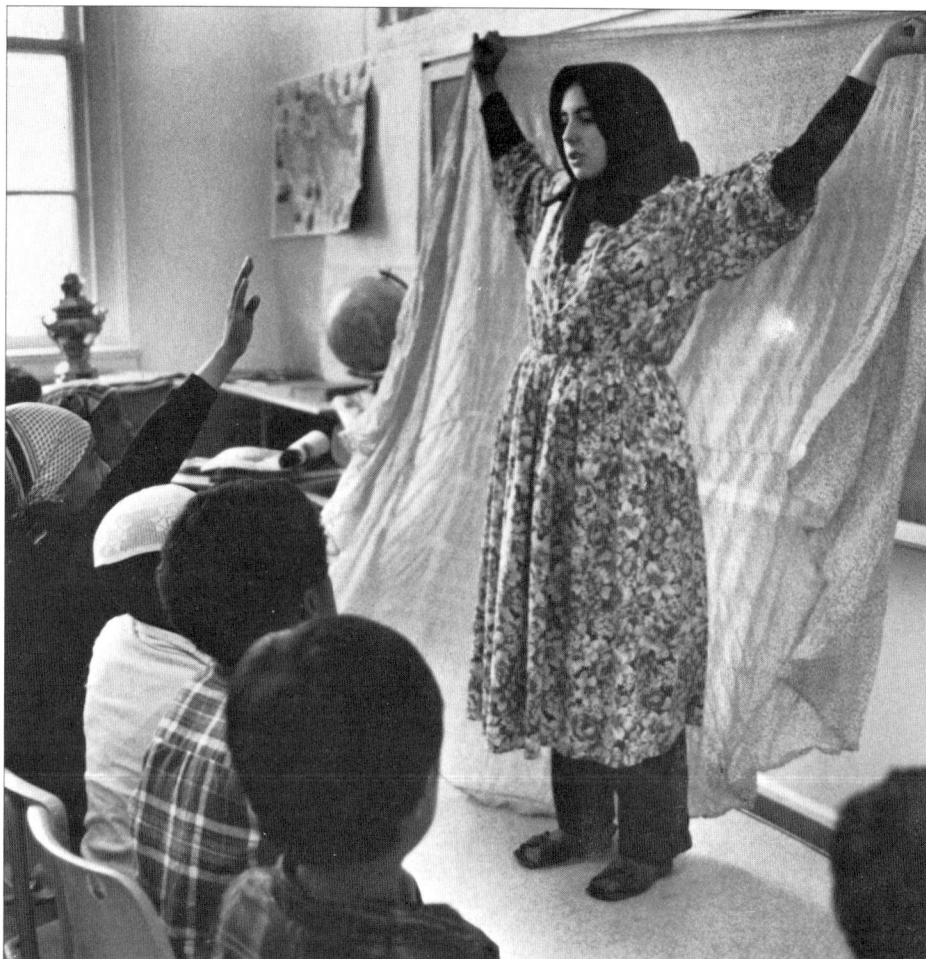

During a social studies lesson on Iran at the Islamic School, Seattle, Washington, Sister Diana Akhgar demonstrates how to dress in a *chaddor*, the outer garment of Iranian women. (ES82-196610-4-24A) Photo by Susan Dwyer-Shick

school—its history, personalities, and circumstances. To grasp underlying commonalities and differences among the schools one must read all the essays in their entirety. But it is possible to present some basic facts about all the schools in chart form.

Table 1 lists the schools alphabetically by ethnic group, followed by the school's location, founding date, and meeting schedule. Table 2 provides information on the organizations or institutions with which the schools are affiliated and their curriculum—the religious or secular orientation and the presence or lack of language instruction.

The tables present the bare facts about the schools we visited. The thirteen selected essays which follow fill in many of the details. The remaining project essays are available from the American Folklife Center individually. Taken together the reports encourage some general reflection on the nature of the interaction between adults and children within ethnic communities and within the context of American society as a whole.

The Folklife Center would like to thank the project fieldworkers, all of whose efforts made this publication possible. In addition to those whose reports appear in this volume, we appreciate the work of Scott J. Baird, who studied a Chinese school in San Antonio, Texas; Carole O. Bell, for her work with a Ukrainian school in Woonsocket, Rhode Island; Joann B. Bromberg, who documented an Armenian school in Watertown, Massachusetts; Morton Marks, who studied a Caribbean school in New York City; Susan Mary Nagy for her work with a Hungarian school in New Brunswick, New Jersey; Ricardas Vidutis, who documented a Latvian school in Milwaukee, Wisconsin; and Philip E. Webber for his work with a Dutch school in Pella, Iowa.

We selected a cross-section of the reports for this book on the basis of a number of factors: geographic distribution of the schools, ethnic community represented, meeting schedule, and date of establishment. The reports that do not appear here are available individually from the American Folklife Center.

The information contained in the reports reflects the differing approaches and perspectives of the fieldworkers who prepared them. We did not sacrifice completeness of information for consistency; bibliographies are included, where submitted, and tape citations appear, where provided.

We would like to thank Lisa Oshins for organizing the project files and Cathy Williams and Aldona M. K. Joseph for their assistance in preparing the manuscript.

Table 1: Ethnic Schools Studied

Ethnic Group	Location	Founding Date	Meeting Schedule
1. Armenian	Watertown, MA	1970	all-day
2. Cambodian	Houston, TX	1980	after-hours
3. Chinese	San Antonio, TX	1927	weekend
4. Czech	Cedar Rapids, IO	1870	summer/1 month
5. Dutch	Pella, IO	1880s*	varied
6. German-Russian	Strasburg, ND	1918*	supplementary
7. Greek	Birmingham, AL	1902	after-hours
8. Greek	Buffalo, NY	1916	weekend
9. Hebrew	Nashville, TN	1896	after-hours/weekend
10. Hungarian	New Brunswick, NJ	1960	weekend
11. Hupa Indian	Hoopa Valley, CA	1870s*	supplementary
12. Islamic	Seattle, WA	1980	all-day
13. Japanese	Los Angeles, CA	1928	weekend
14. Korean	Silver Spring, MD	1977	weekend
15. Latvian	Milwaukee, WI	1950s	weekend
16. Lebanese	Birmingham, AL	1915	summer/weekend
17. Polish	Chicago, IL	1951	weekend
18. Portuguese	Taunton, MA	1980	after-hours
19. Turkish	New York, NY	1973	weekend
20. Ukrainian	Woonsocket, RI	1930s	weekend

*Date of establishment of school program, although ethnic heritage curriculum added only in the 1970s. Supplementary means the program is an elective within an all-day school.

Table 2: Ethnic Schools Affiliations

Ethnic Group	Affiliations	Type of Curriculum		
		religious	secular	language
1. Armenian	Armenian General Benevolent Union (AGBU)		X	X
2. Cambodian	Catholic Charities of Houston Khmer Village		X	X
3. Chinese	local organizations		X	X
4. Czech	local organization		X	some
5. Dutch	church, as well as private and public education systems	X	X	
6. German-Russian	Roman Catholic Church		X	
7. Greek (Birmingham)	Holy Trinity-Holy Cross Greek Orthodox Cathedral		X	X
8. Greek (Buffalo)	Hellenic Orthodox Church of the Annunciation	X		X
9. Hebrew	West End Synagogue United Synagogues of America	X		X
10. Hungarian	Hungarian Alumni Assoc.		X	X
11. Hupa Indian	local organizations		X	X
12. Islamic	Islamic Center of Seattle Muslims Students' Assoc.	X		X
13. Japanese	Senshin Buddhist Church Buddhist Churches of America American-Japanese Language School Assoc.	X		X
14. Korean	First Korean Baptist Church		X	X
15. Latvian	American Latvian Assoc. St. John's Evangelical Lutheran Latvian Church		X	X
16. Lebanese	St. Elias Maronite Catholic Church	X		X
17. Polish	Polish Teachers Assoc. of America		X	X
18. Portuguese	Taunton Sports Club Government of Portugal		X	X
19. Turkish	American Turkish Women's League Government of Turkey		X	X
20. Ukrainian	St. Michael's Ukrainian Orthodox Church	X		some

Introduction

by Elena Bradunas

In societies where interaction with other cultural groups is minimal, people do not often comment on the question of their ethnic identity. They simply live their culture and do not reflect upon it in a self-conscious manner. Language, traditions, rituals, skills, and traditional knowledge are taken for granted as important components of life and are passed on to the younger generation through continuous daily interactions. Immigrants to America become more aware of their ethnicity, however, as a result of cultural dislocation and contact with mainstream American culture. Thus ethnic identity becomes a more conscious component of a person's self-image, to be accepted, rejected, or adapted to new circumstances.

Ethnic schools are a manifestation of immigrants' special adaptation to the American environment. They demonstrate a group's conscious perception of itself as a distinct group with a cultural legacy to be passed on to the next generation. Ethnicity becomes something to be studied, valued, appreciated, or believed in because the old way of life of the cultural group is in many ways no longer feasible. First-generation immigrants or their children, as new Americans, have the choice of whether or not to maintain ties of identity with their communities of origin. There was no such choice to be made in their homelands. Ethnic schools are an attempt by ethnic communities to keep open the option for their children of identifying themselves on a cultural continuum with their parents. Cultural continuity can be maintained by other means as well, but the schools are a concrete manifestation of that desire.

On a trip to Oakwood Cemetery, in the Dutch community of Pella, Iowa, fieldworker Philip Webber points out a gravestone inscription to student Shane Sikkema. (ES82-13050-15-2A) Photo by Barbara Cech

If one were to summarize what ethnic schools are all about, the simplest answer would be that they are about ethnic identity or, even more generally, ethnicity. The curricula of the schools studied during the Ethnic Heritage and Language Schools Project shed light on what each community

13

perceives to be important components of their ethnic identity. Language, religion, history, and other "ethnic subjects" (particularly appreciation of ethnic arts) seem to be the primary educational categories of the classes taught.

Besides the overall concern for ethnic identity, the one concern mentioned by almost everyone with whom we spoke was language. Of course, the intensity of the commitment to language instruction varies from group to group. Language drills are rigid and demanding in some cases, almost nonexistent in others. Even the daily use of language varies tremendously. Some schools, such as the Islamic and Polish schools, use language extensively. Others confine its use to a few words—the names of several religious objects in the Ukrainian school, or the recitation of the United States Pledge of Allegiance in the native language, a tradition that spans four generations in the Czech school.

Even when language instruction is minimal, there remains a strong feeling among community members that language is important. Many mentioned language instruction as one of the main reasons for the school, though it was clear that the goal of teaching the children a foreign language was not being met very effectively. The constant references to language and the persistent attempts to keep some words and expressions alive reinforces among the adults and transmits to the youngsters a sense of a moral imperative—the language must be kept alive, if only symbolically, to mark the group's distinctiveness and its connection to a particular culture. Recognition of this "sense of obligation" helps explain some rather paradoxical behavior. Parents who do not speak the language at home and often have only a minimal grasp of it (sometimes because of having attended similar schools in their youth) explain that they send their children to the school "so they will learn the language." Children who often speak English with their peers and complain of being hostages in the schools also answer that when they grow up they will send their children to Saturday schools to learn the language. Why? "So they will know who they are." Thus even limited language exposure provides identification with the mother tongue and its culture. It is not so much the achieved result as the demonstrated effort, therefore, that stands as an expression of their seriousness with regard to cultural continuity.

Although members of ethnic communities often emphasize the importance of language, their idea of language proficiency does not necessarily correspond with the proficiency exhibited by native speakers. For some members of an ethnic community "knowing the language" may mean being able to answer the prayers in a church or synagogue, exchange greetings, intersperse a few words in a conversation conducted in English, read a paragraph in a foreign newspaper, or understand the gist of a simple conversation. They perceive language as a symbol of ethnic identity. They do not expect it to exist to the same degree in people's lives as it once did in the homeland or among the first generation of immigrants. Many members of an ethnic community register a commitment to language not by how thoroughly and how often they speak it, but by how well they demonstrate general familiarity in the appropriate settings. This observation is important to bear in mind when we appraise the effectiveness of language instruction in the schools.

Another clearly delineated component of the curriculum in a number of schools is religion. Religious instruction becomes part of the curriculum whenever a group perceives religion to be uniquely and intimately connected to its cultural and social history. In our sample the Greek, Hebrew, Ukrainian, Lebanese, and Japanese schools all stress the religious component of their cultural legacy and do not separate it from ethnic identity.

In most cases language is tied to the liturgy, providing an additional motive (perhaps the major motive, as in the case of the Hebrew schools) for language instruction. Even if community members do not speak the language at home or at social gatherings, they use it in the place of worship. The connection between language and religious ritual can erode with time, however. For example, both the Greek and Lebanese communities in Birmingham are debating the pros and cons of using English in their services. The Ukrainians in Rhode Island have already made the shift; consequently, the children no longer receive language instruction during their weekend classes.

Other groups do not seem to connect their ethnic identity to religion in the same degree. For example, the Korean school does not incorporate religious instruction, although it is partially supported by the First Korean Baptist Church and many of the children come from families belonging to that congregation. The Islamic School in Seattle, on the other hand, rests its entire cultural affiliation solely on the faith of Islam. The racial and national identities of the children who attend are irrelevant as long as the families have accepted the Islamic faith. Because of Islam's connection to the Arab world, however, the children learn the Arabic language and identify with the social and cultural history of Muslim countries.

An important component of ethnic identity is the sense that the culture to which one feels an allegiance has persisted. By being a member of the group one connects to others in the past who spoke the same language, worshipped in the same way, and practiced the same customs. Thus it is not surprising that in all the schools we found some references to the history of the group. Such references underline the importance to an ethnic community of the persistence of ethnic identity through time. The past may be presented with some selectivity, emphasizing the group's accomplishments and injustices suffered at the hands of others. Refugee groups who immigrated after World War II often romanticize and idealize life in the homeland, since their departure was not a contemplated emigration but a hurried flight due to political turmoil. Those groups whose ancestors immigrated several generations ago, such as the Dutch and German-Russians, focus on the role of the ethnic group in New World regional history, demonstrating a fascinating melding of ethnic and regional identity.

In a number of schools the children memorize important historical dates, names, and stories of cultural heroes, and study the meaning of calendrical holidays and celebrations. Recitations and dramatic presentations are often part of the classroom. The children present formal programs to parents and the community at large on holidays and at convocation ceremonies. Learning songs and dances and making crafts and other display objects intensifies as the performance day approaches, and children often seem to have the most fun when engaged in such activities.

Within the confines of an ethnic school, children have an opportunity to learn and practice cultural behavior that is significantly different from mainstream American life. Asian children, for example, interact with teachers and adults according to culturally specific rules of etiquette, and Turkish children learn to kiss the hand of the teachers when accepting their diplomas. This collective recognition of particular traditions helps validate the parents' culture in the eyes of the children; traditions need not be confined to the privacy of the home but can be shared with others who acknowledge their worth.

As forums for learning and presenting songs, dances, crafts, and other traditions, schools play an important role in formulating and defining what

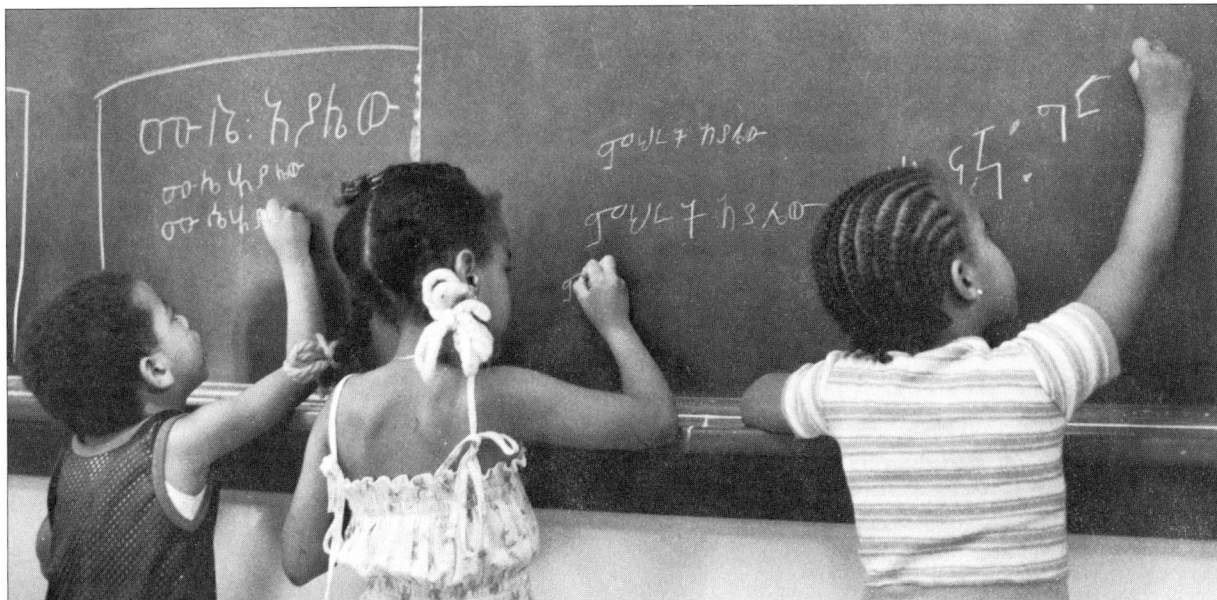

Practicing lessons at the blackboard, Caribbean School, New York, New York. (ES82-196611-1-23) Photo by Jefferson Miller

constitutes ethnic cultural expressions for the youngsters. The songs, dances, and crafts are identified as part of their cultural trousseau and, because they are learned in the school setting, are automatically accepted as authentic and real. If the children are ever asked to present something from their culture to outsiders, most likely they will choose a song, dance, or craft which they have learned in the school. Such cultural expressions taught and sanctioned by teachers and the community at large may even take precedence over other traditions learned at home.

The result can be a kind of standardization of cultural expressions. The transmission of culture through formal means like the schools or dance and choral ensembles may seem stiff to those who would like to see traditions flourish in a more natural and fluid state through family life or informal community activities. Often, however, such home-grown traditions do not hold a strong enough attraction for the youngsters. Some parents do not even expect their children to pick up those traditions, feeling that they are not appropriate or relevant to a successful life in the American mainstream. Ethnic community members are painfully aware of how quickly de-ethnicization can take place when ethnicity is allowed to flourish only within the confines of individual families. They know that collective affirmation of selected values and traditions provides a slightly better guarantee for their longevity. The specific contents of that collective cultural information bank are not always of primary importance to the group. It is the importance of having the children sing songs in their language—and not necessarily just folk songs—that prompts teachers to print song sheets and drill the children for performances.

Whatever the emphasis of the curriculum, ethnic heritage schools seem to convey a sense of ethnic identity quite apart from any specific subject taught. They create this identity by filling children's time with activities shared by others of the same background—time that is not spent watching television, playing football, or engaging in other non-ethnic pursuits. Specific subjects, though important in creating shared symbols and in-group knowledge, may have less importance in developing ethnic consciousness than the mere fact of association.

One characteristic shared by all the schools (except the two all-day schools and among high-school students) was the children's complaint about the tediousness of the experience. Yet almost all of them said they liked meeting with their friends, and it was clear that strong social bonds were being established. Thus no matter how well or poorly the schools fulfill their varied goals, they imbue the children with a sense of community. The experience of togetherness, even if at first based on shared complaints about the drudgery, prepares the child for future adult membership in the community.

In selecting schools to visit we tried to include representatives of all the types of schools Joshua Fishman had described in his book *Language Loyalty in the United States*. Table 1 gives the time schedule for each school. Our project included only two all-day schools—the Armenian school in Boston and the Islamic School in Seattle—in which the ethnic or religious instruction permeates the entire curriculum. Three other all-day schools were visited—the Hupa language classes for children on the Hoopa Indian Reservation, the German-Russian heritage program in a ru-

ral Catholic high school in North Dakota, and the Dutch cultural-enrichment programs in a few regular schools in Pella, Iowa—but attention was
paid only to the special ethnic classes which were offered as free electives for the students. In all three cases the ethnic community is in a relatively rural environment, and its population registers a significant count in
the area's census. The schools have been there for some time, but the
enrichment programs were developed only recently. The rest of the
schools were either after-hours programs or weekend schools.

We had a certain bias toward the after-hours and weekend schools because of their evident support and commitment from the ethnic community. The private all-day schools need support as well, but because they
also provide the children with an accredited education, one cannot assert
unequivocally that the commitment is solely to ethnic language or heritage instruction. The three supplementary cultural-enrichment programs
in public or private schools seemed to have come about because of the
commitment of particular teachers rather than a demand on the part of
the community at large.

To establish a sequence for the essays in this volume, we considered following Fishman's categories. The three categories were unevenly represented, however, making it difficult to correlate our findings with some of
the subtle differences Fishman detected among the categories. For example, his claim that language learning is more effective in the all-day
schools because it is drilled for five consecutive days rather than once a
week was difficult for us to test. Thus, although the categories helped us
at the beginning of the project to focus on the variety of programs in operation, we did not find them as useful afterwards in analyzing and presenting our findings.

When we were selecting our sample we did not know the history of the
schools, so their ages were not a criterion for selection. When we received
the final reports and tried various ways of sequencing them, a chronologi-
cal arrangement proved useful and interesting. One can group the schools
under three headings based on their history: (1) schools founded after

1970; (2) schools founded after World War II; and (3) schools founded from the late nineteenth century to the 1930s. The roster is as follows:

Post-1970

Ethiopian	1981
Cambodian	1980
Islamic	1980
Portuguese	1980
Korean	1977
Turkish	1973
Armenian	1970

Post-World War II

Lithuanian	1960
Hungarian	1960
Polish	1950s
Latvian	1952

Pre-World War II

Ukrainian	1930s	
Japanese	1928	
Chinese	1927	
German-Russian	1918	(enrichment program started in 1970s)
Greek (Buffalo)	1916	
Lebanese	1915	
Greek (Birmingham)	1902	
Hebrew	1896	
Dutch	1880s	(enrichment programs started in 1970s)
Hupa	1870s	(language program started in 1970s)
Czech	1870	

By presenting the description of the schools we visited according to their age we hope to alert readers to certain points. First, the idea of teaching youngsters about their ethnic heritage has been around for some time and is not just a result of contemporary interest and fascination with "ethnic roots." Second, by viewing the phenomenon through time we may be able to discern similarities and differences, changes and consistencies, that tell us more about the place of ethnicity in America.

When comparing the older and newer schools one can quickly note some similarities: the stress on the importance of identity, an acknowledgement of the significance of the native language, a propensity to organize a school-like structure for educational programs, similar problems with teachers and curriculum materials, and the same headaches concerning enrollments and finances. These characteristics can be said to typify all the schools in the sample.

Some differences which can be noted at present may not have always been there. For example, more recent schools, such as the Lithuanian, Polish, Hungarian, Turkish, Cambodian, Portuguese, and Korean schools, seem to stress the importance of language above all else. On the other hand, the older Japanese, Ukrainian, and Greek schools seem to place less emphasis on language instruction. When listening to older people recount earlier times in the older communities, one gets the impression that language was once considered of prime importance. With time, language proficiency diminished. At the same time, almost in inverse proportion, attention to the other "ethnic subjects" increased. The Chinese school, according to a current description, seems to focus solely on a few ethnic arts. The German-Russian and Dutch programs focus more on the social history of their community in its particular locale.

Starting with the accounts of the newer schools, one notes that the recently established programs are being founded about ten years after the immigrant group's arrival in this country, a time lag that allows the group to organize itself as a community. The commitment of organizers and teachers to the new schools seems phenomenal, and the entire community membership is supportive of the venture. This is best demonstrated by the high enrollment of students. In the reports of the older schools one sees a number of changes. The commitment to language is not strong,

Visvaldis Rumpetēris giving an oral exam to Mara Erkmane at the Milwaukee Latvian School, Milwaukee, Wisconsin. (ES82-197009-2-15) Photo by Ričardas Vidutis

factionalism within the community becomes more evident, and enrollment tapers off. One wonders if the newly established schools will follow the same pattern of development.

Will the present-day social climate favoring ethnicity affect the newer immigrants' tenacity in preserving their language and culture? Or will the almost inevitable forces of acculturation and assimilation bring about loss of fluency and cultural transformation? Is the ethnic school a phenomenon that grows out of the experiences of the first and second generations of an immigrant group, happening only rarely during the third and fourth generations? Does a school's function change depending on which generation it services? Does class play a role in a group's desire to preserve or reject its ethnic identity, and how does the eventual climb up the socio-economic ladder correlate with the desire to pass on a sense of ethnic identity to the children? Our findings do not answer all these questions, but they are worth keeping in mind as one progresses chronologically through the essays.

The schools are also characterized by their affiliations. Some of the schools operate in almost complete isolation, connected to no religious network or national ethnic organization which could put them in touch with educational efforts in sister communities elsewhere in the country. In this category of "lone stars" we have examples from older communities, such as the Czech and the Chinese schools, as well as from new arrivals, like the Cambodian school.

At the other end of the continuum, some schools are clearly connected to sister communities and other educational programs through the services of well-organized umbrella organizations. Schools like the Greek and Hebrew schools in our sample have sophisticated religious institutions providing support and guidance in everything from training teachers to curriculum materials. Post-World-War-II refugees, such as the Latvians, have a centralized "council of education" to ensure consistency among educational programs in Latvian communities throughout the country.

Two groups in our sample, the Hungarians and the Portuguese, have established contact with the mother country for help in preparing educational programs and curriculum materials for their children. In both cases a rather recent immigrant generation initiated the contact, having recognized that their own teaching resources were somewhat limited.

Except for the Koreans, none of the groups we interviewed seem to have had contact with schools in other ethnic communities. For the most part, ethnic communities have little awareness of similar efforts to pass on language and heritage within other ethnic groups.

All-day schools, whether public or private, are connected to mainstream educational systems simply because they have to fulfill certain requirements for accreditation. Their curriculum design and instructional materials are fairly sophisticated, and the children seem to have a positive attitude about the extra learning opportunity. The fact that they do not have to give up a free day for the ethnic experience may have some bearing on their attitude. For the organizers of such schools, however, there are usually many more complicated administrative tasks than for those who set up a program outside the official education system.

All the essays discuss the social dynamics that get a school started and keep it going. Our observations clearly show that a considerable amount of sacrifice, in both time and money, is needed for the school ventures. Parents, teachers, and administrators all contribute their efforts, and although the teachers are usually paid for their services, the fees are token honoraria, often barely covering their transportation costs. Unless there are organized car pools, as among the Koreans in the Washington area, most parents must donate precious hours to transport their children to and from the school. In addition to paying the tuition, which may be minimal, parents are also involved in fund-raising activities for the school, since most of the schools do not have other resources to help defray costs. Even those schools that are affiliated with nationwide ethnic organizations usually receive only guidance and curriculum materials, not direct financial assistance. Operating costs may be less in cases in which the church, a foreign embassy, or a local university provides the physical facility, but there remain other financial concerns.

A majority of the schools are governed by school boards or committees comprising parents, teachers, and members of the church or other sponsoring institution. The school boards are primarily responsible for carrying out administrative duties and overseeing finances. Curriculum decisions are usually left to the teachers, but in a number of cases the boards select the teachers. Thus the organization and maintenance of the schools requires a great deal of cooperation among many individuals. There has to be a consensus on basic issues; otherwise, as in a few cases we documented, splits within the community and high attrition can undermine the education program. When rifts have occurred, the data we collected illuminates the role of dissent in community dynamics. On the whole the schools reflect the collective will of a community and provide a wonderful arena for the study of community values.

Many specifics concerning the establishment of the older schools are now lost to history, with only the founding date known through community jubilee publications or other organizational records. Nevertheless, it is possible to form a general idea of how they developed from the recollections of former students. Sometimes the memories are a bit hazy, and one must also remember that they are recollections of the world viewed from a child's perspective. The detailed descriptions for recently established schools are more useful. Because many of the recent schools have a similar genesis, it is likely that the patterns discerned in their histories apply to the older schools as well.

All the schools founded within the last three decades came into existence because some members of the communities felt a need to organize a formal means by which the children could learn something about their ethnic heritage. The fact that they formed schools implies that those community members thought a formal school setting would do something for the children which could not be done in the privacy of their own home. This expectation may have stemmed from their own experiences with education in their homelands, or simply from the desire to validate their own culture in the children's eyes by presenting it as worthy of the same kind of attention as subjects taught in other public and private schools.

By organizing and maintaining a school the parents collectively reaffirmed their own commitment to their heritage. They expected, no doubt, that their children would see that the cultural knowledge being transmitted was valued by other adults like themselves. In some cases the parents felt the school would provide instruction that they themselves could not provide for one reason or another. Because reading and writing a language was something most of them learned through formal education in their homelands, they felt that only a formal school setting could convey that knowledge to their children. The idea that only properly trained individuals could be effective instructors inhibited them from taking on the role of educators in their own homes.

Regardless of the actual reasons behind their establishment, it is clear that the schools are seen as important and necessary ventures. Otherwise, why bother with all that effort? Some examples of school dedication that communities exhibit include the successful effort made by the Muslim community of Seattle to raise the money necessary to buy an abandoned building and convert it into a comfortable school facility. Taunton Sports Club members dedicated many weekends and after-work hours to construct the addition to their clubhouse which was to house the classrooms for the Portuguese school in Taunton, Massachusetts. The Armenian community near Boston is trying to raise the funds necessary to become independent of the 50 percent subsidy it now receives from the Armenian General Benevolent Union.

Examples of such efforts among the newly formed schools most likely approximate the energy and vigor demonstrated by the founders of the older schools. Realizing that the earlier immigrants may have been even worse off economically than the more recent groups, it is truly impressive that they raised the funds not just for their schools but for churches and halls as well.

Although establishing and maintaining schools requires collective support and cooperation among community members, the actual initiative can often be traced to a few people or one individual. Sometimes, as with our Lebanese and Ukrainian examples, a parish priest started the program. Several other case studies underscore the importance of specific individuals who seem to be almost totally responsible for initiating and carrying out a successful program. The Chinese school, which has a long and complex history, seemed to have flourished under the directorship of one dedicated and competent woman. The elective course on German-Russian heritage offered to high school students in Strasbourg, North Dakota, is available for students only because of the creative ingenuity of one young teacher. The same can be said for the few teachers committed to the ethnic enrichment courses in Pella, Iowa, where students learn more about their Dutch community's local history than about "old world" cultural details. The special programs for young members of the Hupa Indian tribe in California also rely heavily on the expertise and dedication of one older native woman, who teaches the children words of a language that their parents never learned or had forgotten.

Parents' Visitation Day at the pre-school, West End Synagogue, Nashville, Tennessee. (ES82-196112-4-27A) Photo by Bob Gates

The concern for teaching children the traditions of the homeland goes back almost to America's first immigrants. The concern has continued with nearly every immigrant wave that came to America, often manifesting itself in the establishment of formal school programs to teach children language and culture (including religion). Why has there been so little attention to the phenomenon in its historical and contemporary contexts?

One possible explanation is that ethnic groups never made a great point of advertising ethnic education programs beyond their own neighborhoods. For the communities themselves the school may be an inner sanctum where the ritual of cultural transmissions, though formal, is shielded from outsiders among whom it may not be properly understood. Such misgivings may have been much stronger in the past, when the formal pressures for becoming an American were quite strong, especially at times when activities with a high ethnic content could be viewed as un-American. At present, when ethnicity is considered a positive commodity, that fear need no longer persist. It is not easy, however, to attract the interest of outsiders, whether journalists, scholars, or educators to something that is not inherently colorful and attractive, as are the usual "eth-nic-knacs" which draw the outsiders' attention at fairs and festivals. Language drills are tedious.

The fact that the linguistic achievements of these schools remain somewhat dubious probably explains why even sociolinguists have not responded to Fishman's call for more thorough research. Although anthropologists are interested in culture contact and in the ways sub-dominant groups try to preserve their identity vis-a-vis a dominant culture, they have not fully turned their magnifying lenses onto ethnic groups in America. Folkorists, more preoccupied with informal cultural transmission that occurs without institutional mediation, have perhaps seen ethnic schools as too formal a setting for informal cultural transmission to take place. We hope the reports that follow will arouse more interest from scholars in these and other academic fields. There remain many questions, and each field can provide unique perspectives on the phenomenon.

Educators who are especially concerned about public bilingual and bicultural curricula and who are aware of the persistent problem of "transitional" versus "retentive" programs should not neglect assessing the value of privately maintained culture-retention efforts as an option, particularly in the face of complaints that the public bilingual and bicultural classes are not satisfying community expectations. One wonders why the official education establishment hardly recognizes these community educational programs, especially when a number of official reports bemoan the general ignorance of foreign languages and cultures among our youth. The schools may not produce fluent speakers of a particular language, but they do enlighten young people about other cultures and languages.

Private, community-based ethnic schools and programs have been functioning for quite some time now, and will probably continue to do so, regardless of official education policy and governmental activities. The schools do not seek or expect to receive public funds, but they will benefit from greater outside recognition of their efforts. We hope that our investigation of ethnic schools through this project is understood to be a recognition of their importance in helping America retain its multicultural profile. Much more study of their functions and their contributions is warranted and we invite others to follow.

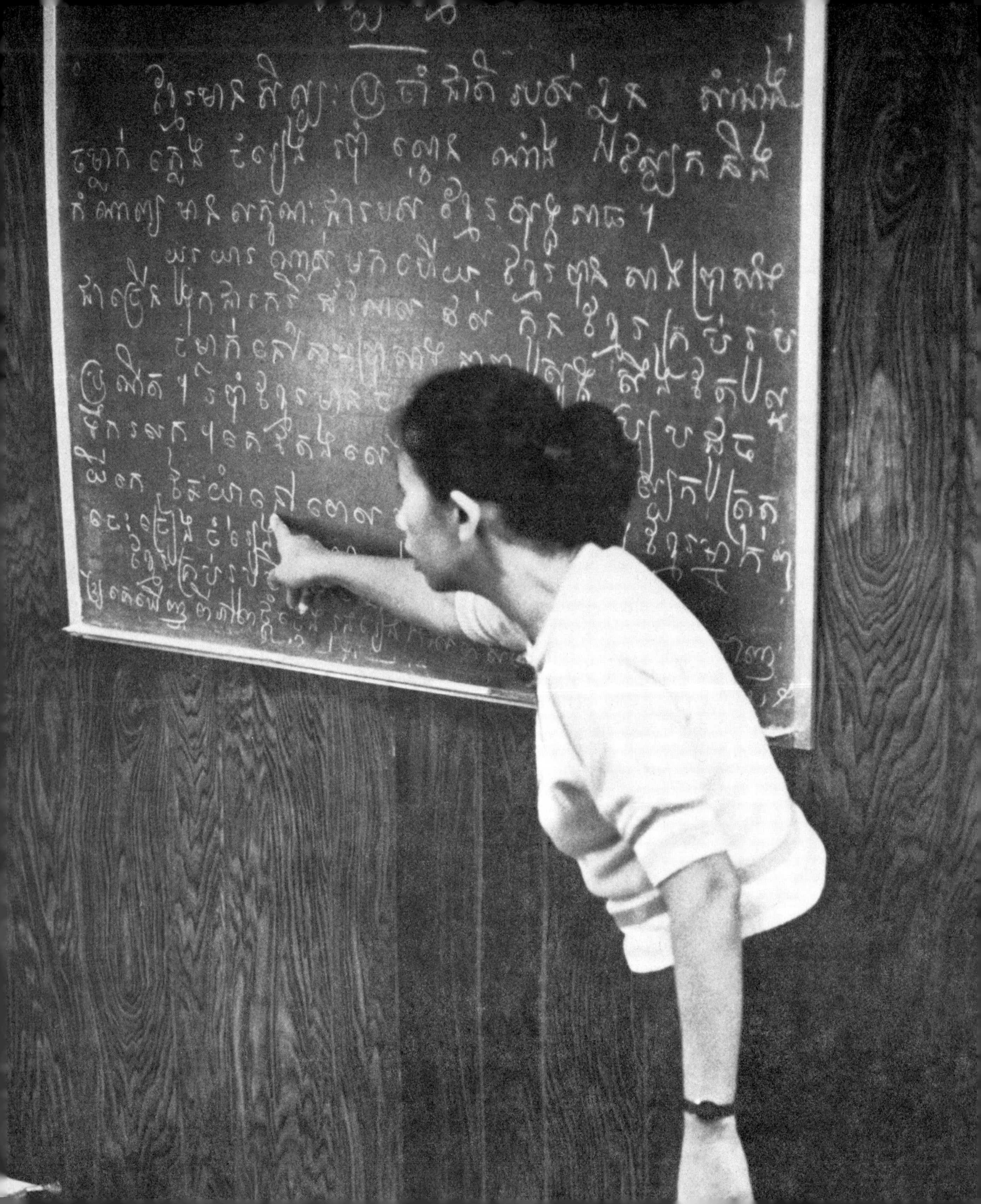

The Cambodian School
Houston, Texas

Frank Proschan

Near the intersection of U.S. Route 59 and Interstate 610 in northeast
Houston is a court of twenty-three houses known as the Khmer Village,
home for about 150 Cambodian-Americans. One of the two-bedroom
houses at the center of the compound is used not as a residence but as a
school. In that building, located at 6779 Bonita Street, adult residents of
the village learn English. In addition, women are instructed in health and
nutrition, while children study Cambodian reading and writing. The story
of the school is the story of the remarkable community it serves and, in
large part, the story of one remarkable woman.

Yani Rose Keo's nominal title is Job Placement Officer for the Catholic
Charities of Houston, an organization which has actively assisted Cambodian and other Indochinese refugees since 1975. In fact, her responsibilities are much broader, encompassing not just employment, but every aspect of social services for the more than two thousand Cambodians who
have arrived in Houston under the aegis of Catholic Charities. On a typical day she might go to see the principal of an elementary school, visit
sick Cambodians at the hospital, pick up a family arriving at the airport
(providing lodging for them in her own home until permanent housing
can be found), make funeral arrangements for a deceased refugee, go to a
job site to clear up a misunderstanding involving a Cambodian worker,
teach an adult English-as-a-Second-Language (ESL) class, settle a domestic dispute at one of her housing sites, and then return home to hand
stitch a traditional Cambodian wedding dress. Nor is her work restricted
to those refugees sponsored by Catholic Charities; any Cambodian in need
who calls on her will be assisted, to whatever extent possible. She is a
modern-day Jane Addams, motivated by an intense commitment to help
her Cambodian countryfolk become self-sufficient, productive, and happy
in their new homes.

Madorom Huot at the
blackboard of the Khmer
Village School in Hous-
ton, Texas.
(ES82-197001-9-35) Photo
by Frank Proschan

The Khmer Village is the first Houston experiment in "cluster housing" for Indochinese refugees. One of the common patterns of immigrant settlement among recent refugees, especially those in large cities, is to cluster in older neighborhoods and older apartment complexes. Such a pattern of unplanned ghettoization has both advantages and disadvantages which cannot be discussed adequately here.

The cluster housing designed by Yani Keo is different in important respects from unplanned clustering. Cluster housing brings together between thirty and two hundred members of one ethnic group in a carefully prepared and planned manner. They all live in one place, either in a complex of houses or garden apartments. The clusters create islands of one ethnic group living within a larger community of another ethnic group—in this case, blacks. Maintenance of critical mass allows the residents of the cluster to gain the benefits of living together with people like themselves, while simultaneously avoiding problems of ghettoization. The cluster communities are relatively small and are carefully spaced, so that no single neighborhood is saturated. For example, all of the children at the village attend the same elementary school. There are enough of them that they do not feel isolated and the teachers and staff are able to learn about their needs and be responsive. There are not so many in one school, however, that the teachers' resources and energies are overburdened, or that the Cambodian children lose the benefit of close contact with American children of other cultures.

Cluster housing maximizes the advantages and minimizes the disadvantages of the less deliberate refugee settlement patterns prevalent in other parts of Houston. In Yani Keo's view it is intended to help preserve the culture, especially for the young and the old, and to minimize problems with culture shock. Friends protect one another and in an emergency, "they know how to help each other." (Keo, ES82-FP-C10, Side 1, 110) Cluster housing is especially desirable for widows with families, many of whom could not even have come to the United States without the support system inherent in the housing pattern.

The Khmer Village is the prototype of cluster housing. Its general description (if not the particular history) applies as well to the three other sites Yani Keo has established elsewhere in Houston. The twenty-three houses had been built as low-rent housing in the 1960s, but had not been very successful. As Charles Thomas, a colleague of Yani Keo's, explains, the renters "became disenchanted, and as the landlord phased out that program with the low-rent agency, they would just damage the place, dilapidate it, tear it up so badly the landlord got a little disappointed and then never bothered about trying to fix the place up and re-rent it again. That's how we were able to get this place." (ES82-FP-C10, Side 1, 220)* Part of the arrangement negotiated with the landlord was that the twenty-third house was provided rent-free to be used as a school; they would pay only for utilities and furnishings (later donated) for that building.

The first task was to make the structures habitable, since when taken over, "the brick walls were still there and that was the extent of it," says Thomas. (ES82-FP-C10, Side 1, 212) In February 1981 a few families that had been living elsewhere in Houston moved in. "I chose the ones that had low incomes, large families, family problems [or were living in bad neighborhoods]," says Keo. (ES82-FP-C10, Side 1, 267) Soon families specifically intended for cluster housing, such as those with widowed mothers, started arriving from Thailand and the Philippines.

The ideal cluster combines newly arrived refugees with others who have been in the United States for up to two years, but not with those who arrived in 1975 or soon thereafter. "We're trying to put them together based on their background, their experience, their economic status ...," Thomas explains. (ES82-FP-C10, Side 1, 365) Those who have been here for more than four years usually have jobs, cars, and good English skills; they can manage well in more expensive (and more remote) housing. They would be out of step with someone who had just arrived, and perhaps disinclined to assist them. Yet it is helpful to have some residents who are in their second or third year—those who have cars, employment, and sufficient English to assist the newer arrivals. Each cluster has a few key contacts, "anchor persons that we can communicate back and forth with," notes Thomas. (ES82-FP-C10, Side 1, 395) Then, adds Keo, "when husband and wife have a job, I move them out, find a better place." (ES82-FP-C10, Side 1, 405) That may be a larger apartment, a rental home, or even a purchased house.

---

*Charles Thomas is personnel director for Standco Industries, a Houston firm that employs about one hundred Cambodians and as many or more Laotians and Vietnamese.

For the residents of the Khmer Village education is not constrained within the four walls of the school building or the local public schools. It ranges from practical orientation, such as how to count change or use American fixtures and appliances, to instruction in English and other academic subjects, technical training in schools and on the job, learning or improving literacy in Khmer, and informal transmission of cultural traditions by neighbors and family members. While this report concentrates on programs within the village school, they must necessarily be seen in the large context. Village residents arrived there along various paths, with widely divergent skills and experiences. No single program can meet all of their educational needs. Therefore, a range of alternatives is made available. Underlying the entire educational program, however, is the idea of survival—providing the knowledge and skills needed to survive, flourish, and prosper in a new homeland.

The most common classes in the village school building are "survival English" for adults and some older teenagers. These English-as-a-Second-Language (ESL) classes are funded by the Houston Community College (HCC) system, which pays for two teachers—one American and one Cambodian. The American teacher instructs the more advanced students, while Samphup Kou (Yani Keo's son-in-law) teaches those with no knowledge of English. Some of the refugees were fortunate enough to be able to begin learning English in the camps in Thailand or the Philippines, but for many of them such classes were unavailable. The routine procedure recently has been for refugees to go from Thailand to the Philippines for several months of orientation and ESL. Some, however, come directly from Thai camps where teaching English is sometimes prohibited, or where lessons must be paid for. In any case, the ESL classes in the camps are only for adults; children are restricted to learning Cambodian. (Huot, ES82-FP-C6, Side 1, 400)

The ESL classes, currently serving some thirty students, meet Monday through Thursday evenings from around 6:00 P.M. to 9:00 P.M. Books are provided on loan from Houston Community College. Students are drawn from the village and from a nearby residence on Shreveport Boulevard which houses some twenty-five new arrivals. Yani Keo also supervises ESL classes taught by volunteers at a church across from her Weaver Street cluster. In addition, several evenings a week she herself teaches ESL classes at 2800 Main Street, attended by students from the Schroeder Street cluster and the Elgin neighborhood. Advanced ESL for adults is offered at other HCC facilities. Some village residents attend General Educational Development (GED) classes, also offered by HCC.

The village classroom is used on an irregular basis for women's classes. Yani Keo teaches women's health and hygiene, nutrition, child care, money management, driver education, rape prevention, and birth control, sometimes assisted by volunteers from the YMCA and, more recently, by staffers from the Red Cross. (Keo, ES82-FP-C10, Side 2, 250) She is training villager Madorom Huot to take over these classes soon.

Turning finally to the classes in Cambodian literacy for children, we must again backtrack for a moment. Yani Keo, schoolteacher Madorom Huot, and the parents in the village share a commitment to the maintenance of Khmer fluency and literacy—a commitment similar to that which characterizes many ethnic language schools. A more immediate problem, however, relates to the special circumstances which preceded the refugees' arrival in the United States. Many of the refugee children (especially those born after a certain date and those from rural areas) never attended school in Cambodia. Rural schooling in most Cambodian provinces effectively ended before 1970; after 1975 there were no schools anywhere in Cambodia. As Keo explains, children born in 1963–64 in rural areas have never been to school (ES82-FP-C10, Side 2, 010), and those born anywhere in the country after 1968 probably did not attend school. Those from rural areas, even if their parents had some literacy, were rarely taught to read or write during a period when sheer survival demanded constant work and education was an invitation to be murdered. Some educated parents, for instance Mouk Phon and In Man (both of whom had taught school in Cambodia), managed to teach their children in Cambodia or Thailand; most children were not so lucky.

Cambodian language schools were established in some of the Thai camps, so some children who had not previously attended school were able to achieve at least partial literacy in Khmer. Those who never learned to read and write their own language are at an enormous disadvantage when trying to learn English. Therefore, initial experience with reading and writing Cambodian is a primary short-term goal for them. "If you don't know the alphabet you cannot go far," says Yani Keo. "You don't have a strong root. That's the Cambodian way to say it, 'strong root.' If you don't have that strong root, you cannot go far. You will give up very soon." (ES82-FP-C10, Side 2, 040)

Huong Chung, Soknay Hong, Sokalay Hong, Chinda Meas, Poeurn Huon, Sophear In, and Bun Vichet In at the Khmer Village School in Houston. (ES82-197001-8FP-32A) Photo by Frank Proschan

Literacy in Cambodian helps these students learn English, in part because the very idea of literacy (that there can be a correspondence between audio and visual signs) is important. If one sees how it works with one's own language, it is far less mysterious when learning a second language. More practically, as Madorom Huot explains, "I think that if the kid can understand Cambodian, knows how to write and how to read Cambodian, they can learn English fast because some words in English they can write [i.e., transliterate] in Cambodian. If they don't know how to read and write Cambodian, what can they do for English? Not at all." (ES82-FP-C6, Side 1, 461)

Consequently, the Cambodian classes that Yani Keo taught in the village during the summer of 1981 were limited to six children, aged seven to fifteen, who had never been to school; the classes were to prepare them to enter the American public school in the fall. Review classes are scheduled intermittently throughout the year, however. The 1982 summer classes included both new (illiterate) students and those who just need to maintain and improve their literacy. There has been an increase in the number and type of students served by such classes because it is no longer necessary for Yani Keo herself to teach all of them with the arrival in the village of the experienced teacher Madorom Huot.

The classroom sessions that I observed featured lessons drawn from textbooks prepared in the late 1960s by the Buddhist Institute of Phnom Penh. This set of three graded books was used throughout the country for language instruction. The series was reprinted recently by the United Nations High Commissioner for Refugees to be used in the refugee camps in Thailand. It is not uncommon for these books to be highly prized by those in the camps—I have seen families arriving in the United States who brought with them a few pounds of rice, perhaps some treasured family photographs, and copies of their Khmer and beginning English schoolbooks.

The younger students used the first book. The lesson I observed involved learning to recognize letter shapes, with students drilled to pronounce the letters correctly or to step to the blackboard to write the letters that Madorom Huot pronounced. The older class used the third-level book for a more complicated lesson on spelling. The Cambodian writing system overlays an Indic-derived script on a sound system that diverges from those Indian languages for which the orthography is better suited. Consequently, as with English, there are various ways to write the same combination of sounds, and complicated spelling rules determine why one combination of letters is preferable to another. Madorom Huot copied a long text onto the blackboard with empty spaces awaiting missing words. She would then read the proper word and students would respond with the proper spelling.

Madorom Huot, a widowed mother of three, arrived in the Khmer Village in the fall of 1981. Her family had lived in the capital city of Phnom Penh for many generations. Her father was a district mayor, so she and her sister were encouraged to study. She graduated from high school and completed one additional year of teacher training that qualified her to teach physical sciences (chemistry and physics) at the high school level. As a student during the last years of the French protectorate, she studied French throughout her schooling and English for five years. When she herself started teaching science in 1966 the textbooks were in French and classes were conducted in Cambodian. A government translation project managed to produce Cambodian texts for the first eleven grades before it was terminated in 1975, however, so that her later teaching usually relied upon Cambodian-language textbooks.

Madorom Huot fled Phnom Penh on April 22, 1975. For the next four years she "worked like a farmer" under the Pol Pot regime. Escaping from Cambodia finally in November 1979, she eventually made her way to Mairut Camp in Thailand, where she and three other Cambodian teachers established a primary school of twelve classrooms. She became principal after the first principal emigrated to New Zealand. Under her direction the school grew to twenty classrooms and a staff of about fifty people. The camp school taught Cambodian, math, health, physical education, dance, and music. United Nations authorities wanted them to teach history, but they declined. Huot wanted to teach English and French, but was prevented from doing so by Thai and United Nations officials; their official policy was that refugees were being prepared for repatriation to Cambodia rather than emigration to the United States or France.

Yani Keo describes some of Madorom Huot's activities now that she has come to this country as follows: "Right now she's teaching Cambodian, she's helping me with the women's program, and volunteers at [Terrell Middle] school, where we don't have any Cambodian aides, or teachers, or translators. She goes to school in the morning to prepare her GED and comes back, [then] goes to the public school to help." (ES82-FP-C10, Side 1, 305)

Huot's work during the school year at Terrell Middle School is voluntary. In addition, she tutors her own children to insure that they do not fall too far behind Americans of the same age. For Madorom Huot has made a decision that illustrates the dilemma that confronts many Cambodian parents: she decided, with the advice and encouragement of Yani Keo, to start her eleven-year-old daughter in the second grade instead of the sixth grade. "I want her to understand more English, and I will teach her the math. When she's able to understand English, I don't worry about [her catching up in] math. I don't want her to stay a long time in elementary school, but if I put her in junior high, she can't understand at all—even math." (Huot, ES82-FP-C6, Side 2, 225) She shares the expectation expressed by Yani Keo, "I had experience when I was teaching in 1976;

some students were put in second grade, third grade, but they can skip. When they get the English, they catch up like this." (ES82-FP-C10, Side 2, 076)

The problem of students' having to be placed in lower public school grades points out another valuable benefit of the Cambodian lessons in the village: students who are embarrassed or uncomfortable in the public school, who feel lost or too old, can gain a feeling of pride and accomplishment in the Cambodian classes. The village school offers a haven in which they can feel productive, to offset the alienation they sometimes experience in the American schools, despite the best efforts of concerned American teachers. Yani Keo notes, "When they go back home they say, 'I know how to write in Cambodian!'" (ES82-FP-C10, Side 2, 440)

Another American educational system is also attended by a number of Cambodian adolescents as an alternative to local public high schools—the Gary Job Corps Center, a residential, technical institute in San Marcos, Texas. Gary Job Corps seems to be especially well suited to young people from fifteen to twenty years old who never attended school in Cambodia. Were they to enroll in a public high school or junior high they would be lost, if placed with Americans of their own age, or it would take them forever to finish, if they started at a lower grade than their age group. Also, these are young people whom parents may perceive to be of employable age, capable of contributing to the family economically instead of going to school. Gary Job Corps provides both technical training and academic instruction, including intensive English for foreigners. The students are lodged and fed without charge. Thus, even though they are not themselves contributing to the family's resources, they are at least not draining them. Moreover, they are being prepared for remunerative occupations. Girls can be admitted to Gary Job Corps anytime. Boys must sometimes wait as long as a year, during which time they attend public school and begin to learn English. When they do go to Gary Job Corps, they can often make better progress than they would have if they had stayed in the public high school.

The immediate benefits of the village school—introducing literacy, permitting transliteration, and giving students encouragement—are especially important and unusual because of the personal biographies of the refugee children and the particular circumstances of their forced flight from their homeland. The long-range goals and benefits of the school fit in more closely with what we expect of ethnic language schools, and it is to those long-range goals that I now turn.

The goals of preserving and maintaining language and culture are the ones cited most often by parents in explaining why they teach their children Cambodian and send them to the village school. Even through the filter of translation, the explanations are compelling. Chung Huon states through an interpreter that if his children asked him why study Cambodian, "he would explain to them why they have to learn Cambodian: he loves his country, so he'd like his children to learn Cambodian." (ES82-FP-C12, Side 2, 178) Musician Mouk Phon tells why his daughter is eager to learn Khmer, also through an interpreter: "She wants to learn all languages—Cambodian, English. She is a Cambodian, so she has to learn Cambodian. The father knows about music, so the daughter has to learn about music." (ES82-FP-C7, Side 1, 450)

The valuation of education by the parents with whom I spoke reflects two convergent attitudes. The first is one in which education is valued for its own sake, and the second is one of civic and social responsibility in which education is seen as one of several ways that people can contribute to both their immediate community and the larger Cambodian and American cultures. To understand these attitudes we must know something of the refugees' educational background at home.

Most of the adult men and fewer of the adult women had attended enough school to have at least some literacy in Khmer. Schools at home were of two types: the *wat* (pagoda) school, sponsored by the Buddhist church but usually offering secular subjects taught by lay persons, and the public schools. Evidently, the curricula covered in the two types of school overlapped, although it was perhaps more standardized and uniform in the public schools. Then as now, schooling might have to be sacrificed if a child had to help support a family. Mouk Phon was forced to withdraw from school when his parents and older brother died. Some of the older teenagers here, who would perhaps benefit greatly from continued schooling, must also seek work instead. The problem of priorities is especially pronounced for those in their twenties who would like to attend college, but who cannot because their work demands too much time.

As to the education of women, my impression is that most urban girls and many rural girls had access to education; but the older a woman, the less likely it is that she went to school. These women are nevertheless staunch in their conviction that their daughters should attend school and that it is just as important that they learn as that their brothers do. Except for Yani Keo, who attended college in France, none of the people I interviewed had attended college. Madorom Huot did receive a year of teacher training, however. Lack of higher education among village residents is not surprising, considering the fact that most of them were farmers or soldiers from rural areas. Refugees with advanced education are more likely to have been among the first to immigrate to the United States, leaving the ones without education or family ties with other United States residents to immigrate later.

The other attitude concerning the value of education held by many of the parents with whom I spoke appears to emanate from their sense of civic and social responsibility. The parents demonstrate a responsibility to their neighbors in the village but also, more broadly, to Cambodian culture as a whole. In Man taught French and Cambodian at the elementary school level for several years, until he joined the army; he then resumed teaching in the refugee camp. Prior to 1975 Mouk Phon taught Khmer adult literacy classes for several hours each evening and then gave music lessons until late at night. These same people and their families helped sweep the village for the New Year's celebration which took place on April 24, 1982, built the stage for the band, and served refreshments. Although they are no longer able to serve their homeland, they are able to help preserve its culture. Further, although they are discouraged about their own ability to contribute productively to American society, they want to be sure that their children gain the skills necessary to allow them to be productive citizens.

The broader commitment to the preservation of Cambodian culture is encouraged by the cluster housing arrangement of the village itself. Within the village all of the children are fluent in spoken Cambodian, even if they are not all literate. Yani Keo explains that sometimes "these children forget what they were before. I have experience. The children who came in '75–'76 don't speak Cambodian anymore, and they don't dance Cambodian dance." (ES82-FP-C10, Side 2, 267) Perpetuation of the spoken language is assured through the village experience. Instruction in the written language acts to validate it and encourage the students to want to remember it, even after they leave for other housing. Nevertheless, it should not be assumed that all of the children are eager to learn Cambodian. Children resist the Cambodian lessons because they represent school, and children everywhere have always disliked school. Madorom Huot says, "If the parents say, 'Go to school and study something,' the kids don't want to.... I have to force, sometimes, my children, too. But the older [ones are] not difficult for me to force them. But the small one, I have to tell him all the time, everyday, to learn, learn English, learn Cambodian...." (ES82-FP-C6, Side 2, 485)

Language is the foundation of the cultural edifice that the school and village are dedicated to preserving because it is the most vital link between the young Cambodians and their families and elders. Charles Thomas recounts an anecdote that demonstrates the resistance and rejection that exists on the part of some young Cambodians:

One Sunday Yani and I were over at the village ... and this mother came in with her two little children [aged 5 and 7]. And the mother could not speak any English at all, and the two little children spoke English. And they were being kept by this family at the Lutheran Church. And they were rude to the mother, so the mother was crying. And she brought them to Yani for Yani to help her work with them. So I said to Yani, "What is the problem?" She said, "Well, it's a very simple problem, that the children have outgrown the mother, and there's the problem. She can't communicate—they don't speak Cambodian and she doesn't speak English. They speak English and they don't speak Cambodian." So I said to her, "Yani, it's a shame, but we always expect children to outgrow the parents; but when they're this age, we don't expect that to happen, because when they're young they become unmanageable." (ES82-FP-C10, Side 2, 295)

The Cambodian lessons in the village school are central to the endeavor of transmitting cultural knowledge, and language is the most crucial connector; but the classes do not exhaust the efforts toward cultural preservation. Thomas amplifies on this point: "What we're doing now is we're using the adults as often as we possibly can. We have affairs within the village, and it brings Cambodians from all over the city, outside and within the village. And there we demonstrate cultural things—dance, games, singing, and even, to some extent, religion—to try and keep the younger people in touch with what their ancestral background and what their cultural past was." (ES82-FP-C10, Side 2, 295) Yani Keo cites the New Year's celebration as an example of the cultural reinforcement offered by events at which Cambodians gather. "The aged people, they are very happy to see the games, like at the New Year. We have the games that they used to play, because the children don't care, but the parents care. (ES82-FP-C10, Side 2, 379)

Formal training in literacy is the keystone of the cultural preservation efforts organized by Yani Keo; but that keystone does not hang unsupported in midair. It is held up by an arch of formal and informal programs by which Cambodian children are educated in their rich traditions. The keystone in turn serves as the foundation upon which future programs will be based. For instance, Keo dreams of having the villagers publish a Cambodian-language magazine or newspaper. (ES82-FP-C10, Side 1, 084) Charles Thomas adds, "We're thinking about developing, if we can, a larger type of complex that will have more than twenty-three houses. And within that [we] will have some shops that will cater to them and their needs, and, of course, it will give them the kinds of opportunities [needed] to express, to train, and also develop among themselves." (ES82-FP-C10, Side 2, 355) Keo would also like to teach Cambodian literacy to refugees elsewhere in the city, some of whom have already asked if they could enroll their children at the village school. "In the future my plan is that I will talk to the [public] school, to teach them at school, like they teach Spanish. If they teach Spanish, why don't they speak the other languages?" (ES82-FP-C10, Side 2, 285) No one who knows Yani Keo's drive and commitment, her inexhaustible energy, and her simple eloquence would doubt that her dream will come true, just as her visions of cluster housing and a school in which to teach Cambodian have already been realized.

* * *

The foregoing has been a report on the school and the village. What follows is more in the nature of a report on the research. The Khmer Village school is a school in the birthing, not one with a long history or established traditions. It is less stable, less established, and less institutionalized than many other ethnic language schools. Often, no boundary can be drawn between activities that are properly the school's and other activities undertaken by Yani Keo; no board of directors or fiscal officer is around to say what is an official school project and what is not. Many of the questions posed in the instructions and guidelines provided by the American Folklife Center were simply inapplicable to this school. In addition, the particular circumstances by which these refugees arrived in

Houston imposed an additional set of questions and problems to be investigated, some of which are included in the report but others of which are not. I have endeavored, both in the research and in the report, to keep the school and the activities within its walls at the center of my interest. At the same time I needed to look back in time and place to these people's former lives and at their total educational opportunities today.

In talking to villagers, both in formal interviews and in informal conversations, I found it easy to get answers on two topics: what their education had consisted of in Cambodia and what educational activities they were pursuing here at present. In fact, a perfect conversation opener was "Where did you learn English?" or "What grade are you in?" When inquiring into the villagers' past lives, I was confronted with the inevitable problem of the horrors most of them had experienced. My approach was as delicate and tentative as possible. As long as we were talking about education, it was relatively easy to avoid painful topics, or, once touched upon, to move beyond them. I avoided many of the customary questions of personal biography that I would have liked to ask or that I might ask in the future, once I know them better. When I talked to a widow, for instance, I did not feel inclined to interrogate her on tape about the circumstances of her husband's death. Although such topics came up many times in my informal conversations with people, I did not pursue them in formal taped interviews. Likewise, with those whom I have known since last year and with whom I have discussed such topics, I did not want to cause them to reiterate painful stories. As a consequence, the "Key Contributor" forms are not as complete as might be desired—only living children are listed, for example.

Another problem was inherent in the situation of interviewing with a translator. It must be remembered that many of these people pride themselves on their attempts to speak English, at the same time that they apologize for their inability. When someone answered me in English, I deemed it impolite to ask them to elaborate in Khmer, although a translator was there who could assist. I felt that it demonstrated respect for their English abilities to accept a tentative or incomplete response in English rather than demanding a fuller reply in Cambodian. This was especially true when posing questions to the children, who lost all of their brash self-confidence when the tape recorder was turned on. Even if their English response was monosyllabic, I was disinclined to make an implicit criticism of their abilities by suggesting that they respond in Khmer. Madorom Huot was there to act as translator when they did not understand my question or when they chose to respond in Khmer; but if they volunteered English, I did not reject it. Mouk Phon, for example, probably speaks better English than he was inclined to demonstrate, but he felt very comfortable working through translation and the two interviews with him worked very well.

The question of individual interviews versus group interviews may also have influenced the choice of language used. If I were to go back to the families and interview one person at a time, I would probably rely more on translation and push the questioning further. For the initial interviews, however, I think that the group approach was better—it represented less of an imposition on the people, their time, and hospitality. That is, by going into their homes and speaking with everyone who was there, I interfered less with ongoing activities than I would have if I had demanded uninterrupted time with each person, supposing that such uninterrupted time were even available.

In my logs of the taped interviews I have reported the on-the-spot translations by Madorom Huot and Moni Kou. It would, however, be productive to return to the salient portions of the tapes, transcribe the Khmer responses, and then translate them in more detail, rather than relying on the more summary on-the-spot translations.

A final word must be inserted on the proper use of quotations from the taped interviews. In my tape logs, transcriptions, and the quotes excerpted in this report I have frequently transcribed English statements in a way that certain scholars might find improper: I have taken the liberty of correcting the English words of my informants on occasion. This has been done neither casually nor carelessly. After careful deliberation I have taken the step with the following considerations in mind. First, in the area of pronunciation, Khmer speakers characteristically do not release the final sounds of words (in contrast to America-English speakers, who frequently emphasize final phonemes, even to the point of exaggeration). Additionally, certain of the final consonant clusters that are common in English are difficult for Cambodians to pronounce, particularly the consonant clusters which serve in English as verbal inflections or plural markers. As an example, Cambodians might not distinguish in pronunciation between "look" and "looked"; but this does not mean that they are unaware of the difference, or would not make the distinction in writing or in deliberate speech.

I have, consequently, conjugated verbs or indicated plurals correctly wherever the meaning was unmistakable, in spite of the pronunciation. At a level of syntax, Cambodian does not inflect or conjugate verbs for number or for tense (past and future being indicated sometimes by compound verbs, but just as often not being indicated at all, except by context). I have occasionally corrected the tense of English verbs, or corrected person-number inflections. Again, this has been done only where the sense was unmistakable. Because the research and the report are intended to communicate the ideas and intentions of the speakers, not to provide linguistic data, I believe this procedure to be sound. The tapes themselves are the final document, should someone eventually wish to use them for linguistically oriented analyses; but for general informational purposes, the "corrected" transcripts should be used.

Finally, I offer a few suggestions for continuing research. As I have remarked several times above, the village school's instruction of Khmer literacy can only be understood in light of the total range of formal and informal educational institutions and channels by which cultural knowledge is transmitted from old to young. If work were to continue in the Khmer Village, it should be designed to investigate that total range of activities. That would include, for example, mothers "instructing" their daughters in cooking (conventional gender roles still apply for many tasks), or musician Mouk Phon teaching younger villagers to play traditional instruments. The first might be more amorphous and unstructured, while the second would likely be more formal and regularized. Research would include parents telling their children the traditional heuristic tales of Judge Rabbit, or showing them how to garden or harvest. It would involve more detailed observation of children at the public schools and Gary Job Corps and of adults at ESL classes. In sum, continued research would more profitably investigate "education within an ethnic community" rather than an isolated "ethnic language school." The school itself would surely figure centrally in any such research, but to limit our curiosity to the physical boundaries of the school building's four walls would be to constrain our possible understanding.

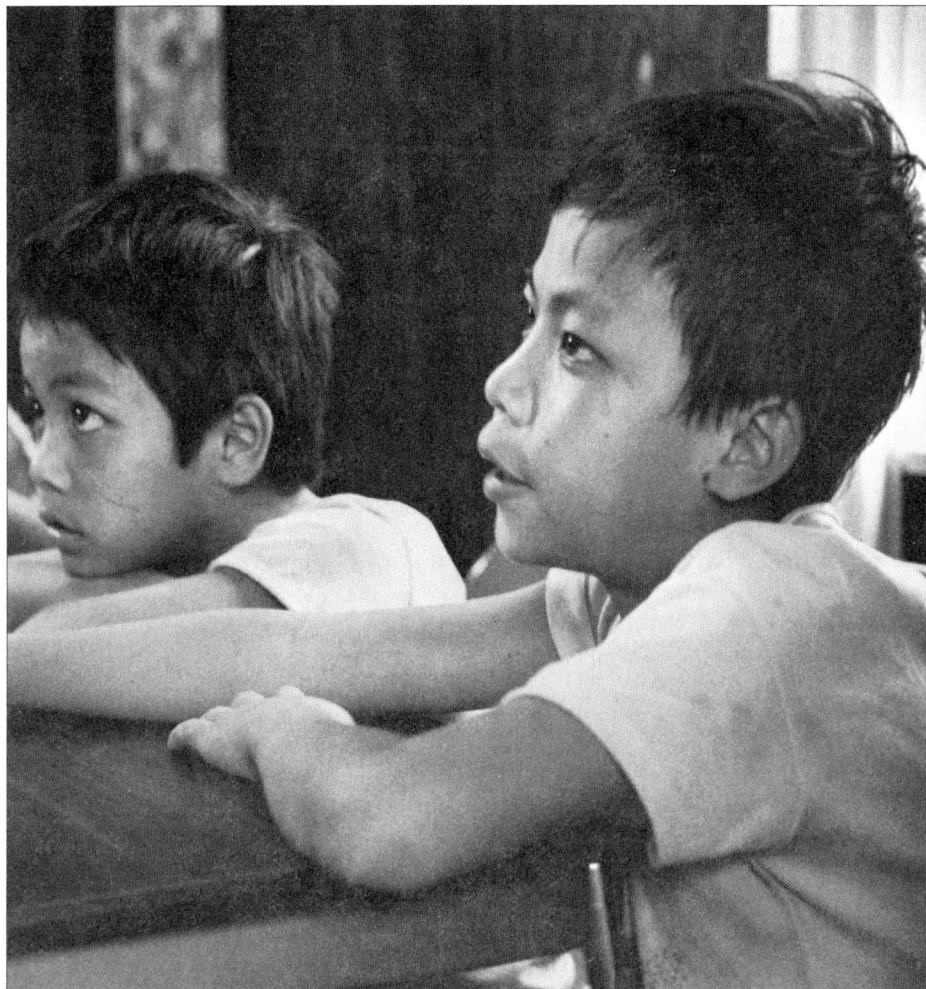

Penh Van and Viseth Van at the Khmer Village School. (ES82-197001-7FP-33A) Photo by Frank Proschan

Postscript—March 1983

Returning to the Khmer Village almost a year after the beginning of fieldwork for the Folklife Center's Ethnic Heritage and Language Schools Project in the spring of 1982, I found that formal classroom instruction in the Cambodian language had been suspended. I noted that the word "suspended" was chosen carefully instead of "terminated," for it is hoped that classes can be resumed by the summer of 1983. What factors produced this turn of events and what lessons can we draw from it?

The major problem with the school has been economic—both strictly in terms of money and also in terms of time. Madorom Huot has taken a job, so the time that she can devote to volunteer teaching has been curtailed. She has also enrolled in Houston Community College to pursue a degree in chemistry, and study time for those classes is yet another demand on her time. Finally, I report with great pleasure that her household has grown, through circumstances at which we can only marvel. When she spoke to me previously about her three children, she referred to them as her three living children. I did not ask further about others, who were presumably dead. In December 1981 Madorom's oldest daughter (now sixteen) made her way finally to Mairut refugee camp in Thailand, where Madorom had been principal of the school. She had been taken care of by another family since 1975, and had almost forgotten the name of her mother, whom she had last seen when she was only seven. At Mairut someone casually mentioned to her that she looked like Madorom. "What was that name you said?" she asked, and the person repeated, "Madorom." It did not take them long to determine that she was Madorom's daughter. She has now joined her mother and siblings in Houston, accompanied by members of the family that had adopted her in the interim. Obviously, these new responsibilities take precedence over Cambodian lessons for the time being.

The school building continues to be used daily for adult ESL classes. During my last visit Yani Keo was rehearsing a group of young girls in the classical dance style. When Madorom Huot or another teacher is able to devote additional time, formal classroom Cambodian language lessons will likely resume.

A similar pattern—for a school to operate for a few months and then discontinue—seems to occur quite often when Indochinese refugees have attempted to establish language schools. Mong Heng told me that he held Khmer classes at St. Anthony Church in Falls Church, Virginia, for several months at the beginning of 1982, until other demands on his time forced him to stop. The two Lao language efforts I have found out about—in San Francisco, California and Murfreesboro, Tennessee—also proved to be short-term projects that ended when their organizers could no longer devote time to them.

The most permanent lessons about which I have heard are the Khmer language lessons run by the Venerable Oung Mean at the Cambodian

Buddhist Association temple in New Carrollton, Maryland. He has conducted language and religion classes regularly every Saturday for more than two years. Although the classes are regular, the attendance is not always stable, primarily because of transportation difficulties.

Finally, there is one additional literacy effort at present which is quite different from the Lao and Cambodian classes. It is organized by the Kmhmu, a highland ethnic group from Laos, now living in Stockton, California. They have been conducting classes twice weekly for three months in the Kmhmu language. Kmhmu was unwritten until the mid-1950s, and even after missionaries devised a Latin-based alphabet, the Kmhmu were prohibited from learning it by the central Laotian government. Since only a few of the twelve hundred Kmhmu in the United States are literate in their own language, they have made it a priority to increase literacy among adults and children. An additional problem for them is to develop teaching methods and curriculum materials as they proceed since they do not have a written heritage and there are no available textbooks. The Kmhmu lessons, including both adults and children, are held in someone's home, with a piece of painted plywood serving as an improvised blackboard, and notebooks and pads which the students bring from home.

These various endeavors, along with the Khmer Village activities, remind us of the necessity of minimizing our preconceptions when we search for ethnic language and heritage education. It will likely be a long time before any of the Indochinese refugees are able to establish formal schools with stable and permanent facilities, faculties, and attendance. The exigencies of their economic situation prevent them from devoting the time, energy, and money which would be necessary to establish permanent schools. Yet language training and cultural education proceed in these communities, perhaps not enclosed within a school building or occurring within a set time period every week, but important nevertheless. Studies of cultural education among America's ethnic groups must consider the total range of formal and informal educational institutions and channels by which cultural knowledge is transmitted from old to young. Our studies should not be limited to those activities which meet some external standard of formality or permanence, even if such established institutions might be our primary focus. Such schools would surely figure centrally in our research, but to limit our curiosity to the physical bounds of a school would be to limit our greater comprehension of community education.

The Islamic School of Seattle
Seattle, Washington

Susan Dwyer-Shick

History of the Islamic School of Seattle

From three families and a handful of unmarried students in the early 1960s, the Muslim community of Seattle has grown to between seven and nine thousand persons in the 1980s. The community experienced its greatest growth, accompanied by a dramatic increase in the number of its school-age children, in the past decade. On February 3, 1980, a small group of Muslim women from the Seattle area met officially for the first time to found a school. Upon incorporation of the Islamic School of Seattle on February 24, 1980, these Muslim parents and educators became the Board of Directors.

The *Parent Handbook*, a twelve-page booklet written by the Muslim administrators and distributed to the school's families, articulates the aims of the Islamic education provided by the school. The school's goals are:

1. To provide our children with an atmosphere, as close to the Islamic ideal as possible, in which they can grow and learn as whole individuals, intellectually, spiritually, and physically.
2. To strengthen them to meet and to effectively deal with the challenges of living in the modern American society.
3. To instill in them a pride in their heritage by enabling them to approach knowledge from a Muslim point of view and by presenting a balanced education with as much emphasis on the Muslim world as on the West.
4. To offer the ultimate in academic excellence so that our children are prepared to take an active and dominant role in the world in which they live.
5. To foster lasting fraternal bonds with their Muslim classmates.
6. To enable them to master the Arabic language so that they may have ready access to the original sources of Islamic knowledge.

Sister Mary Abdi talking over homework assignments with Rohymah Toulas and Lanya Abduljabbar.
(ES82-197518-1-34A)
Photo by Susan Dwyer-Shick

The pilot project, a modified Montessori preschool and kindergarten, opened on September 2, 1980. During its first year the Islamic School of

49

Seattle shared facilities with the Islamic Center of Seattle, both occupying a house owned by the Islamic Center in the city's South End at 4919 31st Avenue South. Children between the ages of two-and-a-half and five were recruited by the school's founders. These women telephoned every Muslim family in Seattle with children in that age range, told them about the new school, and urged them to enroll their children. For Ann El-Moslimany, a parent of three teenage children, and the other founders the approach was straightforward: "We knew all the families in that category." Those contacted responded positively to the solicitations of the school's founders, says Sister Ann, since "mothers of Muslim children know our children need the support of Muslim peers and Muslim education" to keep them from being pulled in two directions.

The success of the school's initial, limited offering provided encouragement and enthusiasm for acquiring an appropriate facility, expanding the existing classes, and extending the program to include the upper grades. During the spring of 1981, the school's founders gave serious consideration to the pros and cons of building a school at a new site or buying an older building. They finally located a solidly built, two-story schoolhouse in Seattle's Central Area. The architecturally impressive structure at 720 25th Avenue, built in 1930, was first occupied by the Hebrew Academy. In the 1960s the city leased it as a public education and youth services facility. During the 1970s, however, it stood empty, a target for vandals. The building was in sad disrepair when Seattle Muslims purchased it for $350,000.

"I was in Kuwait when they called me about finding the building," recalls Sister Ann.

It was a lot of money, all in cash, and due in three weeks. I was asked if I thought I could raise the money. I didn't know, but upon talking with a family friend who knew more about these things than I did, it was agreed that I should try. I telephoned back the decision. The deposit of $50,000 was made and we raised what we needed, although it was closer to six weeks by the time all the money was raised and the paperwork done.

Before opening for the 1981–82 academic year, the school's founders repaired the lovely red tile roof of their new building, painted and put new flooring in two classrooms on the first floor, and made all the changes necessary to comply with city and state health and safety codes. Although professional contractors, some of whom were themselves members of the Muslim community, completed the major structural work, volunteers recruited from among parents, students, and the Muslim community as a whole pitched in on some of the other tasks. During the 1981–82 school year yet another group of volunteers renovated a third, larger room for the preschoolers. Repairs and renovations have continued as funds and resources have become available. In addition, community members have regularly donated their skills and materials. For example, artist Jamshid Kavoussi handpainted verses from the Qur'an in graceful Arabic script at child's-eye level along the building's main hallway and the name "Islamic School of Seattle" in English and Arabic above the main entrance.

In December 1981 the Washington State Board of Education granted full state approval to the preschool and elementary programs offered by the Islamic School of Seattle, finding that the school met all fire, health, and safety codes and provided qualified teachers for its classes. At the close of the 1981–82 school year nearly fifty children between the ages of two-and-a-half and twelve were enrolled in the school's three sections: the preschool, the kindergarten–first-grade class, and the second-through-sixth-grade class. The latter two classes constitute the school's elementary program.

Members of the Muslim community throughout the United States and abroad (especially in Kuwait, Qatar, and Saudi Arabia) assisted the Seattle Muslim community with the purchase of the school and have supported its continuing renovation and operation. The Arabic word *zakat*, which literally means "purification," has no precise English equivalent. It is a Muslim's worship of God by means of his wealth through an obligatory form of giving to those in need. *Zakat* funds may also be spent in the cause of God for the construction of mosques, religious schools, or hospitals and for the salaries of those involved in the propagation or study of Islam whose work keeps them from having time to earn a livelihood.

Besides the payment of the obligatory *zakat*, Islam also urges Muslims to give voluntary charity, to the extent they can afford, to those in need. Indeed, charitableness is among the most stressed tenets in Islam. Since Muslims are supposed to be always responsive to human need and distress, Muslims regard their wealth as a trust from God which is to be used not only for themselves and their families, but for other human beings in need as well. The proper Muslim attitude is set out in the Qur'an:

> Never will you attain to the highest degree of virtue unless you spend in the cause of Allah out of that which you love; and whatever you spend, Allah surely knows it well. (3:93)

> They also ask thee what shall they spend. Tell them: Whatever is spare. (2:220)

Consequently, donations that have been made to the Islamic School of Seattle must be understood not as the largess of wealthy individuals but as an act of worship required of all Muslims in the practice of their faith. For example, Jodi Shahabi, a volunteer at the school, and her husband are students at the University of Washington. They have a small daughter who will attend the preschool in September 1982. Like most student couples raising a family and going to school, they experience financial constraints. Nonetheless, Sister Jodi assumes her responsibility as a Muslim and designates her *zakat* to the Islamic School.

Islam is a complete code of life; Muslims must seek knowledge of the basic tenets of Islam and relate them to all aspects of their individual and social life. In addition, Muslim parents are responsible for the spiritual instruction of their children. The Islamic community has an obligation, therefore, to educate its children in the path of Islam. When the Seattle Muslim community is unable to fulfill this responsibility alone, it is Islamically correct for Seattle Muslims to approach the worldwide Muslim community for assistance. Such an appeal for assistance may have other than monetary aims. Husein Saleh, the Arabic teacher in the elementary school program, is teaching in response to a sense of obligation. "I am not trained in teaching Arabic," he says. "My wife is a linguist and she has helped me prepare many of the materials. My training and interest is in many fields. For example, I have my master's in urban planning. But, it is my obligation to teach Arabic. Each day I ask if they have found another teacher. How can I not teach the students Arabic? It is our language of our religion. It is my duty."

To meet its financial obligations the Islamic School of Seattle has relied heavily on donations from Muslim individuals and organizations. The school has encouraged individuals and groups to plan fund-raising activities. It also charges its students tuition. In addition, the school has initiated educational projects that will provide income and has begun planning for an endowment fund to ensure its financial well-being and continuation.

In addition to monetary donations, offers of supplies and volunteer labor from Muslim parents, students, and community members have frequently helped stretch funds even further. A community-wide effort was put forth to shape up the new school building for the first day of class last September, and a similar effort readied the new preschool room for its February opening. In addition, members of the community have aided the school over and over again by donating needed items. "Twice our needs have been met even before we asked," notes school secretary Diana Akhgar. "On the very day that we had to place an order for additional tables and chairs for the classroom, Brother Sami Amin, who deals in salvage, called to tell us he had two hundred to donate. On another occasion we decided to announce at Juma' [Friday] Prayer service that we needed tricycles and other riding toys. Before the announcement was made we were presented with several such toys from a family who was moving. Allah is the knower of all things!"

Two local Muslim organizations, the Islamic Center of Seattle and the Muslim Students' Association, University of Washington Chapter, have also subsidized the school in the past. The Islamic Center provided the school's first home in 1980–81 and substantial loans when the school's present building was purchased in March 1981. Currently, the vice-president of the Officers of the Corporation, one of the school's two governing bodies, is also the Islamic Center's president. Recently the center held a summer camp benefit in the school gymnasium. In September, just as the school was opening in its new building, the local branch of the Muslim Students' Association contributed $9,000 to the school's scholarship fund.

During the 1981–82 academic year the school collected tuition from all children enrolled in each of the ten-week instructional quarters according to the following formula:

Fee Schedule on a Quarterly Basis

	Full-Day Tuition 8:45 A.M.–3:15 P.M.	Half-Day Tuition 8:45 A.M.–12:00 Noon
1st child	$250	$125
2nd child	$200	$100
3rd child	$150	$75
4th child	$100	$50
5th & additional	-0-	-0-

The school required tuition payments in full by the end of the third week of any quarter, although deferred payment contracts were available. Families with financial hardship are eligible for partial tuition reductions through the scholarship fund, a limited resource which is dependent upon donations designated for this purpose. While the school's administrators hoped that tuition would cover the salaries of the instructional staff (excluding medical insurance payments), in actuality such revenue rarely covered more than one-third of that cost in 1981–82. The school also offered daycare for any child from 7:00 A.M. to 8:45 A.M. and again from 3:15 P.M. to 4:30 P.M. at a cost of $1.00 per hour.

School Administration

The administration and governance of the school is handled by two separate, but related, entities: The Board of Directors and the Officers of the Corporation. Members of the Board of Directors helped to raise funds within the Muslim community to start the school and remain the overseers of the school's assets. Four Muslim women, Zainab Ubaidullah, Ann El-Moslimany, Rafia Khokhar, and Suzette Kakar, have been members of the Board of Directors since February 1980.

In addition, to remain responsive to the community, the school has selected an administrative board, the Officers of the Corporation, from interested community members. This administrative board meets weekly to establish future policies, set priorities, and consider day-to-day problems. It is in charge of all personnel, curriculum, and budget matters, as well as building plans. Board members consult with the school's teaching staff on a monthly basis and with other individuals as needed. Currently, six individuals are serving on the school's administrative board: Abdul-Raouf Mannaa (president), Faizullah Kakar (vice-president), Suzette Kakar (secretary), Ann El-Moslimany (fund-raising chairman abroad), Abdullah Abduljabbar, and Mohammad El-Moslimany. The position of treasurer, formerly occupied by Abdalla Shamia, is vacant; those duties are currently being handled by the board as a whole.

The school's administrative or office personnel staff currently includes two positions. Diana Akhgar was hired in December 1981 as administrative secretary to take charge of the day-to-day, on-site needs of the school in conjunction with the Officers of the Corporation. Decisions about the misbehavior of a child, the taking of class photographs, and the work of a particular contractor are all considered during the weekly meetings of the board. Daily concerns considered during the weekly meeting may effectively crowd out those that are less immediate. Time that might be spent in profitable discussion of long-range goals, such as the securing of contributions to establish an endowment fund, can easily be diverted by hearing about an isolated classroom incident involving one or two children. Because there is as yet no individual at the school with the authority to make decisions and carry out policy on a daily basis, there is considerable latitude for administrative confusion and breakdowns in communication between and among teachers, staff, parents, children, and community members. Consequently, when the school reopens in September 1982 the board hopes to have secured an administrator who would have such authority and yet remain responsible and accountable to board members.

The Islamic School of Seattle, Washington. (ES82-198624-1-26) Photo by Ruth Crum

Irene Junejo has been driving the school's econoline van since the Islamic School of Seattle opened two years ago. She is employed directly by a group of parents to provide transportation for their children along an established route. In addition, Sister Irene drives the van on school field trips, such as the hayride to the Aqua Barn & School for the preschoolers in May, and provides transportation for those in the school's new Women's English Program. The custodial or service personnel staff has three members. Mohamath Toulas, father of two of the older grade school children, is the school's custodian. Mohammad Javaharian and Yaghoub Ebrahimi occupy small, remodeled rooms in the school's basement in exchange for carrying out the responsibilities of security personnel.

The employment of these individuals is not insignificant. Indeed, a recent fund-raising "news update" called attention to it: "An important spin-off of the school has been the jobs which we have been able to provide to Muslims from within the Seattle community." At the time of that newsletter Muslim employees included "two preschool teachers, one elementary teacher's aid, one Arabic teacher, one secretary, one director of the Women's English Program, one school bus driver, and one custodian." The newsletter also points out that employment at the school offers special benefits to two specific groups. "Muslim women who find it necessary to work are now spared the difficulties of working in a non-Islamic environment," and members of political refugee groups with limited knowledge of English and of American society and culture, who need to support their families, can work within a more "supportive and familiar environment."

Parents

The Parent-Teacher Association (PTA) schedules one Saturday afternoon meeting a month at the school. Children take home announcements of these meetings and their parents are encouraged to attend to get to know the other parents and their children's teachers. Meetings of the school's PTA are chaired by a president elected by the parents. Other officers include secretary, treasurer, publications officer, and bazaar chairperson.

The agenda for the January 30, 1982, meeting included: transportation, the new Arabic teacher, the new elementary school teacher, the new preschool director and room, the school's recent accreditation, upcoming PTA elections, and fund-raising. During the school year the PTA's Parents

Committee held a series of rummage sales, raising more than $1,000 toward the purchase of playground equipment.

Participation in the PTA has been estimated at approximately 10 to 15 percent of the parents, a level comparable to that achieved by other PTA groups. With under fifty students in the school and several families sending more than one child, even universal participation would not produce more than a handful of active PTA members, however. Moreover, since many of the school's families come from non-Western countries and are often uncomfortable speaking English, the involvement in their children's education and the participatory role expected of them as parents is still unfamiliar. Nonetheless, the *Parent Handbook* emphasizes parental involvement: "We believe a child's learning experience is complete when the school and home make a cooperative effort. The school and the home are extensions of one another; our interests are the same, so our actions need be also."

Teachers

The Islamic School's teaching staff changed frequently during the 1981–82 academic year. Between December 1981 and April 1982 five individuals joined the full-time faculty, bringing the total faculty to seven. The teaching staff of the school includes:

(1) Mrs. Ruth Crum, director of the elementary school program and teacher of grades two through six, became a member of the school's faculty in December 1981. She holds a B.A. from Seattle University and certification from the state of Washington at the elementary and high school levels. She taught for twenty years within the Bellevue [Washington] School District. Most recently Mrs. Crum spent a year in Peru and three years in Yemen, teaching primarily English-as-a-Second-Language (ESL) in local schools.

(2) Mrs. Carol Thorne, kindergarten–first-grade teacher, was hired in April 1982. She earned her B.A. from the University of Washington, Seattle, specializing in elementary education. Before coming to the Islamic School Mrs. Thorne taught for several years in a suburban Roman Catholic school and was a substitute teacher for the city of Seattle.

(3) Ummil Khair Ishfaaq joined the staff as director and teacher of the preschool in December 1981. Sister Ummil earned her A.A. in early childhood education from Seattle Central Community College. Before joining the faculty she operated a successful Montessori preschool program in her home. It was the first Muslim preschool in Seattle—predating the efforts of the Islamic School of Seattle—and many children attended the school specifically for the Islamic atmosphere that Sister Ummil created. She is currently taking additional Montes-

sori classes during the summer at a local community college with the financial assistance of the Officers of the Corporation.

(4) Husein Saleh, Arabic teacher for the elementary school program, has been at the school since January 1982. Untrained in foreign language teaching, he draws upon his own experiences in learning English as a second language and his wife's expertise as a linguist in preparing his lessons. Brother Husein, who is a native speaker of Arabic, came to the United States from Jordan four years ago to study for an M.A. in urban planning at the University of Oklahoma.

(5) Mohammad Nasser Jappee, preschool Arabic teacher, joined the faculty in May 1982. A native of South Africa, he learned Arabic as a student in Saudi Arabia. Before coming to Seattle he taught Arabic to English-speaking students in Johannesburg, South Africa. In addition to Arabic language instruction, Brother Mohammad has taught calligraphy on occasion to the school's second-through-sixth-grade students and has assisted Samia El-Moslimany in teaching them Arabic songs for the Islamic Center Camp benefit.

(6) Azhar Ibrahim, teacher's aid in the preschool, is the only member of the present faculty to have started in September 1981, when the Islamic School of Seattle opened for its second year. Sister Azhar, who has an M.A. in Persian studies, is frequently called upon to share her knowledge of religion, the Qur'an, and Islamic history and culture.

(7) Mary Abdi, who is a teacher's aid in the kindergarten and elementary school classes, became a member of the teaching staff in November 1981. She is an undergraduate student in anthropology at the University of Washington, Seattle, and has a special interest in elementary education. Sister Mary works with Mrs. Crum and Mrs. Thorne, assisting with reading groups, homework assignments, and review exercises while the teachers work with the other students. More recently, Sister Mary has been conducting social studies and religion classes.

The faculty is paid on a monthly basis, according to the following schedule: director of the elementary school, $1,111; director of the preschool, $700; kindergarten-first grade teacher, $700; and teaching assistants and Arabic teachers, $4.75 per hour.

Volunteers from Seattle's Muslim community augment the teaching staff. For example, Samia El-Moslimany, a college student and daughter of Sister Ann, has been teaching Islamic art and music classes in the elementary school program, and Sister Jodi has recently begun assisting with reading and special reviews in the kindergarten–first-grade class. Also, before her marriage and subsequent move to Indiana last fall, Zainab Ubaidullah, a member of the Board of Directors and its "Perpetual President," taught religion to the kindergarten and elementary school students.

Children

When the 1981–82 school year ended on June 11, 1982, forty-seven children between the ages of two-and-a-half and twelve were enrolled in the three classes: preschool, twenty-three; kindergarten-first grade, ten; and second through sixth grade, fourteen. Boys outnumbered girls, but not by much. More than two dozen families were sending their children to the Islamic School of Seattle. These families represented at least six different ethnic or national backgrounds and spoke as many native languages. Some of the families are in the United States only temporarily, planning to return home when a job or degree is finished. For others, America has become their new home. Perhaps a quarter of the children were from black or Afro-American families. What do these children and their families have in common? The acceptance of Islam, the pride in calling themselves Muslim, and the desire to learn Arabic, the language of their faith.

Classes and Curriculum

The preschool curriculum includes Arabic, primarily vocabulary building; pre-reading and pre-mathematics (sometimes using Montessori equipment); physical activity (organized games and free play in the gymnasium or outdoors); and religion (memorization of Qur'anic verses and discussion of Islamic manners or stories of the prophets). Preschoolers regularly participate in the daily requirements of their faith: the teachers instruct, help, and show them through example "to make *wudu*" (wash) in preparation for *salat* (prayer or worship). While the children usually have *salat* in their own classroom, they often also go to the gymnasium to participate in prayer along with the older children, faculty members and staff, women enrolled in the Women's English Program, and Muslim visitors to the school.

The curriculum for the elementary school program includes Arabic reading, writing, and conversation; spelling; religion; Islamic art and music; and social studies from an Islamic viewpoint. Not all of these subjects are taught every day. During the final quarter the second through sixth graders traveled to the public library on Tuesday afternoons, studied Islamic art on Wednesday afternoons, and learned about Islamic music on Thursdays. The kindergarten-first grade had a similar schedule: social studies from an Islamic viewpoint Wednesday afternoons, handwriting on Thursday afternoons.

The elementary school children also have regular periods for religious activity. Each school day opens with the recitation of the *Fatiha* (seven verses that must be recited at the beginning of a prayer ritual). Later in the morning teachers devote time to helping children memorize Qur'anic verses through collective and individual recitation. The afternoon instruction includes *wudu* and *salat*, often with one of the older boys serving as the *imam* or leader of the service.

The time scheduled for each subject or group of subjects varies. For example, the daily religion class in the kindergarten-first grade is a half hour, while religion class lasts twenty minutes each day for the second-through-sixth-grade group. *Wudu* and *salat* add another forty minutes to the time set aside in the afternoon for Islamic practices. Generally, the time periods in the elementary school range from thirty to seventy-five minutes. Arabic instruction takes up at least thirty-five minutes of each school day, excluding the time spent on the language as part of the daily religion class, *salat*, *Fatiha*, and *surah* recitation (a *surah* is a chapter, part, or book of the Qur'an). Moreover, during the 1981–82 school year the scheduling of subjects changed to reflect alterations in teaching staff and volunteers, availability of audio-visual materials and equipment, and concerns raised by Muslim parents or board members.

Some of the curriculum materials come from major publishers in the United States. The social studies texts are published by Macmillan as part of their series Places Near and Far. Other texts are donated by Muslim countries through their official government or educational channels. For instance, the Saudi Arabian Educational Mission to the United States contributed Arabic-language textbooks. In addition, the school uses texts developed, published, and distributed by Muslims through their own publishing concerns, bookstores, and organizations. For example, the Islamic Foundation of Leicester, England, produces The Muslim Children's Library, a series of small, well-produced books to help a Muslim child "develop a fresh faith, a dynamic commitment, a strong identity, and a throbbing yearning and urge to struggle—all rooted in Islam." The preschool uses *Muslim Nursery Rhymes, Assalamu alaikum* (Peace be with you), and several other books from the series.

The six members of the administrative board currently establish and supervise the curriculum, but certified teachers and trained educator-administrators who have accepted Islam may be given more authority over curriculum development in the future. Due to the lack of such trained

Muslim personnel at the present time, however, these tasks have been the responsibility of the board members. In establishing the school curriculum they have sought advice from certified teachers and other educators outside the Muslim faith, examined curriculum libraries in this country and abroad, and considered undertaking their own publishing program. The first book, tentatively expected to be available in October 1982, will be a combination workbook and reader for the elementary school children who are not native speakers of Arabic. Board members feel this book and others planned for the series could also be used profitably to teach Arabic to young, native speakers of the language. Once this project is successfully under way, at least one member of the board would like to see the publishing venture expanded to include social studies texts and other materials.

In emphasizing the need for such publications, Ann El-Moslimany remarks, "Maybe 30 percent of the countries the children will be studying are Muslim countries, and they are always presented badly, always. I've never, ever, *ever* looked at a textbook that presented a Muslim country in a way that I felt was fair." How could social studies lessons that are unbiased be incorporated into Arabic readers? "We feel that we could use characters, especially, that the children in our school, or other schools—there are other Islamic schools in the U.S.—would identify with," responds Sister Ann. "Children who have, maybe, Pakistani origin, who go back to visit Pakistan. And this is a good place to show what these children would see in Pakistan, what ways they would see that are different from what they do in the U.S. And we could do it with various nationalities; just have a few of these children as the characters in the book." In addition to providing Western-style books, incorporating illustrations and other stimulating and interesting presentation techniques, for their own and other Islamic schools, the venture should also return profits directly to the school fund.

The school provides the textbooks and the children purchase their own workbooks. Earlier in the year *Iftah ya sem sem* (Open Sesame), an Arabic version of the popular children's program *Sesame Street,* assisted teachers in presenting Arabic instruction. Produced in Kuwait, the program made Arabic more accessible to the preschoolers, while making the Arabic-speaking children feel a bit more at home, since the program contained familiar sights, sounds, and people. When Mrs. Crum joined the teaching staff as director of the elementary school and teacher of kindergarten through sixth grade (later, second through sixth grades), she initiated the weekly walks to the public branch library just a few blocks from the school. A bookmobile regularly visits the school so that Ummil Khair Ishfaaq, director of the preschool, can select appropriate books for her children.

All of the teachers rely on handouts to reinforce their lessons. For example, Brother Husein prepares sheets with pictures of familiar animals and objects, followed by the Arabic name, leaving a space for the children to practice writing the correct identification. Sister Mary found that the children in the kindergarten–first-grade group remembered and understood the topic of a religion lesson better when she included a supporting exercise, such as a worksheet to complete or an assignment to "draw and color what we have been talking about." Later, several of these sheets were assembled into religious booklets made by each child as part of one religion class project. Mrs. Crum and Mrs. Thorne rely on similar handouts, as well as on colored construction paper, recycled computer print-

Sister Ummil Khair Ishaaq, teacher and director of the Islamic pre-school, distributes a morning snack of crackers and carrots, while Brother Mohammad Nasser Jappee, pre-school teaching assistant, helps a pupil.
(ES82-196610-1-16A)
Photo by Susan Dwyer-Shick

outs, and other assorted materials to encourage the children and stimulate their imagination. Due to limited resources, the teachers and the children have had to be creative. In the preschool Sister Ummil has introduced the children to "manipulatives" associated with the Montesorri method of instruction. She has also encouraged the children to explore the objects in the classroom and has played "word bingo" to increase their vocabulary skills.

The children are tested and graded on a regular basis. The school year is divided into four quarters and report cards are distributed to the parents at a scheduled parent-teacher conference held at the end of each quarter. Each "card" is actually an 8 ½ × 14-inch, five-page, pressure-sensitive form. This format permits a quarterly report and permanent record of the academic (reading, language arts, spelling, handwriting, mathematics, social studies, science, Arabic language, religion, art, and music) and personal ("listens attentively," "follows directions," "shows respect for authority," and "works independently") development of each child. An evaluation of the effort expended by the child is also possible, since teachers have space under each academic subject to indicate how they compare the child's effort to his or her own ability. The card also shows the "achievement grade," which compares the child's achievement with other students at the same grade level. The "key" or ranking procedure is the same for both effort and achievement: "good," "satisfactory," and "needs improvement." At the bottom of the grade form is a space for teachers' comments and a place to indicate promotion or grade assignment. Each teacher who works with the child fills in the appropriate items, giving an evaluation of the child's work during the quarter. Parents and teachers are encouraged to request a conference at any time during the year. Interpreters are often present during such conferences, whenever a language problem might arise.

Purposes of the School

The founders and the administrators of the Islamic School of Seattle have sought to provide an Islamic environment for their community's school-age children, not a school for Muslim children in which all of their subjects, except religion, are divorced from their Islamic faith. As Sister Ann explains, "It's not that we are trying to pretend that the non-Islamic world doesn't exist, but we'd also like to show our kids that Islam is everywhere. And to let it [Islam] pervade every aspect of what they are studying." It is this emphasis on an Islamic atmosphere, more than the teaching of unusual or religious subjects, that distinguishes the Islamic School of Seattle. Islamic religion and Arabic classes are part of the curriculum at every level. Formal classes in the Qur'an, Islamic studies, and classical Arabic are required of all students in the elementary school program. During school hours all children participate in *salat,* taking their places among peers and teachers.

Those seeking admission for their children are reminded by the *Parent Handbook* that at the Islamic School of Seattle "education is provided within an Islamic framework, and parents should bear in mind that Islam is not only a part of the curriculum, but it is the essence of the school's being." It is this commitment to Islam as a total way of life that provides the framework for the development of the school's specialized education program designed to meet all the children's needs—physical, emotional, educational, and spiritual.

There are differences of opinion about the importance of specific subject matter and the amount of time spent on different subjects, however. For example, there has been discussion about extending the school day for the older children beginning in 1982–83. Instruction during the day could then be divided equally between the study of Arabic and the study of subjects in English. The school board members anticipate resistance to such a change from the two non-Muslim teachers. "To them, of course, this isn't so important. I mean, they can't see the importance; but it is important, and it's our school," explains Sister Ann. For their part, the non-Muslim teachers fully support the religious premise of the school, finding it compatible with their own deeply held Christian beliefs. The non-Muslim teachers are, nonetheless, concerned about the amount of time allotted to "the basics," the core courses required by the Washington State Department of Education, for which, as certified teachers, they are directly responsible.

Yet, even in teaching these basic subjects, both teachers consciously include religious principles and the presence of Allah in their lessons and in their interaction with the children. During a morning science class, for instance, Mrs. Crum helped her second-through-sixth-grade class understand the earth's rotation on its axis, the planet's movement around the sun, and the relationship of these activities to day, night, and seasonal changes. Using a globe and flashlight she and the children portrayed the seasonal changes and talked about the effects on the children's lives. "When the days are longer, I can play outside more," realized Mubarak. "The time for *salat* changes," recalled Rohymah. Then, bringing an interesting and informative science lesson to a close, Mrs. Crum reminded the children that such things are not an accident but "part of Allah's plan."

Still, the ranking order of the important subjects and the allocation of time to different classes remain potentially serious areas for misunderstanding, even conflict. To be a well-educated Muslim one has to know Arabic. Although the "total immersion" Arabic-language plan for the preschool is as yet unrealized, and the "truly bilingual, Arabic-English" elementary school program has not been established, the board remains committed to those programs to generate Arabic fluency among the Muslim children. During the final quarter of the 1981–82 school year, board members supported some changes in the teaching day to accommodate more Islam in the subject areas, particularly in those associated with the humanities and social sciences. Samia El-Moslimany began coming to the school in the afternoons to lead the classes in art and music, emphasizing Islamic influences, characteristics, and appreciation. In one art project the elementary school children practiced calligraphy, writing the name "Allah" and then braiding colored streamers to paste onto the decorative handwriting. Mary Abdi, an assistant in the elementary program, assumed full responsibility for the social studies portion of the curriculum during the same quarter. On Fridays Sister Mary would present social studies from an Islamic perspective, often focusing on a different country from the Muslim world each week.

The children aged seven to twelve in Mrs. Crum's class know why they go to the Islamic School of Seattle: their parents send them. They are also quite certain why their parents want them to go: "Here I am with other Muslims." "At this school I am able to pray." "I can learn Arabic. I can learn to be a good Muslim." "The teachers here are good. They are Muslims, like me." The response to my question, "What classes do you like the most?" was immediate and unanimous—"Arabic!" In our conversations several children suggested other favorites, for example, "Recess!" This response prompted delighted giggles from other classmates who were trying vainly to be serious while being recorded by their now-familiar visitor. This distraction aside, all the children focused upon those subjects unique to their school: studying Arabic, memorizing Qur'anic verses, and working on Islamic art projects. Eager to show me how much Arabic they had learned and to hear their voices on the tape, many of the children volunteered estimates of the size of his or her Arabic vocabulary.

As to why they like studying Arabic, Lawrence, an eight-year-old boy new to the school responded: "I like Arabic because Allah made this kind of language." Do they practice Arabic at home? "Yes, it's the language of our religion," several stressed.

All but two of the children now enrolled in the elementary school program had attended one or more schools before coming to the Islamic School of Seattle. Consequently, many of them could offer comparisons of their experience in those schools with that of being a student at the Islamic School. "At this school we learn English," said Ibrahim, a boy who previously attended school in Saudi Arabia. Mubarak, an Afro-American, emphasized that at the Islamic School he knew that he would receive "right lessons." Rohymah, a Cham refugee from Southeast Asia and the oldest girl in the class, observed quietly: "We come to learn to be Muslims."

For most of the children school hours provide virtually the only time to see one another. With the exception of the Chams, who have largely been settled together in city-owned apartment buildings in Seattle, and some of the families residing in university or college housing units, most of the children and their families are scattered throughout Seattle. One family lives in suburban Kent, necessitating a trip of sixty miles each day by car so the children can attend school. Several of the children participate in "Sunday school" at the mosque, learning Arabic and religion in classes with some of their classmates. There they are joined by other Muslim children who are not students at the Islamic School of Seattle. Although there is no official relationship between the mosque school and the Islamic School, many of the same people are involved in both. For instance, Sister Samia teaches Arabic to the children in the mosque school on Sundays, and Sister Ann proudly reports, "Our children are the star pupils!"

In the final analysis, how do the children feel about attending the Islamic School of Seattle? Certainly, they are glad to be there. During one discussion Jamilla and her younger brother Ibrahim spoke excitedly about the school, saying, "a few more weeks and we'll be off probation." Referring to the official trial period of six weeks for all new students, they were literally counting the days until the school would be truly theirs. "Just sixteen more days and we'll be real students!" Jamilla enthusiastically reminded her brother. Asking the children to help me understand what attending the Islamic School of Seattle means to them, I suggested that they attempt to think about how each of them might describe their school to a new child, a child of their own age, coming to their school for the first time.

Jamilla: "Coming to the Islamic School would be like coming to a new world."

Ibrahim: "I would teach him to pray."

Mubarak: "I would teach him the Arabic alphabet."

Jamilla: "We have different subjects."

Mubarak: "We're Muslims and they're not, but we can still teach them to be good Muslims."

Rohymah: "I would show the girls how to cover their heads, so they would be comfortable."

Escola Oficializada Portuguesa do Taunton Sports Club
The Official Portuguese School of the Taunton Sports Club

Taunton, Massachusetts

Marsha Penti

Eastern Massachusetts, particularly southeastern Massachusetts, has been the site of substantial Portuguese settlement since the nineteenth century.[1] New Bedford and Fall River, Massachusetts are well-known as the largest Portuguese communities in the United States. Taunton, Massachusetts, with a population of just over forty-five thousand in 1980,[2] has been home to the third major Portuguese community within the Bristol County area since before World War I.[3] Informants estimated that Americans born of Portuguese parentage and Portuguese immigrants in Taunton number from 50 to 60 percent of its total population.

The Taunton Portuguese community has grown dramatically in the past two decades as a result of a recent wave of immigration. Older community members remember the days when the Portuguese were a minority ethnic group in Taunton; in 1960, for example, the Portuguese population was 5,695.[4] Today the Portuguese form the largest ethnic community in the city. The existence of a sizeable community base is a prime reason that the Escola Oficializada Portuguesa do Taunton Sports Club was founded in 1980.

The Taunton Portuguese school is sponsored by the Taunton Sports Club. It is housed in an addition to the club building located on the south side of Taunton, in a section known as "Weir Village." As its name suggests, this club is organized around athletics, namely soccer. Apparently a concern with soccer is a consistent feature of Portuguese communities throughout the world and numerous Portuguese soccer clubs exist in the United States. Taunton Sports sponsors three soccer teams—the Portuguese school team, a junior team, and an adult team which plays in the First Division of the Luso-American league (LASA).

Claudina Nunes teaching a class for the youngest pupils at the Portuguese School.
(ES82-198072-6-17A)
Photo by Victoria Westover

69

Each night I visited the school there was a large number of cars in the parking lot. The cars belonged to waiting school parents, soccer players, and club members enjoying the fully licensed bar or participating in functions in the club hall. The club holds periodic fund-raising dinners where Portuguese dishes, such as *carne de porco a alentejana* (fried pork with clams), are served; dancing often accompanies the dinners. On weekends the bar's kitchen is open to serve snacks, such as *linguiça* (Portuguese sausage) sandwiches. Members' wives attend the club dinners and dances, although women are not active in the club. Antonio Amaral, former club president and now school president, explains why.

Portuguese women usually never get involved in social affairs. To them it's not right for a lady to go into a club. The American way is different. We have a Portuguese-American club here in town which has an auxiliary group composed of ladies; but the immigrants normally, I'm not saying generally, but normally, they don't believe in women socializing into clubs like that. We would like to, and try to [have them participate], but they just don't go.

The club also sponsors some calendrical celebrations. In February before Lent there is a *carnaval* dance at the club. In the summer there is a *festa* or festival on the club grounds during which ethnic foods are served and dancing takes place. At Christmas there is a party for school students and children of club members during which children under thirteen receive a gift from the club.

In addition to the soccer teams, the club sponsors a folklore group—Rancho Folclorico do Taunton Sports—which performs traditional dances from all parts of Portugal with music provided by its own band. The group performs at the club's festa and other Portuguese functions in the area, as well as at non-Portuguese events, such as picnics of local businesses.

History of the Taunton Sports Club

The Taunton Sports Club began as a soccer team affiliated with the Ward 5 Athletic Club in 1959. In 1961 the team became independent, renting its own club on Weir Street. The club purchased its own building on Oak Street in the early 1970s. In 1978 the club purchased its present building on Baker Road.

There are approximately three hundred dues-paying members of the Taunton Sports Club; a larger number participates in club activities. According to Antonio Amaral, the membership is "one hundred percent Portuguese immigrants." While many Portuguese clubs in America, particularly in nearby New Bedford and Fall River, are defined by regional Portuguese origin, Taunton Sports has a membership representing all areas of Portugal—continental Portugal, the Azores, the Madeiras, and even the former territory of Angola. There appears to be a general consensus that such a varied membership is preferable because it counteracts discrimination and allows for greater community cooperation. Even non-Portuguese can join.

The other major Portuguese social club in the city—the Portuguese-American Civic Club (PACC)—requires Portuguese descent or marriage to a Portuguese for membership. It is described as directing its attention toward the Portuguese born in America, the Luso-Americans. Both clubs share certain responsibilities toward Taunton's Portuguese community.

The Taunton Portuguese Community

Before proceeding to a discussion of the school itself, some background on the Taunton Portuguese community and its institutions is necessary, since the school is community based. School and club members repeatedly emphasized that today the Portuguese live throughout the city. There remains, however, a major area where Portuguese traditionally settle called "The Portuguese Village" or simply "The Village." It is located in the School Street area, north of the city center. The PACC building, several Portuguese markets, such as Matos Variety and Joe's Superette, other businesses, and St. Anthony—the main Portuguese parish—are located in this area. A second Portuguese church, Our Lady of Lourdes, is in the Weir Village south of the city center, where the Taunton Sports Club is located.

The Portuguese markets and businesses throughout the city help to maintain Portuguese traditions. The traditional elements of the Portuguese diet—*linguiça* and a variety of baked goods produced here, as well as imported dried fruits, canned sardines, and so forth—are easily found in a variety of local Portuguese stores and in the supermarket chains.

In addition to the Taunton Sports Club and PACC, there are several other Portuguese clubs in the city. The Portuguese-American Civic Club is the largest, with approximately five to six hundred members. The smallest club, with a membership under a hundred, is the Taunton Eagles, a soccer club which developed out of Taunton Sports. The Holy Ghost Club, a religious organization in East Taunton, has one hundred members. The most recent organization established to promote Portuguese culture in Taunton, both inside and outside the ethnic community, is the Taunton Organization for the Portuguese-American Community (TOPAC). Since 1981 its 120 members have assisted newly arrived immigrants through citizenship classes and other activities. Membership in these clubs is non-exclusive and Taunton Sports members may be members of other clubs. The Portuguese Continental Union, a national Portuguese organization, also has a Taunton lodge.

A major aspect of Portuguese community life occurs during the summer when festas crowd the weekend calendar. A festa may be a simple picnic without calendrical or historical significance, or it may be a festival with religious meaning. Families attend the local festas and travel to ones some distance away. The major festa in Taunton is St. Anthony's, sponsored by the local St. Anthony parish. The festa consists of a church mass, followed by a religious procession through the surrounding streets of the Portuguese village. Afterwards there is a secular segment during which ethnic and American foods are sold and carnival events take place. Our Lady of Lourdes holds a festa in June and the Holy Ghost Club has one in July. The Taunton Sports Club holds its festa in July too.

The major secular celebration of the year occurred during the course of the fieldwork—the Day of Portugal, which honors Portuguese culture while commemorating the great Portuguese poet Luís De Camoẽs. The actual holiday occurs on June 10, but the occasion is marked by week-long festivities. In 1982 the festivities began on Saturday, June 5 with a flag-raising ceremony on Taunton Green in the city center, followed by a show by local Portuguese artists. A festa was held in the Portuguese Village on Sunday. The Rancho Folclorico do Taunton Sports and four other invited folklore groups from southeastern Massachusetts and Rhode Island performed. Three soccer games took place on Wednesday evening at the Taunton Sports field, during which the club's three teams participated. Finally, on Thursday, June 10 a dinner and fado performance was held at the PACC. The school children commemorated the occasion with an end-of-the-year project of essays and drawings.

History of the Taunton Portuguese School

The Portuguese school was founded in 1980. Antonio Amaral, president of the school since its inception, played an integral role in its creation. Amaral says that he had thought of founding a school when he was Taunton Sports Club president in the mid-1970s, but was prevented by the lack of proper facilities. He finds his interest in a Portuguese school natural, being the father of four and wanting his children to learn his culture, language, and background in an academic way.

An organizational meeting was held during February or March 1980 to discuss the feasibility of the school and assess the means of operation and the number of possible students. Some twenty-five parents, directors and officers of the Taunton Sports Club, and bilingual teachers attended the meeting. The teachers included Joselino Guerreiro, who has continued her interest as present school secretary, and Isaura Amaral, director of both the club's and the school's folklore group.

The Escola Oficializada do Taunton Sports Club began classes on November 5, 1980. The first year's enrollment numbered forty-two students. They were divided by age into two classes, taught by Claudina Nunes and Claudina Borges.

During the first year one class met in the main club hall and the other met in a small adjacent room. The unsuitability of the situation inspired the construction of a classroom addition to the club during the summer of 1981. Parents built the school. Antonio Amaral reminisces, "every afternoon we used to go there after work, and every Saturday." School vice-president José Gonçalves even spent his summer vacation on the construction. Some of those involved in the work put up some of their own money to purchase initial supplies. The only hired help was an electrician. As a result of the parents' involvement in the construction, costs were kept to $17,000. Funds were raised, and will continue to be raised, through raffles, dances, and dinners. The school remains in some debt. Antonio Amaral estimates that it will take two years to repay this. Afterwards only general operating expenses, such as electricity and heating, will remain. The school pays no rent.

The school addition was inaugurated officially on June 25, 1982, during the visit of the Portuguese secretary of emigration, Dr. José Adriano Gago Vitorino. The children's $10 per month tuition fees should cover utility expenses, as well as each teacher's monthly salary of $100. The school texts, supporting materials, such as maps of Portugal for each classroom, and the academic guidance of Emilia Mendonça are provided free of charge by the Portuguese government. Students are only required to supply their own notebooks; the school even provides pencils.

The facilities are excellent: three bright classrooms are furnished with suitable desks, chairs, and blackboards donated by a local school. A fourth room is used as a meeting room and for the storage of texts and school files. An outdoor stairwell is the main entrance to the school, although the addition is connected internally to the main club building.

The school's organizers decided from the beginning to make the Taunton school an official school or Escola Oficializada Portuguesa, seeking support and recognition from the Portuguese Ministry of Education. The Portuguese government offers aid to Portuguese schools in the United States, which includes monetary support, free textbooks, and guidance from a trained coordinator living in this country. Emilia Mendonça is the current Inspectora do Ensino Elementar employed by the Service of Basic and Secondary Education for Portuguese Overseas. Working out of the Portuguese consulate in Providence, Rhode Island, she is the first person to have held this position, having been in the United States for two years. There is no cultural agreement between the United States and Portugal which allows her to act as an official inspector. She merely acts as a coordinator for the various official Portuguese schools throughout the United States, including schools in Massachusetts, Rhode Island, Connecticut, and California. She visits the Taunton school about once a month, meeting with teachers and administrators.

Mendonça said that the first program for Portuguese living abroad was begun in France in 1975, and a program started in the United States about 1977. Portuguese schools in America voluntarily choose to accept Portuguese government aid or to remain independent and private. "It is not the Portuguese government who's imposing these schools," says Mendonça. "It's the freedom of the parents that are interested in the education, to learn the Portuguese culture and language, that makes the Portuguese government aware that they should be interested and help these

schools to go ahead in the right way. It's an answer to a call, to the need."
The Taunton school has used these services since its inception. As Antonio Amaral notes, "Anything that we need for our school they [the Portuguese Ministry of Education] will give to us, within reason."

Emília Mendonça is a trained elementary school teacher and administrator. She taught in elementary schools in her native Azores for ten years, and then worked as an administrator in continental Portugal, after taking an advanced course to become an inspector. She makes periodic reports to the Ministry of Education in Lisbon throughout the year, and visits Lisbon once a year to make a direct in-service report.

Mendonça visits the Taunton school on Wednesday, attending classes and meeting with teachers for two hours after class to introduce supplementary material to the teachers. The texts sent to official schools from Portugal are the same texts used in homeland schools. Apparently no Portuguese teaching materials are published in the United States. The materials Mendonça presents bridge the gap between the old country texts and the American setting. Mendonça writes the supplementary materials herself to explain to the teachers how to teach the youngsters. Since Portuguese is their second language, they have to be more precise and direct than if it were their first language. The method used, called "direct teaching," relates lessons to daily, realistic situations. For example, during the April meeting Mendonça presented a lesson plan consisting of a map of a Portuguese city showing places, such as the post office and museum, to aid students on visits to the old country. Previously she had given a lesson in which students described their homes in America, comparing them to houses in the homeland, based on knowledge obtained from their parents. Mendonça commented that such lessons combine the teaching of Portuguese language, history, and culture.

An official school must fulfill certain requirements in return for Portuguese government support. Seventy-five percent of the school's teachers must be educated in the Portuguese system. Apparently, it has been difficult to find such teachers. The most recent teacher hired is not a local man, and has to drive a considerable distance to class. To gain the approval of the Ministry of Education, the school has to forward teachers' credentials and resumes to Portugal via the Portuguese consul in New Bedford. Two of the present teachers are certified and experienced in

Portuguese elementary school teaching. The third has attended a teacher-training school and has taught in Angola, but is not certified. The school is also required to submit periodic reports to the Ministry of Education in Lisbon on such things as student enrollment. The local Portuguese consul makes occasional visits to the school in an official capacity.

Not only does the school receive the benefits outlined above from operating as an official school, but its students may also take an official examination whose successful passage would allow them to enter high school in Portugal. No student has qualified to take this examination as yet, but some may do so in the spring of 1983.

Administrators, teachers, and parents consistently praised Portugal for the support it has given the school. Faced with the task of opening a new school, the founders were happy to accept the supervision and guidance provided by the homeland, as well as the financial support (this year's grant amounted to just under $1,500) and textbooks. One parent noted that he was "touched" to see "the poor Portuguese government" wanting to "help us keep our culture and pass our culture to the next ones." He wondered "how can they have the courage to do it?" Another parent contrasted the excellent facilities of the Taunton school with the crowded classrooms of his boyhood school on Fayal, where sixty to seventy students of all ages were taught in one room by one teacher, questioning how the Portuguese government could manage to support schools in the United States. The teachers especially are grateful for the help provided by the coordinator from the Ministry of Education. As Fernando Morais, teacher and principal, commented on his relationship with Mendonça, "We are in constant touch with each other. That's why I say it's very useful." If he discovers, for example, that a certain lesson does not succeed in class, he will call the coordinator to ask for her suggestions on other methods of approach.

Antonio Amaral explains the interest of the Portuguese government as follows:

Portugal is a country of immigrant people, from the beginning, since the Discoveries. And a lot of people have a tendency to look for better days outside, even though sometimes they could have the same opportunity in the country. I guess it's in our blood. And so they immigrate to all over the world. And the Portuguese government, knowing that, they would like to continue the culture of those immigrants outside the country. So they promote the culture and the teaching of the Portuguese language and culture outside of the country.

He also points out that the Portuguese government receives benefits in return for its policy. "But you have to keep in consideration that the immigrants are a big part of income for the country. By tourism and by improving the relationship between the immigrants and the generations, actually they are improving the tourists in the future. That's one of the reasons I have; perhaps there are others."

School Administration

After the initial 1980 meeting a committee was formed to begin work on the school. In the fall of each school year the parents meet to elect the school's administration, reflecting the philosophy articulated by Antonio Amaral: "The ideal is to have a school run by the parents." Amaral is president of the school. He is assisted by José Gonçalves, vice-president. The school treasurer is Joseph Fresta, a leader in the local Portuguese community who, in his retirement years, is able to devote considerable time to the school. The only non-local administrator is the secretary, Joselina Guerreiro, a bilingual teacher. All of them have been elected school administrators each year since the school began.

The administration also includes five elected school directors, many of whom are parents. The entire administration meets about once every three months, although pressing needs are addressed without a meeting. The administration is responsible for everything, including the collection of the $10 tuition fee from each student.

Officers are often in attendance on school nights. Gonçalves is always present to open and close the school, as well as to take care of school business, such as correspondence with the Ministry of Education in Lisbon. Perhaps he will even call parents of absent students. The school principal, Fernando Morais, is appointed by the school administration and the Portuguese consul. He assumes responsibility for the educational aspects of the school.

Parents

Parents of school children have been most supportive of the school. Antonio Amaral sees their interest as essential to the future of the school. "It's to make sure the school goes ahead. Nobody else, more than the parents, will be interested in the kids' education. Right? We are there now; one of the reasons I'm there now is cause my kids are there now.... Some day ... it will be the other parents' turn."

There is no formal, PTA-like organization at present, although there are plans to have one in the future. Parents frequently stop to talk with teachers after class. The teachers say that they enjoy speaking with them. As Principal Morais, who also teaches, said, "That's how I get my information. That's how I learn a great deal."

The parents receive periodic information on their children's progress through report cards. This close contact is maintained because, as Morais says, "I inform the parents of everything that goes on. Everything! I don't want any surprises." Antonio Amaral observed that, since Portuguese is spoken in the students' homes, parents are aware of the children's progress. "I believe it's easy to keep an idea.... All the parents speak Portuguese, and I believe they can recognize the progress of the young kids."

Transportation, tuition expenses, and home supervision are the parents' principal obligations toward the school. Such obligations can occupy significant time. The reasons some parents do not choose to send their children to school include a lack of tuition money or time to transport their children to and from school. The administration has considered running a bus service to assist transportation.

Another explanation for lack of participation on some parents' part is that recent immigrants are concerned only with the adjustment to American life and the learning of English. A general apathy toward education was cited. Another frequent comment was that student attendance reflected regional differences. Immigrants from mainland Portugal are more interested in culture and education. The majority of the students' parents were born on the continent, whereas the majority of Portuguese in the community are from the Azores.

All parents interviewed were born in Portugal or a Portuguese territory. Asked why they sent their children to Portuguese school, most parents responded that they wanted them to learn the Portuguese language and to study Portuguese culture and history. One father saw it as an obligation to send his children, saying, "As a father I *should* send my children to the school." Another father remembered his first years in America during the late 1950s, when he could not find someone easily who could speak both Portuguese and English; he hoped his children, as bilingual speakers, might be able to help new immigrants. He also viewed his children's bilingualism as assisting them in finding better jobs.

Another common impetus cited for sending children to the school was so that they could communicate with non-English-speaking relatives, both in the United States and in the homeland. The occasions for speaking Portuguese in America most often mentioned were at the dinner table, in the presence of grandparents,[5] or at celebratory Portuguese events, such as weddings and festas. Many students have visited Portugal or are intending to make a visit. One father spoke of his desire to take his children and wife to look at the house on Fayal in which he was born to celebrate his twenty-fifth wedding anniversary. He felt his children's Portuguese education increased the likelihood of a memorable trip.

Classes and Curriculum

The school operates Monday and Wednesday evenings from 5:00 P.M. to 7:00 P.M. During the 1981–82 school year there were sixty-two students enrolled in the school. The students come primarily from Taunton, although a few come from neighboring Raynham. A couple of students began classes in the middle of the year, and a few dropped out; but the basic enrollment has remained constant.

There are three classes—beginning for students from seven to eleven years old, intermediate for the eight to twelve age group, and advanced for the thirteen to seventeen year olds—taught respectively by Claudina Nunes, José Malhinha, and Fernando Morais. The students are divided by age, rather than simply by language ability.

During the course of the fieldwork I attended a session of each class. Classes emphasized Portuguese language training, with the chosen texts being analysed word by word. There were also written exercises, including spelling and dictation. Conversation was encouraged as well. The exact lesson content and teaching methods were determined by the level of the students and the judgment of the teacher.

The beginning class was devoted to language study—reading aloud, writing texts, spelling words, and conversation. Nunes noted that her greatest problem was to teach her students to speak Portuguese well. As a result, she tried to draw students into conversation whenever possible, either during the study of the text or through a discussion about the children's families in Portugal.

The intermediate class was based directly on the day's text, with students reading the text, taking dictation, and working on spelling. Comprehension and grammar were emphasized; students also conjugated various verbs and nouns used in the basic text.

In the advanced class the lesson, based on the day's text, aimed at comprehension of the subject matter, grammatical understanding, and proper spelling. Morais tried to draw his students into Portuguese conversation throughout the class because he feels student skills in this area are most in need of attention.

My observation, corroborated by interviews with teachers, revealed the major emphasis of the school to be Portuguese language training. Because most students lacked Portuguese fluency, the class level in Portuguese school was lower than in American schools. History and other subjects were taught in the school, but they typically constituted an indirect approach to general language instruction. In the beginning class, for example, there was a discussion of a project in which students would write letters to their families in Portugal. Students drew comparisons between elements of life in Portugal and the United States throughout the discussion. "All we do here is to compare America to Portugal . . . ," says Claudina Nunes. "Something we got in America, we got in Portugal. You know, they are just kids, but I choose the easier way to take them to Portugal—in thinking." On the night I observed the class such comparisons were made by students who actually had visited Portugal.

Again in the intermediate class actual language learning was emphasized and other subjects entered the lesson obliquely. For example, Malhinha explained some basic science concerning the sun as part of text comprehension. He also made a comparison to the homeland while discussing the text, noting that one could not see the sea in Taunton, but that in the Azores "all the time we see the sea around us." He explained that subjects such as mathematics were left for American schools, and Portuguese history was done in the advanced class; in this classroom history was mentioned only to elucidate a particular text, because teaching Portuguese history is difficult. "We have a big problem with Portuguese history, 'cause it's more than eight hundred years."

Fernando Morais, teacher of the advanced class and school principal, elaborated on the subjects taught in the Portuguese school. He emphasized that the basic subject was language itself. Each class includes reading, spelling, conversation, and social studies, which he defines as "The way the people live in Portugal ... where the population is ... the Portuguese climate, the main products grown, the main source of Portuguese income." Only the advanced class studies Portuguese history as a separate subject.

As previously noted, the texts are provided free of charge by the Portuguese Ministry of Education, except for a few purchased in a New Bedford Portuguese bookstore when the school began. Many bear a Taunton Sports stamp—ESCOLA OFICIAL DO ENSINO PRIMARIO DO TAUNTON SPORTS CLUB, INC./BAKER ROAD/TAUNTON, MASSACHUSETTS 02780—and the Portuguese Ministry of Education stamp—OFERTA/ INSTITUTO DE CULTURA E LINGUA PORTUGUESA SERVICOS DE ENSINO BASICO E SECUNDARIO PORTUGUES NO ESTRANGEIRO. The paperback texts are colorful, recent publications from the late 1970s and later. All of the texts are used in schools in Portugal as well.

Until just before my fieldwork began there had not been sufficient texts for each class. Trying to treat each school equally, the Portuguese consulate forwarded only three to five copies of a text, forcing the teacher to use several texts in one class, or to make offset copies for each student. The teachers are encouraged that there are now finally enough copies of texts for each class. The Ministry of Education also has provided a map of Portugal, dictionaries, and literary works for each classroom.

Those interviewed emphasized that all teachers are free to choose the text and specific lesson they wish. Sometimes teachers proceed sequentially through a particular book. At other times they may skip from text to text.

Fernando Morais noted that he chose suitable lessons which would be understandable to his students. For cases in which aspects of the lesson were foreign to his students, he acted as a bridge between the Portuguese setting of the book and the American setting of the students. Morais gave the example of encountering texts which mentioned birds native to Portugal but not to the United States, which he described before proceeding with the text.

Just as the teacher acts as a bridge between text and student, the Portuguese Ministry of Education coordinator, Emilia Mendonça, also is faced with the job of adapting curriculum to the American setting. At the monthly meeting with teachers she presents materials she has written for Portuguese schools in the United States. During the April meeting which I observed she explained several sets of duplicated pages to the teachers, including a map lesson to familiarize students with a typical Portuguese environment and an exercise which allowed them to purchase a stamp or bus ticket.

Teachers are actively involved in the process of selecting appropriate books. Fernando Morais showed me one book, *Imagens de Portugal*, which had impressed him as particularly valuable. "In other words, by reading this book the person is going back home, like on a trip." There

Broadway Bakery, Taunton, Massachusetts. (ES82-198072-3-3A) Photo by Victoria Westover

One of the drawings of the local community made by a student for the Portuguese School's "Day of Portugal" program. (ES82-198072-4-7A) Photo by Victoria Westover

are only a couple of copies of this book available; as a consequence, he has been able to use it only in a limited way. He is ordering copies for each of his students for next year, as well as for interested parents. The book describes each part of Portugal, presenting traditional recipes and songs.

Several of the books sent by the Portuguese Ministry of Education are not actual texts, but are books on subjects such as the selected texts of the famous poet Luís De Camoẽs. In the future the books sent from Portugal may serve as the basis of a Portuguese library for students, parents, and interested members of the community.

The three teachers stressed the difficulty of teaching only four hours a week at a time of day when the children are tired. The students come to Portuguese school having already spent a full day in American schools, attending the school at their customary dinner hour. Nunes and Morais both said they worked to gain students' attention through games. Claudina Nunes, for example, divides her class into two teams which compete in a dictation exercise at the blackboard. The children obviously loved the exercise and cheered when she announced it. Nunes also places examples of the best student work on the classroom walls. "They get so excited, and this way I think I can take their attention to what I am doing," she says of her methods.

Morais ran a week-to-week spelling contest for his advanced students, with each student competing for individual points. The four winners received a copy of one of the general books sent from Portugal. Judging from the intense discussion by students concerning the contest rules, it was clear that Morais captured their attention.

A constant theme expressed by both parents and teachers was the intention that Portuguese school work should not interfere with students' American school work. The Portuguese school teachers never gave any homework assignments to their students until recently. They are now experimenting with limited amounts of homework. For example, Morais asked for four-sentence essays, and was pleased with the results. "Usually I ask them to do things which get them together with their parents on finding out things about the old country—old stories, traditions," he explains. "That way, father and son, father and daughter get together and talk about old ... the things in their motherland. The kids can learn an awful lot by doing that."

Certain special projects are carried on throughout the school year. The advanced class made drawings depicting Portuguese emigration around the world which were sent to the Ministry of Education in Lisbon to compete with those of Portuguese school students outside the homeland. Other projects of limited length included the one undertaken by the beginning class of preparing its own newspaper *O Nosso Journal.*

The major project of the school year was in honor of the Day of Portugal on June 10. This year's theme, announced in Lisbon, was "The Day of Portugal and Portuguese Communities." Principal Fernando Morais selected as the school's essay theme "Please explain in your own words in what way have the Portuguese contributed to the development in our community." Students also made drawings on the theme. The essays and drawings were displayed in the school's hallway for viewing by parents and friends during the Day of Portugal soccer games held at the club on June 9 and after graduation on June 25.

The drawings depicted Portuguese-owned neighborhood markets, garages, and furniture stores; the Portuguese school itself; various Portuguese occupations in the area, such as fishing, farming, and factory work; and Portuguese homes with grapevines in the yard. The essays described how the hard-working Portuguese are employed in local factories or operate their own businesses. They described soccer, festas, and elements of the ethnic community communications system such as Portuguese newspapers, radio stations, and television programs. The pervasive influence of Portuguese food on the surrounding population was also a constant theme. The Portuguese consul was so impressed by the work that he awarded special first- and second-prize certificates for drawings and essays to students from each class during the graduation ceremony.

Steve Almeida, an eighth grader in the advanced class, described the Portuguese community in a prize-winning essay translated for me by Fernando Morais:

The dream of the Portuguese when he goes to a different country is to improve and better his way of life. When he arrives, he works hard, saves his money, and makes lots of sacrifices in order to make his dreams come true. The Portuguese immigrant is a hard worker. He likes to pay his debts, because he is honest and proud. He wants to have nice and beautiful things and he keeps his name clean. Lots of Portuguese buy old houses. They make improvements and they become just like new. Other Portuguese have their own businesses, for instance, Antonio Amaral, Mr. Caramelo, and José Fernandes, and many others. Others go to school and study. Later they become lawyers, doctors, teachers, and priests. One of the most important figures is Cardinal Humberto Medeiros. Others work in markets, factories, and offices. The streets where the Portuguese live keep looking much better. The houses have been improved. There are beautiful gardens, beautiful statues of saints near the beautiful houses. The Portuguese like to maintain their traditions; that's why we have our festas, mostly religious, at Santo Antonio church and Nossa Senhora de Lourdes, at the PACC, Taunton Sports and our school, and the Day of Portugal.

Student Language Capabilities

Students come to the Portuguese school with a previous knowledge of Portuguese. The majority of students have parents born in Portugal and many were born in Portugal themselves. The typical home situation finds students hearing their parents and grandparents speak Portuguese while they reply in English. Antonio Amaral talked about such a situation in his family. "We always speak Portuguese. The kids answer in English. We are so involved that we sometimes don't recognize that they're speaking English back to us. The two languages work simultaneously. We don't try to correct them, that's why they understand. But they're kind of lazy speaking it, 'cause they're afraid it's not coming out."

The primary aim of the Portuguese school appears to be to provide the students with an increased fluency in Portuguese. "In this school that's what we're doing—we're pursuing the improvement in the Portuguese language," says Principal Morais.

We want them to learn and improve. But, of course, we know the Portuguese language is going to be their second language. We want to maintain our culture, and our customs, and everything, but we have to realize that English is the first language and Portuguese will be their second language. But, of course, when they meet Portuguese people, they socialize in Portuguese functions and they are going to use ... the Portuguese language. It won't be lost there. They know how to communicate and they know how to deal with those things.

The students' prime fluency in English intrudes upon the classroom situation and general school environment. One night, while setting up a tape recorder before class, I overheard some girls having an English conversation in the classroom. A boy entered the room, took a look at me, and told the girls, "This is a Portuguese school, not English!" One girl replied that class had not begun and continued to speak English.

Students always spoke English with one another before and after class. During class students continued to address each other in English. Claudina Nunes, like the other teachers, found it impossible to limit classes to Portuguese language usage. "We can never get this from the kids," she says, "because they already have the idea to speak in English, even if they are joking or anything. They just try to speak English ..., they just speak English. All the time I say, 'No English, just Portuguese!' But forget it!"

English fluency creates certain difficulties in learning Portuguese. Advanced students, for example, already have a good knowledge of English grammar, which may confuse them at times. Morais laughed as he told how he would explain certain grammatical rules and students would tell him, "No, you are wrong!" based on their understanding of English grammar.

In his short time at the school the intermediate teacher José Malhinha has seen progress in the reading and writing abilities of his students. Morais, the teacher of the advanced class, gauges the improvement of his students by the fact that he no longer has to remind them continually not to speak English. "At first they were shy [to speak Portuguese]. Now every day they are more and more comfortable."

Students

The students have mixed attitudes toward attending Portuguese school. They frequently explained that they go to Portuguese school because their parents want them to go; yet there are others who were excited about Portuguese school and said they would attend without parental urging. Most teachers and administrators, however, would agree with Fernando Morais's assessment: "I believe a good part of them are there because their parents want them to be."

Since the Portuguese live throughout the city, students may come to school without knowing other students. The children are able to meet new friends at the school and develop a social network with a Portuguese affiliation. "I guess in this school everybody has something in common with you 'cause you're Portuguese and the same thing at home. Whereas in [high] school your culture is different from everyone else's, and you might not have as many things in common," explains Teresa Amaral, a student in the advanced class. Students are enthusiastic about the new friends they have made through Portuguese school, and talked of telephoning their friends or even visiting them at home. Other students said they had the same friends in both Portuguese and American school.

Speaking of what they have learned at Portuguese school, students emphasized language skills, mentioning improvements in writing (especially spelling) and speaking. Steve Almeida felt he had improved in his Portuguese reading and writing skills, but thought his greatest progress was in his speaking skills. Teresa Amaral was enthusiastic about her improved Portuguese skills, especially her ability to write letters to a girl she had met on a recent trip to Portugal. Parents also told of seeing children reading Portuguese newspapers in the home, or of noticing their improved comprehension of the language at functions, such as plays performed in Portuguese.

Teachers

Without exception teachers indicated that they taught in the Portuguese school out of love for teaching and love for their culture. The teachers' salary of $100 per month certainly does not compensate them for their efforts of teaching classes, attending teachers' meetings and school functions, and preparing and grading lessons at home. All of them hold full-time jobs outside of Taunton and have to rush to arrive at school on time.

Fernando Morais expressed the wish that he could teach full time, rather than work as a manager at Christy's Market. "I'll be planning to teach for as long as I can. I love this!" Claudina Nunes, who provides a warm, maternal guidance for her young students, comes to the school tired from a day's work as a machine operator. After class she resumes her home duties by cooking supper. The vitality she exhibits in class fades when she leaves the school. "Over here I'm just excited, I don't feel nothing. But when I get out of here, oh my God!" José Malhinha was happy to accept the position recently offered him by Principal Morais, his former classmate. "I never talk about the money, because I know they don't pay too much. . . . I like to teach again my own language."

The teachers possess the background of teacher's training and teaching experience in the Portuguese elementary school system required by the Portuguese Ministry of Education. All three teachers emigrated to the United States as adults, accompanied by their immediate families. While they have had experience in the Portuguese system, none were familiar with the textbooks now used in the Portuguese school in Taunton. Malhinha explained that there was only one official book for each class before the 1976 revolution in Portugal; but numerous books have been written since.

Despite some adaptation, the curriculum of the official Portuguese school in Taunton is rooted firmly in the Portuguese system. José Malhinha made some interesting comparisons between the two systems, however. Throughout the class I observed he made comments contrasting procedures in Portuguese school with those in American schools. He observed that Portuguese students write in script on standard-size paper, while American students print on all types of paper. He was also surprised that his present students chew gum in class; in homeland schools there is strict discipline. There is, nevertheless, considerable discipline in the

Taunton Portuguese school, reinforced by parental cooperation. One mother was overheard telling a teacher to pull her son's ears if he did not behave, and a young boy commented that the main difference between Portuguese and American schools was that the Portuguese school teachers are more strict.

The teachers meet monthly after a Wednesday class. Emilia Mendonça usually attends these meetings to introduce supplementary materials. Principal Morais leads these sessions in her absence. There is no interaction with teachers from other Portuguese schools in the area.

Considering the American setting, the requirements for teachers are somewhat demanding—copies of teachers' certificates of graduation and resumes must be forwarded to the Ministry of Education in Lisbon by the New Bedford Portuguese consul for approval. This process takes several months and, therefore, the school began without approval. All teachers have been approved to date and the school has not had to give up its official status. Principal Morais feels that finding additional teachers will not be a problem. When one second year teacher was forced to quit suddenly at the end of the year, he located his former classmate Malhinha, whom he knew was qualified.

Purposes of the School

The primary reason given for the existence of the school is language instruction. The teachers are very conscious of the importance of language study. "They should learn Portuguese too. I think it's very important that they learn Portuguese like they learn English," says beginning class teacher Claudina Nunes.

First thing is, this way they can communicate with the family. Because, like you see, we got a lot of kids, they have grandparents here, and it's sad they cannot deal with grandparents 'cause they don't know, you know, they don't speak English.... We think it's sad. And they go, you know, so often to Portugal to visit with the family over there, and [when] they go, they don't speak nothing Portuguese. They don't understand what the family ... means or they talk about. We think this way—the English is ... the first language for everybody, but to learn the second language, their language, is going to be better, for the good.

Malhinha forsees the day when the students, competent in both English and Portuguese, will graduate from colleges and technical schools and will be an asset to the Portuguese community, assisting other community members who are not fluent in English. Fernando Morais feels language preservation is a means of preserving culture. "More or less, it starts with the parents," he says. "The parents come to us, and they say 'We want our son or daughter to learn the language and the history.' Some of these kids were born there [Portugal]. Some were born here. But there is this concern on the part of the parents for the children to learn the language, the correct way to speak fluently, because we want to preserve our culture and we want them to pass our culture to future generations as well." Elaborating from his own experience, he adds:

If the kids are tired, the teachers are tired too [laughs]! We have a whole day's work in our own jobs too. What happens is the children only see the present now. But later in life they will say "I should have learned Portuguese, why didn't I learn Portuguese!?" This is an example I see everyday. I see people from Portuguese descent, and they were born in this country, and they say "Why didn't I listen to my grandmother, grandfather? I could have learned the language with them."

Parents view the purpose of the school in both practical and cultural terms. Cândido Almeida, parent of two school children and a school director himself, spoke of the general enriching experience of learning several languages. Almeida also sees his children's learning "the language of their ancestors" as a basic part of the preservation of their ethnic heritage. He described the preservation of culture as being like constructing a building—you have to start with a foundation or the building will be destroyed—and language is the foundation of culture.

Antonio Amaral, school president and father of three students, sees his children's language training in practical and ethnic-heritage terms. "I like for them to learn the language, first of all, because it's a plus in whatever they become in the future. Secondly, it's to preserve our customs and ways, and that means a lot because, not that *we're* different, but every ethnic group is different. And we like to have things that we'd like to preserve in our culture." Later he elaborated on the school's function. "I think the school helps by teaching our youngsters our essential things, you know. Also, by getting them together with one another, they lose that shyness that they would have if they were not together. In American school, I believe, many of them avoid to say 'I'm Portuguese,' or even to say a word in Portuguese. But by being together with so many that speak the same language or think the same way, they might not be ashamed, and they might be aware of the fact they're also important."

Amaral also sees the Portuguese school as serving the local society and country at large:

But, nevertheless, we're doing a service to this country. In a way we're preparing better citizens for the future, because I'm sure they [the students] are going to stay here for the rest of their lives. And giving them extra knowledge of another foreign language, makes it easier for them to learn French or Spanish in the future, if they want to take those courses in the high school. It will prepare them better for high school also, because they already have experience with a foreign language. And it keeps them, above all, out of the streets in their free time, which is a problem, because most of the kids today don't have anything else to do after school. If they are out in the street, they get into problems. After all, it's a social service.

Reiterating his belief that an ethnic language and heritage school, such as the Taunton Portuguese school, serves the good of the country, Amaral addressed a final interview comment to the American government:

I'd like to know how the American government sees this project in these private schools. . . . They do encourage or don't they? Is that a pro or against the principles? I think that's a fair question. To me, I think it's a pro, because this country is not any longer a melting pot. We all have something different to offer, and the more we offer, the better the country will be. Right? We cannot say just the Irish are the good ones, or the English, the South Americans, or the colored people. They all have something good and something bad. . . .

Twenty-two years ago, when I came, there was the tendency that we all have to be American regardless. We all have to melt into it, you know, it was the idea, that ideal. Then it changed with the bilingual programs and the trying to accept everyone's ideas and cultures, which is good. It's good! That's what made this nation so big, so great—right?—was everybody working to the same goals—a better life for everybody. That's my comments.

The role of the Portuguese school in maintaining the Portuguese ethnic heritage must be judged against the background of the local community. The graduation ceremony on June 25 underscored the Portuguese sense of community. The highlight of the occasion was the official visit by Dr. José Adriano Gago Vitorino, the Portuguese Secretary of State for Emigration, whose department supplies the funds to support official Portuguese schools in the United States. He inaugurated the school addition and gave the key graduation address. The graduation ceremony rang with culturally important phrases, such as "Portuguese community," "our culture," "our language," and "the Portuguese family." Students delivered dramatic interpretations of Portuguese poetry, and the honored speakers—Dr. Vitorino, the New Bedford Portuguese consul, the president of the Taunton Sports Club, a local Portuguese priest, and the school president—praised the community for its work in maintaining the Portuguese heritage through their school.

Future of the Escola Oficializada Portuguesa do Taunton Sports Club

The school anticipates continued growth. After the graduation ceremonies school president Amaral said that next year he hopes to have an additional Tuesday and Thursday session. He also noted that, based on the size of Taunton's Portuguese community, a two-hundred-student enrollment could be expected in the future. Some advertisements of the school will be placed in Portuguese newspapers and churches in the area to attract students, but no concerted campaign will be launched. Amaral prefers to have students come to the school voluntarily. "It's available to those who want it."

Amaral would like to have tape recorders and slide projectors available at the school to take advantage of additional materials offered by the Ministry of Education. He also hopes to develop extracurricular activities in addition to the soccer team and folklore group for the students. "It's a million things we can offer if we have the money and facilities."

Fieldwork Techniques

The informants in this project were most cooperative. I feel that being a native of the area helped to provide credibility for me. I came to this project unfamiliar with Portuguese culture, which I remedied through research, and without the Portuguese language, although I did have my college French. Since all my informants spoke English, I was able to feel comfortable in the field situation and do not feel that my lack of Portuguese was detrimental to the project. Comparing this work to my previous experience of working in a language other than English in which I was fluent, I believe that my unfamiliarity with the Portuguese language and culture was advantageous to the project—it allowed me to distinguish Portuguese ethnic characteristics from the perspective of an outsider.

Acknowledgments

I would like to thank the administrators, teachers, parents, students, and friends of the Escola Oficializada Portuguesa do Taunton Sports Club for their generous cooperation. This project could not have been accomplished without their kind assistance and continuous aid. I would like to offer special thanks to those who provided translation services. I finish this project profoundly impressed with the commitment and energy shown by those involved with the school. It was with great personal pleasure that I came to know and respect the members of the Taunton Portuguese community and to appreciate their efforts in the maintenance of the Portuguese language and ethnic heritage in the United States.

Notes

1. Leo Pap, *The Portuguese-Americans* (Boston: Twayne Publishers, 1981), pp. 44–46.

2. *The World Almanac and Book of Facts* (New York: Newspaper Enterprise Association, Inc., 1982), p. 218.

3. Pap, p. 85.

4. Pap, p. 85.

5. It is common for three generations of a Portuguese family to live in the same household.

The First Korean School
Silver Spring, Maryland

Lucy M. Long

In 1982 an estimated 600,000 Koreans and Korean-Americans were living in the United States, congregated in three major population centers: Los Angeles (with about 200,000 Korean residents), Chicago, and New York. San Francisco and Washington, D.C., have the next largest Korean populations. The Korean Embassy estimates that between 35,000 and 40,000 Koreans live in the Washington metropolitan area, the locale of the school in this study.

The majority of the Korean population in the United States arrived after the 1950s. The Washington, D.C., population is even more recent—there since the 1970s.[1] The first generation of Koreans born in America is now coming of age, and the problems they face are new ones for the Korean community.

Many Koreans immigrating to the United States do so for occupational or educational reasons. Others want to escape what they feel is an overly competitive and restrictive society in Korea. Still others come to provide their children with opportunities they might not have in their homeland. By emigrating, many give up established careers, social status, and economic security. Their first years here are often a struggle for survival, full of long hours at low paying jobs. Even so, most Korean immigrants succeed financially in the United States, often achieving economic stability within five or ten years. Many of them own their homes and businesses and send their children to the best schools and colleges.

Korean School principal, Mr. Han-il Lee, points to the words on a chart as students sing. (ES82-195616-3-30) Photo by Carl Fleischhauer

Koreans have a great deal of pride in their heritage. Their history, which extends back five thousand years, has been a continuous struggle to maintain an identity distinct from that of Japan and China. The small country has nurtured many scholars, artists, and inventors. A respect for tradition and the past, which is reinforced by the contemporary achievements of Koreans, is an integral part of Korean culture. On the whole, Koreans living in the United States have retained their cultural pride; they maintain a distinctive personal ethnic identity and express a community identity through numerous ethnic organizations.

Christian churches, particularly Presbyterian and Baptist, function as the central social organization in many Korean communities. Washington, D.C., has over sixty Korean churches, many of which have their own buildings. They offer a variety of services to the Korean community, including Korean language classes for children. Approximately twelve Washington-area churches sponsor such classes.

In some respects, the Korean population in the Washington metropolitan area is not typical of other Korean communities. Its members have a higher level of education and income than Koreans in other parts of the country, and they tend to be more recent arrivals. They also appreciate the need for language and culture maintenance, supporting a total of twenty-four language schools.[2]

History of the First Korean School

The First Korean School was established on June 5, 1977, by the First Korean Baptist Church of Silver Spring, Maryland. The school became an incorporated institution within the state of Maryland separate from the church on April 10, 1979. As of spring 1982, it maintains relations with the church, but is growing increasingly independent in financial and policy matters. It is also growing in size and reputation.

The school is located in Silver Spring, Maryland, in the annex and basement classrooms of the First Korean Baptist Church. Situated on Georgia Avenue, five miles beyond the Washington, D.C., beltway, the church is surrounded by Maryland suburbs. Korean lettering on a sign in front of the building is the only indication of the church's ethnic identity.

Over 150 kindergarten, elementary, junior high, and high school students attend the First Korean School. A faculty of thirteen teachers and two administrators teach the classes in Korean language, music, dance, and martial arts. The primary emphasis is on Korean language (both reading and speaking), but other subjects are included to attract the children's interest and to expose them to Korean culture and values.

Classes meet every Saturday from 9:30 A.M. to 1:00 P.M. and follow the American public school calendar, with summer and winter vacations. The school celebrates most American holidays, as well as selected Korean ones. Students enroll by semester and receive report cards and certificates of achievement at the end of the school year.

Although the school is nominally independent of the church in which its classes are held, members of the First Korean Baptist Church play important roles in the school's administration. The church also provides classroom space and utilities, but in all other ways the school is self-supporting, earning funds for faculty salaries and supplies from the students' tuition fees.

The First Korean School was created by a small group of Korean immigrants living in the Maryland suburbs of Washington, D.C. Mr. Han-il Lee, the current principal, initiated the idea and spearheaded the organization of the school, aided by church and community leaders.

Before starting the school Mr. Lee sought advice from a number of people involved in ethnic language education. The Washington Korean School created in 1970, the oldest Korean school in the Washington metropolitan area, provided an example of an established school. The Korean Embassy's office of education, which works with Korean ethnic schools throughout the country, supplied other models, as well as official support and a representative to the school board. Mr. Lee also drew ideas from other ethnic communities—specifically, Finnish, Polish, Jewish, Chinese, and Japanese—and their organizations.

Mr. Lee also organized the original financing of the school. He obtained approximately one-third of the funds for supplies and administrative expenses from the First Korean Baptist Church, which considered this aid to be part of its Christian service to the Korean community. The rest was paid for by students' tuitions. The church also provided free use of their facilities and utilities.

The Korean Embassy gave the school free textbooks. Although the embassy provides funding for administrative costs to language programs requesting such aid, the First Korean School was ineligible at first because of its connection with the Korean Baptist Church. The embassy cannot support church-sponsored schools since the Korean government claims to have no official religion. When the school later became independent, its administrators did not request funding from the embassy because they felt the tuition payments sufficed for the school's administrative needs. The embassy later donated a library of some ten thousand books of Korean literature to the school for use both by children and adults. The school plans to organize a national library-loan system by which Korean schools in other areas can borrow from their library.

In the first years of its existence the school was run primarily by Mr. Han-il Lee. He designed the curriculum, class structure, and school schedule. He also printed the handouts used by all classes to supplement their texts in his own print shop in suburban Maryland. He prints all materials for the school at cost.

Mr. Han-il Lee was principal of the school during its first two years. His official duties included budget matters, policy decisions, and faculty hiring. Dr. Lee, associate pastor of the First Korean Baptist Church, replaced Mr. Han-il Lee as principal in 1979. After one year Dr. Lee returned to Korea to a university position; his place was filled by Mr. Hee-Kyu Park, former chief of education at the Korean Embassy. Mr. Park was principal for several months. Then Mr. Han-il Lee returned to the post and remains school principal.

Mr. Lee is currently seeking another principal. He feels that the position should be filled by someone with academic degrees from a prestigious institution, who enjoys community status and respect. He sees the principal as a figurehead who will lend his status and reputation to the school. Although he has been principal several times, Mr. Lee's lack of a university degree makes him uncomfortable in the role.

The job of vice-principal was not formally established until the 1981–82 school year, when Mr. Han-il Lee requested it. The faculty then elected one of its members, Mr. Koh, to the position.

Since its creation the Korean School has had a governing board that makes policy decisions. Mr. Lee and the leaders of the First Korean Baptist Church chose the first board. They established a seven- to nine-member organization that included three official church members: the pastor, the director of Christian education, and the president of the parents association. Representatives from the Korean community, some of whom were specialists in relevant fields, filled the other positions. About 50 percent of the board were church members, and most were parents. The board was also divided evenly between United States citizens and recent immigrants. Although board membership has changed over the years, Mr. Lee has tried to insure a mixture of backgrounds to obtain a broad range of opinions.

Purposes of the School

While the First Korean School identifies itself as a language school for teaching the "mother tongue" to Korean descendents, its administrators state that its primary purpose is to create good Korean-American citizens. They believe that the more a child understands and appreciates his ethnic heritage, the better person he will become and the more smoothly his acculturation into American society will be accomplished. By giving him the opportunity to know his background, the school provides the child with more options to choose from when he begins to develop his own perspective on his ethnic identity. These goals can best be accomplished by teaching the Korean language, using it as a vehicle for transmitting Korean values and beliefs, as well as knowledge about Korean culture and history.

Facilitating communication between generations is another major concern of the Korean School. Language is often a barrier between parents and children, particularly since many Korean families are recent immigrants. Because of their interaction with native-born English-speakers through their schooling, the children usually learn English within a few years of their arrival, while the parents take much longer. Often parents and grandparents never become fluent in the language and speak Korean among themselves and in their homes. As Mr. Noh, the sixth grade teacher and a board member, says:

Their mother tongue, Korean, is needed as a tool of communication between generations. Sometimes, the first generation and second generation . . . find a gap [in] communicating with each other later on. Then, make kind of tragedy in the immigrant family. So we worry about [it]. Their mother tongue is basically a tool for communication in the immigrant family. (ES82-LL-R7)

The language barrier is particularly obvious in homes where grandparents are living with the family.

School administrators are also concerned that differences in values and attitudes may create inter-generational barriers just as troublesome as language. Principal Lee described a representative incident in which a story in a school publication was misunderstood by the students. The story concerned a famous Korean general who often visited a wine shop in his youth. One day, while riding his horse, he fell asleep. The horse continued walking and carried him to the wine shop. When the general awoke and found himself there, he realized that he had become addicted to wine. He then killed his horse and began leading an upright life, eventually becoming a great hero.

Mr. Lee explained that the moral of this story is that one must dispose of bad influences if one wants to succeed in life. The horse was aiding the general's addiction and therefore had to be destroyed. The Korean parents recognized this moral and agreed with it. Their children, however, saw no nobility in the general's actions and felt that he was cruel for needlessly killing his horse. Such different interpretations reflect different values and codes of behavior. Mr. Lee hopes that the school will help the children understand their parents' attitudes and values. He recognizes that the children may not agree with them, but at least they will know what the values are, and may later choose to accept them.

Many of the adult Koreans at the school have a strong sense of their own Korean identity and heritage. They are proud to be Korean and feel strong emotional ties with their motherland. They also feel that an appreciation for Korean ways is a valuable and precious possession, one that should be passed on to future generations. Their involvement in the school is generated partly by these attitudes. "We don't want to forget [our Korean heritage]," explains Mr. Noh. "We don't have to get out of that kind of cultural resource. That means that [it] is a kind of mission of the first generation" (ES82-LL-R7).

The administrators are concerned with both the immediate and long-term welfare of the students and of the Korean-American community. The school offers the language classes not only to transmit knowledge of a cultural heritage but also to provide a central place where Korean-American children can be with others of their background, a place where they can feel comfortable and have a sense of belonging. School administrators hope that the children will maintain the relationships that begin there, strengthening their ties within the Korean-American community.

The administrators are further concerned with the success of the children in achieving their long-term educational and professional goals, most of which are set very high. Along with instruction and guidance at the school, they try to provide role models by exposing the children to ethnic Americans who are successful. In terms of the future welfare of the children, the administration believes that it can help most by encouraging them to set high goals. As Mr. Han-il Lee says:

If you buy a ticket—airplane, bus, train—from here [Washington] to San Francisco, you can get off anywhere along the way. But a ticket to New York, takes you only to New York. In life, [one has] only one chance. If [one has] a big goal, [one] can go far. If have small goals, only go a small distance. So ... Korean school tries to give students big goals. (ES82-LL-R16)

School Administration

The school's administrators include a school board, the principal, and the vice-principal. The board determines the overall budget and policy matters, such as the purpose and emphasis of the school. The principal handles most administrative details—hiring, application of budget, class schedules, school calendar—and develops a broad outline of the skills and knowledge to be taught to each class during each semester. The vice-principal assists the principal in his duties. An administrative assistant also aids the principal, acting as secretary, treasurer, and substitute teacher, preparing the students' morning refreshments, and keeping track of supplies.

In 1980 the congregation constructed a new church building. The completed structure houses the main sanctuary, church administrative offices, a kitchen, reception area, and classrooms for the school's upper grades. The old building was designated as the education building, to be used for Sunday school classes, the Korean school, and other community activities. In addition to school classrooms, the building has a smaller sanctuary and a kitchen.

Having a place of its own has made a tremendous difference for the school. It has the space to accommodate the growing number of students. It can store its teaching and administrative materials there, and also has a room set aside for the library donated by the embassy.

The church grounds include an old house, where the library was stored until fall of 1982, a small playground, and an extensive parking lot. Students often use the basketball hoop and picnic tables by the parking lot during their class breaks.

Except for the facilities and utilities provided by the Korean Church, the school is financed wholly by the students' tuitions. Seventy percent of these funds go to faculty salaries. The remaining 30 percent covers supplies and miscellaneous expenses, such as year-end awards—notebooks, pencils, crayons, books, and certificates—and the handouts used as teaching aids. The Korean Embassy donated the textbooks. Students use them in class, but cannot buy them or take them home.

Each student pays $60 per semester. Families having more than one child enrolled receive discounts: 10 percent for two children and 30 percent for three or more. Scholarships or tuition remissions are available to needy children. Korean children adopted into American or Korean-American homes are also eligible for scholarships. Beginning next year Mr. Lee hopes to offer a reduced tuition to children of mixed marriages.

The school also charges a snack fee to cover the cost of the juice, doughnuts, and fruit served every Saturday morning. Children who ride the school vans pay an additional fee of $5 to $10 each month, depending on the distance from the child's home to the school. Karate uniforms and dance leotards are an additional expense.

Teachers receive an average of $8 an hour for four hours of teaching each Saturday. A sliding pay scale reflects experience and training, but the payment amounts to little more than an honorarium. Some of the teachers double as drivers for the three school vans and receive an hourly wage for their additional work.

The church owns one of the vans and lends it to the school. The other two are privately owned by faculty members. The school also owns its

At the Korean School in Silver Spring, Maryland, Miss Boon-Yi Kwak watches as a student writes an answer on the blackboard. In the background, fieldworker Lucy Long records the session. (ES82-195616-2-13A) Photo by Carl Fleischhauer

own bus, but uses it only when a sizeable number of students need transportation.

The Korean school also runs Scholastic Aptitude Test (SAT) preparation courses for high school students. American teachers brought in from a local high school teach the courses in the evening at the church. Students pay $7.50 an hour for the two-hour sessions held twice a week.

Classes and Curriculum

The focus of activity at the First Korean School is the teaching of the Korean language. Language exercises are, therefore, the most prominent part of the curriculum.

The school originally placed the students into three different levels in accordance with their language skill. The classes cut across age and school grade, placing seventh graders with first graders. The students disliked the mixing, and the school subsequently changed to a system corresponding to the childrens' age and American-school grade. The new system has proven to be relatively satisfactory, and nine grade levels now exist: kindergarten, first through sixth grades, junior high, and senior high.

Another class, the Special Class, provides children of any grade with remedial help in reading and writing Korean and basic vocabulary. Sometimes a child will be placed in a higher or lower grade if he or she lacks certain skills. Some of the children were embarrassed that they were in a lower grade—one said that she had flunked out of the other class. Because the children tend to interpret such actions in this way, the teachers try to keep the children in their respective grades.

No standard tests are given to students to assess their ability or skills. Each teacher is responsible for monitoring the progress of their students. The system of grouping the students results in a wide range of abilities in each class and poses structuring difficulties for the teachers. The school is still searching for a system that would better accomodate the range of skills and abilities displayed by each age group. The principal hopes to get ideas from other ethnic schools. In the meantime, Mr. Han-il Lee has suggested that they divide the class into three levels and give separate assignments to each level, but this is the teacher's option.

These basic classes focus on Korean language skills: reading, writing, vocabulary, grammar, and conversation. Reading exercises are based on handouts, textbooks, and sentences and phrases written on the blackboard. The students usually take turns reading out loud, although some teachers have their students read out loud together.

The reading lessons often include traditional Korean stories. Students in one fourth-grade class chose characters in a story and read those parts out loud. Teachers also use the stories for question and answer sessions to test the students' comprehension.

Writing exercises usually involve copying text from the blackboard and from handouts. Quizzes which combine dictation and spelling are a standard part of most of the classes, and students often receive writing exercises for homework.

Once students have acquired the basic skills of reading and writing, vocabulary and grammar lessons make up a major part of their class time. They receive vocabulary words to learn at home, which they practice in class. Grammar lessons often involve building phrases and sentences out of the new words.

Korean conversation also figures in most of the classes. Teachers often generate conversation by asking questions in Korean. They also encourage students to speak Korean throughout the day, but the children invariably speak English among themselves.

All the teachers use standardized Korean textbooks donated by the Korean Embassy, but most of them feel that they are inadequate for Korean-American children. The students often use texts several grades behind them, since they lack the vocabulary to understand the ones for their own age group, and the subjects, people, and places mentioned in the texts tend to be foreign to their experiences. "Our situation is different—everyday life, thinking, everything is different for students here from the textbooks. So they need something they know," says Mr. Noh. (ES82-LL-R8)

Most of the teachers design handouts to supplement the textbooks. They also write their own tests and quizzes. In this way, while helping the school develop a reservoir of unique teaching materials, they can address the individual skills and interests of their classes. Each teacher also determines the amount and type of homework assigned in class.

From the beginning the school has included music and martial arts along with its language classes. Dance was added several years ago. The evening course to prepare students for the SAT college entrance exams got under way in 1979.

The administration hopes that the extracurricular classes will entertain the students and provide a break from language study. They are concerned that the children, finding the language classes too demanding and tedious, may lose interest in Korean. They also hope that the extracurricular classes will expose the students to additional aspects of Korean culture and values.

All classes informally include Korean history, literature, and culture. Teachers sometimes give lectures on such subjects in the upper grades, but teachers for the younger students try to incorporate history and culture into reading and writing exercises.

Some teachers also include discussions of ethnicity in their classes. Ethnic topics are difficult to fit into the curriculum, since most of the students lack the vocabulary to understand complex ideas in Korean. The administration also hesitates to emphasize such issues, feeling that it is best to provide an environment in which the children can discuss their ethnicity when they are ready and feel comfortable doing so. As Mr. Lee explains:

> We cannot separate culture, or some history, or some custom [from] the language. So, basically, we teaching for Korean tongue. Korean writing is easy, so we push just for tongue. But if we push too much, they hate Korean language. So, first time, I suggest to teachers that you have to do is encourage in what is interesting. Attending here, they make friend of same skin or same color, so they enjoy school. Then, they grow up. If they have good memory . . . just keep tongue. . . . (ES82-LL-R22)

The principal has also found that the students are more receptive to discussions of ethnicity when they come from outsiders rather than members of the Korean community. Accordingly, he has invited two men—one Finnish and the other Polish—to talk to the students about maintaining their ethnic identities. In Mr. Lee's view the response was positive:

> Kids are very interested about that. Because if [I] push myself, they very [much] hate or are against [thinking about Korean identity]. But the other person, they [are] talking about themselves: "We keep our own heritage, we keep own language, then we [are] so proud." [They say], "Why don't you keep your own language and your own heritage?" Then, a little bit, they [the students] understand it. (ES82-LL-R22)

The school day is broken into five forty-five-minute periods, three of which are spent in the language homeroom classes. The other two are used for music and dance or martial arts. Usually girls take dancing and boys take martial arts, but a few girls choose the latter. Students are divided into three groups for their extracurricular classes: kindergarten through second grade, third through fifth grades, and sixth grade through high school.

At the end of the school year, every student receives a report card. The teachers design their own methods for computing a grade, but all of them use the following grade designations: excellent, good, satisfactory, and unsatisfactory or needs improvement. Most of them do not emphasize grades, but feel that the students work harder if they receive grades. The extracurricular classes have their own reward systems. Students who excel in music can join the children's choir sponsored by the Korean Baptist Church. The martial arts class follows a system used by all karate schools in which different colored belts represent levels of achievement, the highest being a black belt and the lowest being white.

Students who have done especially well in their classes receive certificates of achievement. At the 1982 graduation ceremony the names of those students receiving certificates were read to the audience while the students stood and were applauded. One child received an award for being the best student in the school, and another for making the most progress. Students graduate from Korean school when they finish American school, regardless of their Korean language skills. At that time they receive a diploma stating that they have attended the language program.

The school calendar parallels the one used by American public schools. The First Korean School usually starts classes in early September and ends them in early June. The administration plans for forty Saturdays of school, with five or six holidays. American public holidays are recognized but not celebrated by the school as a whole. Christian holidays—Christmas and Easter—are usually marked by some classroom activities. The only holidays celebrated by the entire school are two Korean ones: Chusok, the fall harvest festival, and Korean Independence Day on March 1. The school holds assemblies and parties to celebrate them.

Two issues frequently mentioned by the faculty are the emphasis given to the amount of knowledge a child should be expected to learn and the use of English in the classroom. Both are related to the school's desire to impart an understanding and love for Korean heritage to the students. Most of the teachers feel that language is a way to transmit those feelings and should not be an end in itself. The amount and quality of language skills are not as important as the attitudes a student has toward his ethnic identity and heritage. Classes, therefore, should be enjoyable, interesting for the students, and not too demanding. "They are so busy, and they are just little children. I don't want to give them too much work because, if I do, they will have no time to play, and they will hate Korean school," says one of the Special Class teachers.

The amount of English used in the classroom is resolved individually by each teacher. Principal Lee encourages them to speak Korean at all times, but recognizes that the students' level of comprehension makes it difficult:

If talk completely in Korean, they cannot catch [the meaning and] feelings. So sometimes, [for] important things, we explain in American. But, basically, we have [emphasize] learning the Korean tongue, so, if possible, have to use Korean. (ES82-LL-R22)

Most of the teachers try to speak primarily Korean in class, but find that they need English to explain vocabulary words and ideas and, sometimes, simply to keep the students' interest. "When I speak only Korean, they don't understand, and they get bored and don't learn," says Ok-Kyung Kim. "But when I use English, they are interested and can ask questions. Then they learn." (Interview 5/22/82)

Mr. Lee also feels that it is more important that the students gain an appreciation for their heritage than that they speak the language fluently. As he notes:

Sometimes they [teachers] explain in English, because they [students] cannot catch [understand], and they hate Korean. So if youngest are this way when they grow up, they cannot choose [to appreciate their heritage], and they will always hate Korean. So [we] have to pay attention to make [learning Korean] interesting. (ES82-LL-R22)

Plans for the future of the school include adding more subjects to the curriculum and expanding the extracurricular program. Mr. Lee is presently searching for someone to direct a school and community orchestra. He hopes to offer classes that would provide technical training and teach useful job skills, such as automobile maintenance and printing, and is also interested in starting hobby courses for adults and senior citizens. Several members of the school's faculty are presently working with a national association of Korean educators to design textbooks suitable for Korean-American students. They hope that the books will be ready for publication within the next two years.

Teachers

In its first year the faculty of the First Korean School consisted of six teachers, three of whom are still with the school. The first teachers included Mr. Han-Il Lee, Miss Kwak, Mr. Chang, and Miss Pak, all of whom taught the language classes. In addition, Mrs. Kwun taught music and Mr. Kim taught *taekwondo* (Korean martial arts). Mr. Kim continued with the school, teaching the high school class, and Miss Kwak now teaches the fourth grade. Mr. Lee, the principal, also teaches as a substitute.

The faculty now numbers thirteen teachers, although the number tends to fluctuate during the school year as teachers find they cannot afford the time and energy required, or move away. Appendix I provides information about the teachers employed during the spring semester of 1982.

A large number of the faculty and administration are members of the First Korean Baptist Church. While membership is not a requirement for hiring, the administration is concerned that the faculty share their values, many of which are based on a Christian belief system.

The school does not formally train its teachers or set requirements regarding the experience and background for hiring, but the administration does try to select teachers with previous training and experience. Most of the teachers are highly qualified for elementary and middle school teaching. At least seven have formal training in education from American or Korean institutions, and most of the teachers have had some experience working with children. Those who lack formal training or previous teaching experience compensate with understanding and concern for the students and with their commitment to the school.

Very few of the teachers have specific training for language education. Mr. Park, the junior high school teacher, is the only one involved professionally in teaching the Korean language. Some say that their previous teaching helps them in dealing with the children and structuring their classes, but not particularly with teaching the Korean language. Most find that their task is further complicated by the need to teach cultural values and heritage as well as language.

The principal provides guidelines for the classes, but the actual class development is left to the individual teacher. The faculty meets occasionally to plan the curriculum, discuss teaching methods, and gather teaching materials. The faculty usually meets with the principal briefly after the morning assembly to discuss immediate concerns and to exchange information. Teachers often gather informally during their morning breaks in the administrative office. This free interaction seems to create a good atmosphere among the faculty and administration. No single individual acts as an authority or expert; rather, all work together to develop the best possible teaching methods and materials. The Special Class, for example, resulted from the faculty's recognizing a need and designing a way to fulfill it.

While teaching Korean language is the primary emphasis of the classes, the more immediate concern of many of the teachers is maintaining the children's interest. Some do so by presenting lessons as games, or by changing activities whenever they sense boredom or fatigue among their students. Others try to create a relaxed and cheerful atmosphere. For example, the junior high school teacher purchased Ping-Pong equipment for his class to use during breaks, and another teacher periodically takes her class outside for a change of scenery.

Some of the teachers are concerned about discipline in the classrooms. One felt that the children, particularly the younger ones, lack discipline at home and in American school and need to receive a firm hand at the Korean school. Other teachers tended to be more tolerant in their judgments and expectations. Most agreed that the Korean language is demanding and that many of the children find it difficult. Their restlessness in class, they felt, is due more to the nature of the subject and the fact that it is Saturday than to a lack of discipline.

The second grade teacher, Mrs. Kim, proposed another reason behind her class' somewhat boisterous behavior:

They feel at home here. They're with children who are the same color, and many of them are their friends. Everybody is speaking the language they hear at home. It's not like at American school, where they feel they're a little bit different. Here they can be themselves. That's why they're a little noisy. (Interview 4/3/82)

During my observations of the classes I felt that the teachers were tolerant of students' behavior, but not lax. They usually allowed some degree of play and freedom among the students, but the classes never seemed out of control. If the class did become too noisy, the teachers usually quieted it by clapping their hands and calling for attention, or by speaking directly to the child. Discipline was always administered with good humor and affection.

The teachers' reasons for teaching at the Korean school are primarily altruistic. Some of the stated reasons include a feeling of responsibility toward the next generation, concern for the ethnic identity of the youth and the possible problems resulting from a lack of ethnic identity, concern for the future economic, social, and emotional welfare of the Korean community in the United States, and a love for Korean culture. Also mentioned were a sense of Christian duty to guide youth in the right direction, a calling to teach, and a love for children. Most of the faculty said that they consider their teaching to be a service to the Korean community and that their job is a way to provide role models for Korean values. "The teachers are really volunteers," says Mr. Lee. "The salary doesn't pay for anything—except gas money. So the teachers have to have a real [commitment]." (ES82-LL-R22)

Students

Forty-five students registered for classes in the school's first year. By spring 1982 a total of 151 students from 86 different families were listed in the school directory. All of the students live in Maryland, most of them in middle-class, suburban areas fairly close to the school.[3] The student body includes both members and non-members of the First Korean Baptist Church.

Most of the students at the First Korean School are between the ages of five and fourteen, although there were some who were older and younger. These ages correspond to American public school grades kindergarten through eighth grade.[4]

A large number of the students seemed to be full-blooded Koreans. At least two were adopted and several came from mixed marriages. Most of the children who were not full-blooded Korean attended the Special Class, where they were learning basic vocabulary and grammar. Although no official count has been made, most of the faculty agreed that all of the schoolchildren had either been born in the United States or had spent the majority of their lives here.

All the children I observed spoke English fluently, and many of them consider it their first language. One teacher suggested that perhaps 50 percent of the children speak Korean at home. He also observed that it is more likely for a child to be fluent in Korean if the grandparents live with the family. Among themselves the students usually spoke English. They also called each other by their American names rather than the Korean ones used by the teachers. All of them wore American clothing to school. I saw Korean clothes only at special events, and only a small number of children (usually girls) wore them then.[5]

In general, the students seemed very Americanized. "The children look Korean, have Korean skin color and eyes," says Mr. Kim. "But their thinking and customs are American. [I] think these children [are] not Korean; they're American." (ES82-LL-R11)

The majority of the students said they disliked attending Korean school, claiming that they came only because their parents insisted. Some complained that school was boring; others that it was too difficult. Several said they were tired of classes after five days of American school, and some wanted to watch Saturday morning television. Others had conflicts between Korean school and community activities, such as Little League baseball. Nevertheless, most of them have fun at school. Many were friends with their classmates and seemed to like their teachers. They also appeared to enjoy the non-language classes. Martial arts, in particular, elicited keen enthusiasm.

Most of the students seemed very aware of their "Korean-ness" and tended to accept it matter-of-factly. One teenager said that it was impossible for him not to acknowledge his heritage because his looks are Asian. He feels like an American, eats American food, has American friends, and speaks English fluently. But he recognizes that some aspects of his life differ greatly from the lives of his friends. For example, he likes Korean food and wants to marry a Korean girl so that his wife can prepare it for him at home.

Another teenager wanted to learn Korean so that she could participate in the Korean students' group at the university she planned to attend. She thought that she would feel more comfortable with other Korean and Korean-American students, even though she spoke fluent English, because they would share her cultural background and values.

Korean and Korean-American children tend to fit easily into the American ideals of behavior and success. Many of them excel in American schools and hope to continue their education at prestigious institutions, such as Harvard, MIT, and Yale. Of the Korean-American children I spoke to, approximately 90 percent said they make straight A's on their report cards for American school. The same percentage said they plan on attending college. About half the children said they want a career in one of the medical professions. Striving for success is partly due to respect for their parents' wishes—many see their parents sacrificing for the children's futures—but it also reflects Korean values that encourage hard work, achievement, and material and academic success.

Parents

The parents of the students at the Korean school represent a wide range of professions, as well as economic and educational levels. The school has purposely structured its fees so as not to be a financial burden. It also offers conveniences, such as the van service, so that minimal effort is required from the parents.

The administration and faculty feel that one of their tasks is to educate the parents about the need to maintain and transmit an appreciation for their Korean heritage in the home. The school cannot achieve its purpose without the support of the parents; Korean language, in particular, cannot be taught without some reinforcement in the home.

Parents' involvement with the Korean school seemed to be minimal, often because of conflicting work schedules. According to the faculty, parents often help the children with their homework, but relatively few assist at the school itself. Some help out by substitute teaching, bringing snacks, and forming car pools.

A parents organization associated with the First Korean Baptist Church exists, but is not very active. Most of the parents are too busy to participate. Many of them hold two jobs, or run their own business, often working twelve or more hours a day. Some parents that I talked to said they would like to be more active, but need to get financially established first. The church group meets about once a year to discuss the role of the school and current concerns of the parents.

The reason most often given by parents for sending their children to the school is that it would be a shame for them to not know their own heritage. They worry that the children will lack a strong sense of identity and pride in their heritage, both of which may create obstacles for them in achieving a successful and fulfilled life. The parents are also concerned about the maintenance of the family identity: they want the family name to be honored, and they want the children to know their ancestors. Communication between generations is particularly important, and some parents felt that their children were adapting too well to American values and customs. While Koreans do not officially practice ancestor worship, reverence for ancestors is an integral part of the culture.[6]

Most Korean parents seem to demand a lot from their children. Their high expectations stem from several factors. Traditional Korean values stress achievement and place responsibility on children to bring honor and respect to the family name. Children are seen as the hope of the future; the child will take care of the parents in their old age and will continue the family line, insuring that the family name survives into the future.

The parents recognized that the children complain about attending school and learning Korean, but they felt that the children would appreciate the training when they were grown. Several parents who do not send their children to the school said they were concerned about demanding too much from them. Some felt that their children needed to concentrate on learning English, studying for American school, and participating in other activities, such as music lessons. Others said that forcing their children to attend would produce negative reactions to their Korean heritage.

Conclusions

The First Korean School directly reflects the concerns of the adult generation of Korean immigrants and Korean-Americans in the Washington area. These concerns are not limited to transmission of cultural heritage, but include the immediate and future welfare of Korean-American children. Nor are the individuals involved in the school limited to a select group within the Korean community. The school's administrators and faculty hold a range of educational and occupational credentials, and the larger community displays its support through the continued enrollment of its children.

Since its creation in 1977 the First Korean School has grown to approximately four times the size of its original student body and faculty. At least four factors are responsible for this growth.

First is the commitment and determination of the individuals who organized and developed the school. Their continuing efforts to create an effective educational program have attracted support increasingly from the Korean community.

Elementary school girls dance in a Christmas show at a nursing home in Silver Spring, Maryland, December 1981. (ES82-4-29311-5A-6) Photo by Lucy Long

Another factor is the continued support of the First Korean Baptist Church. The building added by the church in 1980 has enabled the school to expand its classes and accommodate more students, while the free rent and utilities provided by the church have allowed the tuition fees to be used for other expenses.

A third factor in the school's success is the nature of the Washington area Korean-American community and its high degree of ethnic awareness. The community is proud of its heritage and has developed strong networks between its members through a variety of occupational, social, and religious organizations. It has also been settled in Washington long enough for its members to acquire a measure of economic stability, enabling the community to support—both financially and socially—the maintenance of ethnic language. Many have also been here long enough to realize that such language maintenance is not a luxury but a necessity.

A final factor is the school's concern with meeting the immediate and long-term needs of its students by shaping them into good Korean-American citizens. It attempts to achieve this goal by instilling good values and healthy attitudes, by encouraging the children to set high goals for themselves, and by providing an environment in which they can confront and explore their ethnicity. The administration feels that possessing knowledge of their heritage is essential for the children to develop strong, positive self-images, which are vital to their becoming good citizens. The school emphasizes the Korean language as a means both of transmitting a cultural heritage and maintaining strong family ties, which form the basis of social responsibility.

Being Korean in America requires more than simply speaking and understanding the Korean language. Most Koreans consider a degree of acculturation to be inevitable if their children are to succeed in this society. They try, therefore, to expose them to the best of both worlds. They consider an appreciation for the arts, both Eastern and Western, important. The school includes music, dance, and martial arts in its curriculum. The inclusion in the curriculum of such things as the SAT classes demonstrates the value placed on achievement and success, an additional aspect of the Korean-American identity.

In conclusion, the school tries to instill a sense of ethnic identity in its students, while simultaneously assisting them to adapt to American life.

Rather than seeing these as conflicting goals, the school considers them necessary and complementary processes in the children's development into honorable individuals. Furthermore, the school recognizes that the children will never be wholly Korean nor wholly American, but will have to forge an identity for themselves as Korean-Americans. The school hopes its efforts will provide resources for that task.

Profile of Teachers at the First Korean School

Mrs. Wol-Jin Ahn, the kindergarten teacher, has been a principal and elementary school teacher for forty years. She has lived in the United States for four years.

Miss Koh, who teaches first grade, has taught in a day care center and as a substitute teacher. She has been in the United States for three years and is studying education at the University of Maryland.

Mrs. In-Ok Kim teaches second grade and has previously taught in Korean Sunday school. She is a dental technician who has lived in the United States over ten years.

Mr. Young-Woon Koh, the third grade teacher, has taught Korean high school for twenty years. He has a degree in math and is a teacher's aid by profession. He has been here three years.

Miss Boon-Yi Kwak teaches fourth grade.

Miss Young-Ja Kim is the fifth grade teacher.

Mr. Hwang Noh, who teaches sixth grade, taught previously in Korean high school and has been affiliated with the Korean board of education. He works for a private trading company, having arrived in this country five years ago.

Mr. Hee-Kyu Park teaches the junior high school class. He is a teacher by profession and is a Korean language instructor at the Foreign Service Institute.

Mr. Dong-Yull Kim, the senior high school teacher, has tutored students in agriculture in the past. He is a veterinarian.

Mrs. Ok-Kyung Kim teaches the Special Class.

Mrs. Shin Kong Ki, the music teacher, taught music in Korea as well. She is a piano teacher by profession who has lived in the United States for two years.

Mrs. Chang-Soon Lee is the dance teacher.

Mr. Myung-Chul Choi, the martial arts instructor, taught martial arts in Korea. He has a B.A. in sociology and has lived here six months.

Selected Bibliography

General references on Korean history and culture

Henthorn, William E. *A Guide to Reference and Reseach Materials on Korean History: An Annotated Bibliography.* Honolulu: Research Publications and Translations, East-West Center, 1968.

————. *A History of Korea.* New York: Free Press, 1971.

Osgood, Cornelius. *The Koreans and Their Culture.* New York: Ronald Press Co., 1951.

References on Korean-Americans

Choy, Bong Youn. *Koreans in America.* Chicago: Nelson-Hall, 1979.

Gardner, Arthur L. *The Koreans in Hawaii: An Annotated Bibliography.* Honolulu: Social Science Research Institute, University of Hawaii, 1970.

Hurh, Won Moo. *Assimilation of the Korean Minority in the United States.* Elkins Park, Pa.: Philip Jaisohn Memorial Foundation, 1977.

————. *Comparative Study of Korean Immigrants in the United States: A Typological Approach.* San Francisco: R and E Research Associates, Inc., 1977.

Kim, Christopher. *Annotated Bibliography on Koreans in America.* Los Angeles: Asian American Studies Center, University of California at Los Angeles, 1976.

Kim, Hyung-chan. "Koreans." In *Harvard Encyclopedia of American Ethnic Groups.* Stephan Thernstrom, ed. Cambridge, Mass. and London: Harvard University Press, 1980.

————, and Wayne Patterson, eds. *The Koreans in America, 1882–1974: A Chronology and Fact Book.* Dobbs Ferry, N.Y.: Oceana Publications, 1974.

Koo, Hagen, and Eui-Young Yu. *Korean Immigration to the United States: Its Demographic Pattern and Social Implications for Both Societies.* Honolulu: East-West Center, 1981.

Melendy, H. Brett. *Asians in America: Filipinos, Koreans, and East Indians.* Boston: Twayne Publishers, 1977.

Patterson, Wayne, and Kim Hyung-chan. *The Koreans in America.* Minneapolis: Lerner Publications Company, 1977.

Notes

1. For a concise introduction to Korean immigration to the United States, *see* Hyung-chan Kim, "Koreans," in *Harvard Encyclopedia of American Ethnic Groups,* Stephan Thernstrom, ed. (Cambridge, Mass. and London: Harvard University Press, 1980), pp. 601–6. For a more detailed history refer to Hyung-chan Kim, *The Koreans in America, 1882–1974* (Dobbs Ferry, N.Y.: Oceana Publications, 1974).

2. The Korean embassy maintains files on these schools, as well as on language programs throughout the country.

3. Addresses were not provided for all students in the directory, so the following statistics are not complete, but they suggest the geographic distribution of families associated with the school. The following breakdown is by families, not by number of students:

Silver Spring—2	Gaithersburg—4
Rockville—12	Adelphi, Beltsville, Hyattsville—3
Potomac and Wheaton—7	Takoma Park—2
Olney—5	Burtonsville, Derwood, Glen Dale, Kensington—1

There are no statistics available on the distribution of the Korean population in this area, so these numbers cannot be compared to the community as a whole. It is interesting to note, however, that a good number of students come from distances that require a thirty- to forty-five-minute drive. Most of these students ride the three school vans, but some are driven to school by their parents. Some of the van routes are rather long—one starts two hours before classes begin—and the long ride apparently keeps some children away.

Most of these areas are suburban and middle-class. Silver Spring is a pleasant neighborhood of middle-class homes, and has a good number of established Asian immigrants. Potomac is an upper-middle to upper-class area of expensive homes and country clubs. The fact that seven Korean families live there attests to the upward mobility of the Korean population. The areas from which three or fewer Korean families send children to the school are middle-class to lower-middle- and working-class. The distribution of housing may reflect a correspondence between wealth, awareness of ethnicity, and willingness to participate in an organized attempt to preserve and transmit ethnic heritage.

4. Koreans figure age differently. They consider children to be a year old at their birth, and sometimes celebrate a second birthday on the Lunar New Year, when all birthdays are traditionally celebrated. *See* Cornelius Osgood, *The Koreans and Their Culture* (New York: Ronald Press Co., 1951) for more information about these customs. The Western custom of celebrating one's day of birth is becoming more common, particularly among urban, middle-class Koreans. The children at the First Korean School sometimes gave both their "Korean age" and "American age." They seemed to prefer the Korean version, because it made them older.

5. Koreans living in Korea today tend to wear Western clothes more frequently than Korean clothing, particularly in urban areas. The Korean dress for women consists of a short jacket with full sleeves over an ankle-length full skirt. It is still frequently worn, particularly by older women, and by women of all ages on special occasions. The men's costume, which consists of a jacket similar to the women's over full, long pants, is more rare.

6. A point of pride among many of the Koreans I have interviewed in the Washington area is their ancestry. Several have shown me extended genealogies that trace their family for fifty to seventy-five generations.

Atatürk School
New York, New York

Maurie Sacks

Atatürk School is a Turkish language and culture school in New York City which meets on Saturdays. Centrally located, it serves the Turkish community in the Bronx, Manhattan, Queens, Long Island, and Brooklyn, as well as in upstate New York and Connecticut.[1] The American Turkish Women's League, an organization of middle-class and elite Turkish women living in the New York metropolitan area who are interested in serving the Turkish community, administers the school.

The women's league established the school in 1973 at the Turkish consulate in New York. Later it moved to the United Nations School, where several ethnic groups had space for their ethnic heritage programs. Teachers volunteered their services in the early years, and there were few expenses since no rent was paid before the move to the United Nations School. At that point the school began to charge tuition to cover the rent. The practice of charging tuition has continued, with each child paying a nominal fee of fifty dollars per year.

Space was inadequate at the United Nations School, making teachers, pupils, and parents unhappy. In 1978 Atatürk School moved to its present location, where it is again housed at the expense of the Turkish government. It is now on the second floor of a large office building. The large space is divided up into smaller areas through the use of partitions. They are moved into place each week to accommodate the school, creating areas for six classes—kindergarten through fifth grade.

A teacher at the Atatürk School kisses the cheek of one of his pupils at the Closing Day ceremonies. (ES82-197561-4-16) Photo by Lance Tarhan

Preparations for classes, which are held on Saturday mornings, include carrying folding chairs into the class areas and rolling blackboards to desired locations. At the end of the day everything has to be put away; school materials are stored in a small room set aside for the women's league. The room also houses lockers for the teachers, principal, and league president, and curriculum materials. For special occasions the entire floor can be opened up and turned into an auditorium.

Administrators, faculty, and parents all expressed satisfaction with the current location of the school. They feel that it is their own space, that there are adequate provisions for the classes and waiting parents, and that they have sufficient storage space for the school's equipment.

The school began nine years ago with only one class; today it has six, including a kindergarten. There are nine teachers—six classroom teachers, a music teacher, a folk-dance teacher, and a religion teacher—serving approximately ninety pupils aged four through fifteen.

Although there are other Turkish schools in the Bronx, Brooklyn, and Queens, some families from each of these boroughs bring their children to Atatürk School. The Brooklyn school serves a special constituency of Crimean Turks who settled here after World War II and have their own organizations. The Queens and Bronx schools also apparently serve special sub-ethnic populations. Atatürk School offers an education consistent with the culture of the modern Turkish nation and does not appeal to any particular sub-ethnic group. Parents bring their children to the school because they see themselves as mainstream Turks, because of its central location, and because Atatürk School offers an opportunity to connect with the Turkish-American elite.

The first impression one gets of Atatürk School is that it is a place full of life and exuberance. Children race and tumble amidst a cacophonous din before, between, and after classes. Boys wrestle and toss around each other's hats, shoes, or books, while girls wander about in groups of two or three, talking, playing games like "London Bridge," and drawing on blackboards. During classes the demeanor is more decorous, however. Teachers expect the children to sit quietly and copy lessons from the board, take dictation, or listen to each other recite.

School Administration

As stated previously, the American-Turkish Women's League, which is affiliated with the Federation of Turkish-American Societies, sponsors the school. A woman educator started the women's league informally between 1948 and 1950. It was formally registered in Albany, New York, in 1956. According to Münevver Özdil, its current president, the league has several objectives: to foster ethnic awareness and knowledge in Turkish-American children, to administer Atatürk School, and to further friendship and love between Turks and Americans in the United States. The league currently has over two hundred members, but, as in many organizations, the work of supporting and maintaining the school reportedly falls to about a dozen of them.

The women's league raises money for the school budget—about $10,000 per year—selects teachers and a principal, oversees the acquisition of curriculum materials from Turkey, sets tuition fees and salaries, and plans and organizes school functions, such as holiday celebrations. The league raises money by charging entrance fees to some school functions, selling food, and organizing fund-raising events, such as teas and balls. There are conflicting reports as to whether the Turkish government subsidizes the school in any other way than by contributing space. In any case, however, the women's league is independent of the Turkish government and takes full responsibility for the existence of Atatürk School.

Teachers

The teachers at Atatürk School are professional educators from Turkey living in the United States. The school stresses the qualifications of the teachers, all of whom teach at the school because of their concern for Turkish children and love of teaching. They receive an honorarium of twenty-five dollars per week for their services, which merely meets their expenses. One of the school's goals is to eventually raise the teachers' pay.

All of the classroom teachers at the school have teaching certificates from Turkish institutions or are professional educators. One spent his professional life in Turkey editing and publishing textbooks. Another taught school in Turkey and Germany. The music teacher's avocation has been performing Turkish music at public functions for many years, and the folk-dance teacher has danced in a prize-winning Turkish folk-dancing troupe which toured Europe. The religion teacher has two graduate degrees from Istanbul University, a certificate from the High Institute of Islam in Istanbul, and works as a full-time *imam* (priest) and school administrator for a Turkish community in Brooklyn.

The principal of the Atatürk School, Mrs. Karcioğlu, taught biology at the college level in Turkey and has a certificate from Teachers' College at Columbia University. Mrs. Özdil, president of the women's league and a school administrator, taught for many years in a private school in Brooklyn and served as its principal.

Classes and Curriculum

Atatürk School derives its curriculum from books published by the National Education Ministry in Turkey and monthly magazines for each grade published by one of the large Turkish banks. The president of the Turkish-American Society acquires the magazines for the school. Classes use the books and magazines which are appropriate to their grade level. Pupils pay one dollar for each book they take for the year. At the end of the year·they can return the books, if they wish, and get their money back.

Since the school has only a few hours per week in which to make use of the materials, the lessons leave out quite a bit. The school does not teach math or science, for instance. The classes emphasize Turkish language, history, social studies, music, and religion. The nursery-kindergarten class stresses songs and poetry, the first grade emphasizes reading and writing, and the higher grades concentrate on social studies and history. All grades use Turkish. I was unable to obtain lesson plans, but was told that teachers choose their study materials at the beginning of the school year in conference with the principal, making yearly, monthly, and weekly lesson plans.

The school chooses curriculum materials with several goals in mind. Many parents and teachers stress the importance of the children's knowing the Turkish language well. In fact, children have the impression that language instruction is the main purpose of the school. Language is taught as it is taught to schoolchildren of comparable age in Turkey—not as a second language. The fostering of ethnic pride is another emphasis of the school. To this end lessons stress the glories of Turkish history, the greatness of Mustafa Kemal Atatürk—the founder of modern Turkey—and the beauties of the Turkish homeland. This body of knowledge, along with the ability to speak Turkish, is an important marker of Turkish identity.

Atatürk School recently added religion as a subject. To be Turkish in Turkey means to be Muslim, and when someone has converted to Islam, the saying goes, "He became a Turk." (Although being Muslim is so closely associated with being Turkish, many educated Turks do not practice religion.)

In some classes, when the school day begins at 10:00 A.M., students shout a motto after the teacher while standing at attention. It starts, "I'm Turkish, upright, and hardworking," and goes on to mention defending the young, honoring the elders, loving one's people, and uplifting one's nation; in other classes the call to order is more subtle. The teacher then announces a lesson, frequently writing it on the blackboard for the pupils to copy. Lessons might be on Turkish language, "life knowledge" (customs), social studies, or history. Teachers may then expect their pupils to listen to further explication, read aloud before the class, or answer questions.

There is a lunch break at 12:00 noon. Most children bring their lunch, although some parents bring in pizzas at lunchtime and have their children share with their classmates. Although one teacher stays upstairs in the class area on "lunch duty," there is no attempt to enforce orderly behavior at this time—short of throwing food or injuring someone, most kinds of horsing around are tolerated, along with the soaring noise levels. Some children go downstairs to have lunch in the waiting room with the parents. Most of the lunches are American-style sandwiches and drinks. There was no noticeable tendency for children to bring Turkish-style picnic foods for lunch.

When classes reconvene, the children dispose of lunch refuse in overflowing wastebaskets and resume a quieter demeanor. On alternate weeks the music teacher and the religion teacher arrive. The students split into two groups and the two teachers alternate between each half of the school. Sometimes, during the week when the teachers do not come, the whole school assembles and the regular teachers instruct the children in Turkish songs. For example, the teachers taught the children the song "My Mother" in preparation for Mother's Day. The lyrics describe an older child's longing to have mother hold him in her lap and sing lullabies again, like she did when he was small.

School let outs at 3:00 P.M. and the children drift away, except for those staying for the folk-dance class. About a dozen children seem to be involved in the class. They were practicing for the 19th of May celebration during the weeks I observed the school.

Mothers gathering at the
Atatürk School for the
Mothers' Day program.
(ES82-196411-7-17A)
Photo by Lance Tarhan

Atatürk School allows many different teaching styles. The first grade teacher uses warmth, physical contact, and praise to encourage the youngsters to behave well. She rewards good work with red ribbons pinned to the children's clothing and called to the attention of anyone around who might be interested. The second and third grade teachers are more formal in their approach to the classroom and more stern. They use stern voice tone, scolding, and occasional ear tweaking to encourage the children to settle down and do their work. Both of the classrooms have rows of seats facing the blackboard. The fourth and fifth grade teachers are more soft spoken, but also use a stern voice tone to guide the youngsters toward good behavior and good work. The seats in the fourth grade class are in a circle and those in the fifth grade are in arcs around the teacher's desk.

In addition to lessons directed toward language learning and proper Turkish etiquette, Atatürk School provides formal occasions and informal situations in which children pick up proper Turkish comportment. Turks engage in a whole range of polite behaviors which are unfamiliar to Americans. Greeting behaviors, including cheek and hand kissing accompanied by appropriate verbal expressions, are very important. Children should be familiar with those gestures and must perform them in public as signs of their socialization in Turkish culture. On the final day of classes, for example, one of the younger girls went around and kissed the cheeks and hands of some of the "aunts" (as Turkish children are taught to address the adult women gathered in the waiting area off the school lobby) in a formal and polite farewell. Both the recipients of the gesture and the mother of the girl, who beamed with pride at her daughter's good manners, praised and appreciated her behavior.

In addition to being able to communicate in the Turkish language, being Turkish involves being familiar with Turkish history and symbols. This includes knowledge of the history of the Turkish Republic, acknowledgment of Atatürk as a cultural hero, and familiarity with the geography of Turkey. Atatürk School provides its students with this body of information as well.

Parents

Atatürk School serves first-generation Turkish immigrant families living in the New York metropolitan area and the Turkish consular staff serving temporarily in this country. Some of the children were born in the United States, others in Turkey. Many Turkish immigrants represented in the school population are members of the intelligentsia who came here as college students and stayed to practice professions, but workers and small entrepreneurs also send their children to the school. The families whose members I interviewed include several individuals with Ph.D.s, families in which both the father and mother have professional careers, families in which the sole wage earner is a mechanic, building superintendent, engineer, doctor, or diplomat, and others in which both parents run a small business, such as a dry cleaning establishment, restaurant, or tailor shop.

The families interviewed exhibited differences in their commitment to living in America. No one admitted that they never planned to return to Turkey. Everyone had been to Turkey within the last five or six years, at least as visitors. Some are in the United States with short-term goals in mind, such as completing an assignment from the Turkish foreign ministry or educating a youngster. Others are raising their families here because of favorable economic conditions, but hope to return to Turkey. Among the most highly educated families are some who have made a conscious decision to settle in America; but, when pressed, even they do not rule out the possibility of retiring in Turkey eventually.

My observations indicated that the most educated families are the most assimilated and the most secure in their decision to remain in America, except for those working in the diplomatic corps. The least educated tend to remain more Turkish in their language and behavior, to view their stay in America as an economic adaptation to difficult times, and to anticipate their eventual return "home." Many demonstrate the "boxes in the closet syndrome"—whenever they purchase an appliance they save the box, because someday it will be packed up and sent to Turkey!

While school is in session, twenty or more mothers usually gather in the waiting area of the lobby, which has benches, chairs, and a coffeepot. Less than half a dozen fathers may gather at the opposite end of the room from the mothers. The fathers sometimes engage in conversation, sometimes read a newspaper, or just sit quietly. The mothers engage in lively conversation and gossip, making the occasion into an important social event. For some this is the only chance they have to meet regularly with other Turkish women—certainly, to sit with a whole group of them—as is common for women in Turkey to do.[2] Sometimes a mother brings homemade cakes for the gathering. Most of the women who sit in the lobby are homemakers, and my impression is that the core who come most faithfully are wives of blue-collar workers. I have also spoken to wives of professional men, however, who like to visit with the other mothers, at least occasionally. I did not find any career women among them.

The talk, which is in Turkish, revolves around homemaking skills—cooking, sewing, and shopping—ill health and good fortune among acquaintances, problems of adaptation to American life, and events at the school. The gathering is an important clearinghouse for information concerning products available, proprietors worth patronizing, housing, vacations, and coping with American and Turkish institutions. It also serves as an ad hoc PTA for the school. The principal regularly joins the mothers for some time each week, discussing school matters and the contributions expected from the parents, such as preparing the children's outfits and food for special events. Teachers sometimes join in the conversations before and after classes.

At the end of the school day, as parents and children drift away, some mothers stay to make the most of the last few moments of conversation, urging their friends not to be in a rush to leave. There is some Turkish-style kissing on both cheeks among the mothers at parting.

Purposes of the School

The purposes of the school include socialization in Turkish identity for the children, enculturation in Turkish language and world view, formation of a Turkish ethnic group, and provision of a forum where bicultural children can formulate their own value system.[3] Parents, teachers, and administrators give many reasons for their participation in Atatürk School. Underlying all of them is a burning concern that the children acquire and retain a sense of identity and ethnic pride. All are willing to give their time and energy for the rewards of hearing the children speak Turkish, seeing them write Turkish, and having them participate in Turkish events.

College-educated parents show an awareness of "identity crisis" and express concern that their children formulate a sense of identity and know "who they are." They feel Atatürk School can provide this for their children. Less educated parents demonstrate less interest in abstract identity and more concern for their children's continuation of traditions that are familiar to them; they do not want to be cut off from their children and their homeland by loss of the language and culture. One mother, born in America and married to a Turkish-born man, expressed a fear that, if she did not expose her son to an ethnic education, he would one day accuse her of depriving him of his birthright.

Turkish language acquisition for the children seems to be one of the primary goals of the school. All curriculum materials are in Turkish exclusively. The only classroom in which the teacher speaks English frequently is the first class, attended by children less familiar with Turkish. Even there an attempt is made to conduct most matters in Turkish. One teacher eloquently expressed to me the need for the children to be fluent in Turkish so that they would be able to feel at home in Turkey. He likened Turkish children in America without the Turkish language to nightingales in a gilded cage. No matter how beautiful and rich the cage, the inhabitant is still not free. To be free—to return to their homeland if they wish—Turkish-American youngsters must have command of the Turkish language and culture.

Attitudes toward the use of the Turkish language vary with the education of the parents and the degree of their assimilation. Parents who have a career are more likely to report speaking English to their children at home. One family, in which both parents are involved in American careers, employs a Turkish housekeeper to care for the children and speak Turkish with them. College-educated parents emphasize the general benefits which accrue to language acquisition in the business and academic world as part of their reason for sending their children to Atatürk School. Since these parents are also most concerned about assimilation themselves, however, they most often speak English to their children, "to make sure the child understands," to facilitate the child's adjustment to his American peers, or to perfect their own skills in English. Wives of highly educated professionals complained most to me about their inadequate English; they speak English better than the other mothers, but not as well as their husbands. One blue-collar mother reports speaking Turkish to her children at home because her ethnic neighbors told her that, if she did not, her children would lose the language, as theirs had. She feels that she is sacrificing her own opportunity to learn English better for the good of her children.

Münevver Özdil has a more broad-reaching vision for the school. She sees it not only as a language-teaching institution and link between Turkish-American children and their homeland but also as a fosterer of a Turkish ethnic presence in the United States. Fully aware of the small number of Turks living in this country, she is concerned that they be able to unite and make their voice heard and respected. She expects that creating Turkish-conscious youngsters who are educated and aware will contribute to this cause. The children, she says, learn that they are representatives of the Turkish community in their public lives and that they must be careful to set a good example, to be loving and fair to their fellows, so that others will know that the Turks are a loving and friendly people.

Students

There is a difference between the children and their parents over the issue of staying in America permanently. Although many youngsters professed insecurity about their future in this country, most indicated quite strongly that they want to spend the rest of their lives here. No child showed any reluctance to assimilate, to speak English, have American friends, dress in American clothes, and enjoy American foods. This includes children of the consular staff. On the other hand, some children did show a reluctance to stress Turkish behaviors, including use of the Turkish language; but none seemed eager to forget about being Turkish altogether.

Folkdance class at Atatürk School.
(ES82-196411-3-17A)
Photo by Lance Tarhan

The children, like children in most ethnic schools, profess little interest in the issues of such burning importance to their elders, and most would rather be doing something else on Saturday. Boys especially are eager to disclaim any interest at all in their Turkish studies, to assure me that they are hostage to their parents, and to underscore the point that they are "made to come to this school." Most children believe that they are at the school to learn Turkish because their parents do not think that they know the language well enough. The children feel that they do know the language and that they get along fine when they visit Turkey. They do not see the need for learning all the history and social studies, singing, and religion taught at the school. Many who feel unhappy about the school give boredom as their reason. Most also feel bored with their public school education, although some make distinctions between the two. Several girls did feel free to tell me that they enjoy Atatürk School, they like learning Turkish better, and find Turkish history interesting.

The children I spoke with have American friends where they live and do not especially seek out Turks, even when they are in the same school, unless their families carry on relationships with the other families. Some of the children have acquired Americanized nicknames. When asked if they share their Turkish culture with their American friends, more than one child told me that their friends tease them when they act or appear Turkish, and that they want to pass as any other American. Some play on softball or soccer teams, take music lessons, or belong to a YMCA with their American friends. When extracurricular activities conflict with attendance at Atatürk School, they sometimes sacrifice attendance at the school. One girl told me that she had missed several Saturdays because of softball.

Asked what they like best about the school, many children responded "lunch" or "fooling around with my friends," which indicates that, even for the disaffected, the school holds the pleasure of associating with other Turkish-American youngsters in the same situation. Since the children come from such scattered homes, school provides the only regular opportunity for some students to be in a gathering of Turks, to feel that they are not alone or weird, and to create a culture of shared Turkish-American experience.

Conclusions

It is clear that Atatürk School is engaged in creating and maintaining ethnic identity for children of Turkish parents residing in America, whether they are permanent residents, staying here temporarily to raise their families, or on a tour of duty. There are two main aspects to the school's function: (1) the sharing of a body of knowledge which Turks acknowledge as their own and which serves as a marker of Turkish identity; and (2) the provision of social space where students can act out their "Turkish-ness," practice their mannerisms and language, honing them to a Turkish norm (or at least a Turkish-American one), and express solidarity for an appreciative audience. The end product of both functions is an ethnic group capable of behaving as an interest group. This idea has been expressed in scholarly literature by Anya Royce[4] and from the lay perspective by Mrs. Özdil (see above).

Almost all transactions that occur at Atatürk School take place in Turkish, with the exception of the banter that goes on among the children, and even that is sometimes in Turkish. Nothing can establish social boundaries as quickly and emphatically as a shared language. It provides not only a vocabulary and idioms which create a common medium in which those who know the code may communicate, but it also provides a world view.[5] In fact, there is no satisfactory English equivalent for many Turkish concepts. By teaching Turkish as a mother language and not as a second language, thereby avoiding much direct translation, Atatürk School operates within the Turkish world view and passes it on to the children.

Mustafa Kemal Atatürk, the first president of modern Turkey, is the school's namesake and hero. A mural depicting Atatürk's great humanism and quoting his wise sayings dominates the mothers' waiting area. The holidays celebrated throughout the school year were mostly established by Atatürk. On those occasions the children recite his orations, perform songs glorifying his achievements, and listen to speeches which hold him up as a great man to be emulated and revered. A speech being practiced by one of the children for the celebration on the 19th of May depicts him as a leader of the victorious Turks and founder of the nation. The knowledge about the founding of the Turkish Republic, which increased nationalistic pride and self-respect for all Turks, inspires a recognition of Atatürk's greatness. The children at the school learn to respond to Atatürk as the symbol of modern Turkey and the source of modern Turkish patriotism. They also learn to honor the Turkish flag, to sing the national anthem and other patriotic songs, such as "To Be a Turk Is the Greatest Honor," and to recognize Turkish folk costumes and music.

Concerning the religious component in the school's curriculum, Mrs. Karcioğlu told me that parents at the school wished to have religion taught because they are aware of the saliency of religion as a determinant of identity in America. In other words, religion, which for some would not be stressed as an important element of identity in Turkey, where nearly everyone is born into the same religion, becomes stressed in America, where religion is often a component of ethnic identity and sometimes even stands alone as a label or designator of group affiliation, e.g., Catholic, Protestant, or Jew. Some parents, especially those who are most educated and would have stressed religion least in Turkey, feel that their children are getting more religious training here than they would have in Turkey because of the inclusion of religion in the school curriculum. As in Turkey, however, religion is an optional subject.

Although there are parents at Atatürk School who carry over their secularism to the point of celebrating Christmas for their children as a seasonal holiday, others take advantage of the winter holiday season to impress their Turkish identity on their children. One parent pointed out that her child's exposure to Judaism as an acceptable alternative to Christianity in America made it easier for her to present Islam as yet another alternative, and the only appropriate one for Turks like themselves to espouse. Whether or not they practice Islam, children at the school experience a body of religious knowledge which reinforces their sense of being Turkish and differentiates them from other Americans.

Quite apart from the curriculum, Atatürk School is an important source of Turkish identification as a center where Turks can gather and act Turkish. More than one mother acknowledged that, although the manifest purpose of bringing her child to the school is to improve his or her knowledge of Turkish, the more compelling reason is to socialize with the other mothers.

In-gathering is also very important for the establishment and perpetuation of group norms and values. A reference group provides standards against which members measure their self-worth and success.[6] The mothers and children who gather regularly at Atatürk School sort out acceptable and unacceptable behaviors for group members on the basis of the interactions in which they participate. "Turkish" behaviors—the use of Turkish language, gestures, and greetings—are highly rewarded, while un-Turkish behaviors—refusing to sit and visit, or the use of English—are either sharply criticized or ignored. Career mothers may avoid the gathering not only because it consumes so much time but also because they do not live up to the standards of traditional Turkish womanhood that are manifested there. If so, the absence of career mothers is an excellent example of the power of in-gathering to set group standards and eliminate non-conforming behavior.

Besides providing a location for Turkish in-group behavior to be honed and developed for Turkish-Americans, Atatürk School provides a focus for Turks in the area, who are otherwise divided in their loyalties by their socio-economic status, sub-ethnic interests, and commitment to assimilation in the United States. One father pointed out that, although the Turkish-American community has become fragmented during the past few years by a proliferation of associations formed by Turkish interest groups,[7] the members of many of the groups support Atatürk School. Children at the school, therefore, come in contact with a cross section of Turkish society in the United States. The mutual agreement on the part of many groups to submit their children to a single curriculum means that there is a common denominator of Turkish culture shared by all.

For the children Atatürk School is the one place they experience a large number of Turks congregating in a limited space on a regular basis. In some cases it may be the one place outside their home where their Turkish identity is salient and where they get a chance to practice it. The inclusion in the student body of the children of consular staff, "Turkish Turks" (as opposed to "American Turks"), further emphasizes the fact that Atatürk is a school for Turkish children. It also brings out the commonality between the children born in America and their Turkish-born brethren.

Of greater significance for the children, however, is the fact that Atatürk School is not only a place to learn about Turkish culture and behavior but also an arena in which they can act out the tensions involved in being bicultural. Many children spend most of the week ignoring or even denying their differences from other American children, at least in public. Several told me that there is no opportunity at their public schools to share aspects of their ethnic heritage with other children, and several boys assured me that their American friends teased them mercilessly if they let slip a Turkish-ism in their behavior. Some have American nicknames to mask their Turkish names. Yet these very same children will fight, if necessary, to protect the good name of Turks.

Many of the children act out some of the tension involved in being bicultural in their display of dislike for Atatürk School. The children tell me that they are "Turkish enough" and have no use for the enculturation they experience at the school. They are highly sensitive about their Turkish-ness; they do not enjoy having it "rubbed in." One boy provided a clue to the noisy negative feelings expressed by the children by telling me that he would really like to go to a Turkish school in Turkey, but that his parents told him that it is too expensive. He seems to be saying that he would like to be all Turkish in Turkey, or all American in America, but that being both is a strain. After trying all week to be just like any other American kid, it must be difficult for the youngsters to "turn on" Turkish on Saturdays. The one adult I interviewed who could look back on such an experience herself, however, says that she appreciated it and wants her child to have the same experience. Perhaps one of the greatest services Atatürk School offers the children is an opportunity to vent their negative feelings to each other in a safe environment. These feelings, which would be anti-Turkish if shared with American friends or Turkish parents, become part of the culture of Turkish-Americanism. Atatürk School is wise to provide the students with a relatively unsupervised lunch period during which the children can discharge the tensions they feel in a situation in which mutual support and understanding is possible and the disapproval of adult authority figures is absent.

If the manifest function of Atatürk School is to socialize children as *Turks*, one of the important latent functions is to provide an organized vehicle for the formulation of a *Turkish-American* culture. Americanisms in the children's dress (blue jeans and sneakers for many), food (pizza), and use of Turkish language ("I ate breakfast" rather than "I did or made breakfast," which is idiomatic) are readily accepted. Children have unstructured time to share their own values and experiences. The formal structure of the school comprises the use of strictly Turkish curricula, but the informal structure cannot help but model a blend of Turkish and American culture.

Notes

1. Unlike some of the communities documented by the Ethnic Heritage and Language Schools project, the Turks do not have an archive which records the history of the Turkish community in New York or the United States. It has been estimated that there were fewer than one hundred thousand Turks in the United States in the late 1970s. About one thousand Turks per year, mostly engineers and doctors, have been immigrating for the past twenty years. Although there is a plethora of Turkish organizations in the United States, most are small and relatively inactive. See Talat Sait Halman, "Turks," in *Harvard Encyclopedia of American Ethnic Groups*, Stephan Thernstrom, ed. (Cambridge, Mass. and London: Harvard University Press, 1980).

2. Turkish women's visiting patterns have been well documented in anthropological literature. *See* Barbara C. Aswad, "Visiting Patterns among Women of the Elite in a Small Turkish City," *Anthropological Quarterly,* vol. 47, no. 1 (January 1974), pp. 9–27, and Peter Benedict, "The Kabul Günü: Structured Visiting in an Anatolian Provincial Town," *Anthropological Quarterly,* vol. 47, no. 1 (January 1974), pp. 28–47.

3. The importance of establishing criteria for "evaluation and judgement" of behavior pertinent to ethnic group membership is discussed in *Ethnic Groups and Boundaries: The Social Organization of Culture,* ed. Fredrik Barth (Bergen-Oslo: Universitetsforlaget and London: George Allen & Unwin, 1969).

4. Anya Peterson Royce, *Ethnic Identity: Strategies of Diversity* (Bloomington: University of Indiana Press, 1982).

5. *See* Benjamin Lee Whorf, "Science and Linguistics," in *Language, Thought, and Reality,* ed. John B. Carroll. (Cambridge, Mass.: The Technology Press of the Massachusetts Institute of Technology, 1956). Reprinted in *Anthropology, Contemporary Perspectives,* David E. K. Hunter and Phillip Whitten, eds. (Boston: Little Brown and Company, 1975), p. 280.

6. *See* David E. K. Hunter, "To Find A Community," in *Anthropology, Contemporary Perspectives,* David E. K. Hunter and Phillip Whitten, eds. (Boston: Little Brown and Company, 1975), p. 158.

7. Some Turkish organizations include the American Turkish Islamic and Cultural Center, Turkish Cultural Alliance, Kibris Türkane Yardim Ocaği (Association for the Aid of Cypriot Turks), American Association of Crimean Turks, Anadolu Club, Inc., Azerbaijan Society of America, Turkish-American Neuropsychiatric Association, and Turkish-American Scientists and Engineers.

Polish Saturday Schools
Chicago, Illinois
Margy McClain

Patricia Witkowski grew up in South Chicago, a neighborhood on Chicago's far southeast side. From the time she was three, Patricia made a fifty-mile round trip each week to a neighborhood then known as the "Polish Triangle," just northwest of downtown Chicago, to attend Polish Saturday school.

Growing up in the 1960s, Patricia spoke Polish at home and wore pigtails "when it wasn't 'in' to be ethnic." She also attended parochial schools in predominantly Polish parishes, but there the Polish language was not encouraged. The teachers were Felician sisters, a Polish order. They taught in English and scolded in Polish.

Faced with Polish jokes and other images which stressed the negative stereotype of the "dumb Polak," Patricia easily felt defensive about being Polish. So going to Polish Saturday school was worth the aggravation of another day of school. Polish school counteracted the negative stereotypes encountered elsewhere and provided "a sense of history, culture, ethnic identity ... [and the feeling that] hey, I belong to a group of people and they are important." That feeling gave Patricia the confidence to deal with the problem of "being different" that seemed to bother friends who had not been given a strong sense of Polish identity.

Patricia has been active through the years in various Polish organizations, serving at times as Polish-language secretary. She values her fluency in the Polish language, achieved through twelve years of Polish Saturday school study and a noteworthy accomplishment for someone raised in the United States. But more than anything else, she says, Polish Saturday school nourished her sense of self-worth as a Polish-American.

Witold Pawlikowski was just a small boy in 1939 when the Soviet Union invaded Poland and occupied his hometown. His father disappeared without a trace, and the rest of the family was deported to Siberia. After great

Pulaski School principal Jozef Żurczak "guest-teaching" a combined first and second grade class, Chicago, Illinois. (ES82-AF88416-1-35A) Photo by Margy McClain hardships, the Pawlikowskis and other Polish military families were sent to Iran. After World War II they eventually made their way to England, where the Polish government-in-exile had spent the war, and then to the United States. Witold served in the United States Army, then settled in Chicago in 1957 and completed his engineering education.

Because of his childhood experiences of uprooting and loss, Mr. Pawlikowski felt strongly that his daughter Beata should have a good education—"the one thing that can't be taken away from you"—and that she should know her Polish heritage of language, history, and traditions. He wanted her to speak the language at home and to know Polish grammar and read Polish literature. He and his wife Yolantha, the daughter of two teachers who take an active part in Chicago's Polish Saturday schools, cajoled and supported their daughter through twelve years of Polish school. Like Patricia Witkowski, Beata Pawlikowski is a graduate of the General Casimir Pulaski Polish High School.

The Witkowski and Pawlikowski families are members of Chicago's strong Polish-American community or "Polonia," as Polish communities outside Poland term themselves. They and many like them in Chicago's diverse ethnic groups passionately desire to pass on to their children the traditions, values, and symbols of their ethnic identity which have shaped their own lives.

Chicago ethnic communities educate their children as ethnic Americans in many ways, from family training to church activities, lodge events, and formal ethnic schooling. At least twenty of Chicago's eighty-plus ethnic groups, and perhaps many more, support ethnic heritage schools. Chicago Polonia, one of the largest ethnic communities in the area, claims over seven hundred thousand people of Polish descent living in the Chicago area. In 1982 the Polish community in Chicago supported a network of fifteen Polish Saturday schools.

An umbrella organization of professional Polish educators, the Polish Teachers Association in America, Inc., coordinates the Saturday school network. The schools are generally referred to as Polish language schools or Polish Saturday schools, (or, more informally, simply as Polish school). They meet on Saturdays and offer instruction in Polish language and history for students from kindergarten through high school. Polish high school graduates speak Polish fluently and have a command of the written language, literary traditions, and Polish history. Through the schools students also gain a sense of confidence and pride in being Polish-American. Maintaining the schools is a community effort accomplished with relatively little money and a great deal of energy. Over and over again, teachers and parents testified that these efforts on behalf of the schools are labors of love and extremely important to them.

Early Polish Education in Chicago

At the start of the twentieth century, when the great waves of immigration brought thousands of Poles to the Chicago area, Poland did not exist as a nation. Poland had been partitioned in 1795 among Russia, Prussia, and Austria, and ethnic Poles referred to themselves as "Russian Poles," or "Austrian Poles." Language and the Roman Catholic religion, rather than nationality, marked the Polish people.

Early Polish immigrants to the United States defined themselves by language, ethnicity, regional origin, and religion. They were mostly peasants with little formal education. They came for economic reasons, working hard so that their children might struggle up the ladder of success in America. Education was an important rung on that ladder, and education for many of the children began in Roman Catholic parochial schools.

Polish immigrants sought to establish Catholic parishes that were Polish in character. They built many churches and established schools with them. Most of the students in the parish schools came from Polish-speaking homes, and the teaching nuns also spoke Polish. With each school free to determine its own use of the Polish language, the curricula varied greatly; depending on the school, or even the individual teacher, students might study only religious subjects or most of the curriculum in Polish. The Polish instruction in the parish schools, therefore, seems to have arisen more from the fact that teachers and students shared a common language than from an explicit desire to impart to students a mastery of the Polish language or a need to instill articulated values related to the traditions of Poland.

Language instruction in the Polish parochial schools began to decline in the 1930s, although some instruction continued for another twenty years. During the Depression pressures from the Archdiocese (historically dominated by Irish and German clerics hostile to parishes that clung to an ethnic interpretation of Catholicism) to rid the parishes of "foreign" associations, combined with a general pressure on immigrants to assimilate, contributed to the decline in language use.[1]

Polish immigration to the United States came to a halt in the 1920s, due to restrictive immigration laws. Thirty years passed before another significant wave of immigration occurred. Isolated from Poland, the Polish community evolved distinctive Polish-American traditions. A unique "Chicago Polish" dialect arose as American-born children learned to speak the Polish language based on the various regional dialects spoken by their parents and teachers. Immigrants arriving after World War II were surprised to find many archaic words and grammatical constructions preserved in the speech of the established Polish-American community.

After World War II thousands of new immigrants flooded the country from the refugee camps of Europe. The new arrivals were to have a profound impact on the nature of Chicago Polonia. They came from a Poland briefly reunited between the world wars, and had been raised with a strong sense of Polish national identity. Now they were refugees who could not return to Communist Poland. Their strong love of country, fueled by a sense of being disinherited, gave rise to a deep need to keep alive things Polish and to pass on to their children raised in the United States a pride and knowledge of what it means to be Polish.

History of Chicago's Polish Schools

Chicago's Polish schools have their roots in the upheavals of World War II. The founders of the Polish Teachers Association in America, Inc. (PTAA) and a great many of the teachers and parents currently active in the Polish schools were adults or young children in Poland during World War II. After the war many Poles found themselves in either Displaced Persons camps (also known as DP or refugee camps) in Germany or in temporary camps in England for those associated with the Polish Army.[2]

Personal relationships formed in the camps were often longlasting, carrying over to the immigrants' new homes. Polish teachers who set up schools in the camps later helped establish Polish Saturday schools in the countries where they finally settled: the United States, England, and Canada. Polish teachers' organizations formed in the camps were models for later groups.

Thousands of Polish refugees came to the United States in the late 1940s and 1950s under the Displaced Persons Act. Existing Polish-American institutions met many needs of the new arrivals, but the parochial schools, where the heritage of Poland's turn-of-the-century rural traditions predominated, could not. For Poles educated in a united Poland between the two world wars, knowledge of the contemporary, standard Polish language was an important attribute of being Polish. They wanted their children to speak the language well and learn Polish history and national traditions in a more structured way than the home could provide. The parochial schools could not teach modern Polish nor instill a contemporary sense of Polish national identity.

So, while many new immigrants sent their children to parochial schools for their regular education, they also began to create special Polish schools. In the 1950s, as Polish cultural education in parochial schools declined, the Polish Saturday schools emerged.

Chicago's Polish community established two Saturday schools in the early 1950s: General Casimir Pulaski Polish School and Tadeusz Kościuszko Polish School. Both are still in operation, offering a program of Polish education through high school. The schools were located in the Polish Triangle—where Ashland, Division, and Milwaukee Avenues come together on the near northwest side of Chicago—until the early 1970s. They served thousands of students. For example, Pulaski had one thousand students in 1970.

The Polish Triangle was an important Polish neighborhood for many years, boasting numerous Polish parishes. The building of the John F. Kennedy Expressway in the 1950s, however, changed the character of the neighborhood fundamentally. Chicago Polonia fought bitterly and successfully to save two magnificent Polish churches, but Polish residents slowly began to move out as lower-income housing was built. The neighborhood is now primarily Hispanic, although some Polish churches, organizations, and businesses remain. New immigrants from Poland settle in the neighborhood, but even they have found a more comfortable area further northwest along Milwaukee Avenue.

As families moved out of the old neighborhood it became increasingly difficult for students to attend Saturday school there. Some families felt unsafe. School enrollment soon dropped.

Many Polish families who left the inner city settled near each other in new communities mostly in far northwest Chicago neighborhoods and in the northwest and western suburbs. When they could no longer attend the old schools, they established new ones. Nine new schools opened during the 1970s and two have opened since 1980. They joined earlier outlying schools established in Hammond, Indiana (just across the Indiana-Illinois state line from Chicago) and in Cicero, Illinois, a suburb just west of Chicago. Most of the schools now offer only eight grades.

The older schools continued to operate, but they too moved to new locations, following the resettlement of Polish families farther northwest within the city of Chicago. Pulaski and Kościuszko are among the four schools in Chicago that offer all twelve grades, so students come from surrounding suburbs to continue Polish high school.

Polish education remains in demand. In 1980 Polish Saturday schools enrolled around two thousand students. By 1981–82 enrollment had increased to three thousand. The steady growth of newer, smaller schools may have contributed to the increase. The continuing immigration of young parents from Poland may also account for some new students. In addition, the election of a Polish pope and the struggle of the Solidarity Union in Poland have encouraged more positive attitudes toward Polish-Americans, and may have influenced the marked growth in Polish school enrollment.

The fact that all Polish schools are named for famous Poles underscores the independent, national orientation of the schools. The two earliest schools were named for the first well-known Polish-Americans—Revolutionary War generals Casimir Pulaski and Tadeusz Kościuszko. Other schools are named after popular figures from World War II, such as St. Maksymilian Kolbe and General Władysław Anders. The names of some recall famous scientists and artists, such as Copernicus, Paderewski, Sienkiewicz, and Chopin, while Maria Konopnicka School commemorates a much-loved poet. The choice of the names St. Maksymilian Kolbe and Pope John Paul II (there are several named after the Pope) definitely have Polish rather than religious significance; there are no schools named for other saints or popes.

Case Study: General Casimir Pulaski Polish School

General Casimir Pulaski Polish School offers classes from first grade through high school. It is one of four Polish high schools fed by the more numerous Polish grammar schools in the Chicago area. In Polish, its name is Polska Szkoła im. Gen. K. Pułaskiego.

Pulaski's rapid growth during the 1950s attests to the strength of the need it met. Beginning with 200 students in 1954, it grew to 850 in 1961, when high school classes formed. In 1970 1,000 students attended. As families left the Polish Triangle, many Pulaski students went to the newly formed, smaller schools in other neighborhoods and suburbs. Some 350 students were enrolled in the school's twelve grades during the 1981–82 school year.

From the early 1950s until 1978, Pulaski School met in various locations in the Polish Triangle. The move in 1978 to the parish school facilities of St. Wenceslaus Roman Catholic Church, 3415 North Lawndale Street, took the school further northwest within the city of Chicago. The new neighborhood, close to the "new Polish Triangle," a thriving community of newly arrived immigrants, housed many Polish families. Although Bohemian immigrants founded St. Wenceslaus, the current priest and many parishioners are Polish. Ten percent of Pulaski's students also attend the St. Wenceslaus parochial school. St. Wenceslaus occupies an entire city block in a quiet, well-kept residential neighborhood of two- and three-flat apartment buildings. Ample space for playing fields surround the large, substantial brick buildings of the parish school.

Each Saturday at 8:30 A.M. the parish school again bustles with activity, as parents gather in the basement hall before their children run off to Pulaski's morning sessions. Some wait there for their children to finish, setting infants in baby seats while they conduct school business, visit, or read the paper. Coffee and homemade pastries such as *pączki,* a kind of jelly doughnut, are available.

Ten classes meet in the morning and ten in the afternoon. The larger grades, first through eighth, have two sections; one section of grades one through eight meets in the morning and the other in the afternoon. The high school classes have fewer students, so two high school classes meet in the morning and the other two in the afternoon. Students who participate in the arts classes, which include singing, poetry recitation, and dancing, either stay later or come earlier.

Classes and Curriculum

The school's primary goal is to teach the Polish language. To this end all grades stress language skills and all classes speak exclusively in Polish. Reading and writing are the main subjects in first through third grades. The younger students learn some Polish history and traditions, primarily through legends and stories. The intermediate grades refine Polish language skills, continue literature, and begin Polish history and geography. The high school grades emphasize the study of Polish literature and history.

Most of Pulaski's students come from homes where at least one parent speaks Polish and the language is part of the home environment. Although all students come to Pulaski speaking some Polish, command of the language varies greatly. Everyone acknowledges that the students are all most comfortable speaking English. The first grade teacher, Mrs. Helena Sromek, felt that she essentially teaches Polish as a second language. If students persist with Polish studies and graduate from Polish high school, they can speak and read Polish fluently. They write well, too. The high school classes cover high school level material in Polish. The school is particularly proud of its high school graduates.

"Only the dedicated and motivated students really survive and go through high school," says Helena Ziółkowska, PTAA president. "But once they finish you really can converse with them fluently ... they have good knowledge of literature and write a good paper."

The arts classes are called extracurricular activities, because they are considered to be outside the main curriculum of academic subjects. The school acknowledges their importance as enjoyable activities that attract students and help keep them involved in the school.

Students

Polish school parents and teachers recognize that attracting and keeping students involved is vital to the success of the schools. Activities such as extramural school sports and other leisure time pursuits are powerful competition to another day in school and extra homework.

Students at Pulaski seemed to agree about why they attend, at least initially: "My parents made me." Those who stick with it either "just get used to it" and quit fighting the inevitable, or really get interested. The parents' motivation is often the deciding factor.

Older students raised two main reasons for keeping on with their studies. One group wanted to learn the Polish language to enhance their success in college or in a career. Other students had visited their relatives in Poland, and cited the satisfaction of being able to speak Polish with their family and get around in another country. As Patricia Witkowski described her trip to Poland at age thirteen, "Suddenly it wasn't just all this Polish stuff—it was real people and real places."

Polish school is a challenging experience, especially in high school, when the curriculum matches the actual age of the students, who use high school level texts from Poland. Those who complete Polish high school, often fulfilling demanding college preparatory classwork at the same time, find the satisfaction great enough for considerable sacrifice. Some finish two years of Polish high school in one to graduate with their class.

Parents

Parents are the core of the Polish schools. Their motivation for their children to attend Polish school is the prime reason that most students begin classes and stay with them. Sometimes it becomes a battle, and the family member with the most determination wins. As older students continue their Polish studies, parents support them through the increasing difficulties of scheduling, commuting, and meeting increasing academic demands.

Post-war immigrant parents wanted their Polish speaking children to become literate in Polish and to know Polish history and culture. They felt that establishing a formal educational environment would be better than trying to teach such subjects at home. The relative importance of these factors varies, of course, from family to family, as does the commitment to speaking Polish at home and to helping children with Polish homework.

The high priority that Polish school families set on education is reflected in their desire to send their children to college. Clippings in the Pulaski school scrapbook attest to its pride in the higher education achievements of its students.

Parents at Pulaski school pay a modest tuition fee of seventy-five dollars for one child per year, eighty-five dollars for two children from the same family, or ninety dollars for three. They also support the school by volunteering their services for administration and fund-raising activities, and by attending special programs at Christmas and Easter.

Perhaps even more important, parents also sacrifice considerable time and effort, giving up their only day free for shopping and errands. Saying, "My Saturday is shot anyway," they may arrange other classes, such as music lessons, for their children, or attend Polish scout meetings as well. Saturday is a family day.

Teachers

Teachers at Pulaski school range from recent immigrants to Mrs. Żurczak, who celebrated her fiftieth year in teaching in 1982. Only the first grade teacher, Mrs. Helena Sromek, has both Polish and American teaching credentials. One of the high school teachers, Dr. Janina Kras, holds a Ph.D. from Jagiellonian University in Krakow, Poland's oldest and most-respected institution of higher learning.

Because Polish language skills are the heart of Pulaski's mission, the school seeks teachers who have recently come from Poland and know the most up-to-date language. The school is aware that languages change, and even teachers educated in Poland are out of touch with the most current developments after they have been in the United States ten or fifteen years. The new teachers, like their colleagues, have teaching certification from Poland. The school prefers certified teachers who specialized in language arts and have a degree in Polish language for elementary grades. When teachers with a language specialty are not available, a good teacher with a degree in another field may find a place in the school as well.

Classroom discipline is an important theme stressed by parents, teachers, and school officials. In Polish and other European educational systems, maintaining a certain distance between teacher and students is traditionally part of the way students express respect for the teacher. Some Polish parents perceive the American classroom style as lax and believe children do not learn as well in the public schools because of it. Better discipline is cited as a reason for enrolling children in parochial rather than public schools. Continuing the European tradition of classroom discipline is one of the goals of Pulaski School. Classes are quiet and students stand by their desks to respond. Teachers remain affectionate toward the youngest students, however, and cordial with older pupils.

School Administration

Like each school in the network, Pulaski School maintains its own independent school administration. A Parent-Teacher Association elects the school board, which negotiates for space, sets teachers' salaries, and pays the bills.

Tuition covers the majority of the school budget, around fourteen thousand dollars a year. The remaining funds come from contributions made by Polish organizations (channeled through the Polish Teachers Association) and fund-raising efforts by parents. Parents' contributions—service on the school board, sewing costumes for school presentations, organizing, and baking for the yearly fund-raisers—are essential. Administrators stress the difficulties of raising even relatively modest amounts of money and the personal sacrifices of all involved.

The Polish-American community has several large fraternal organizations which help to support various community cultural efforts. Some Polish schools have chosen to affiliate with these organizations, such as the Po-

A Polish Saturday school participating in the Polish Constitution Day Parade, Chicago, Illinois. (ES82-AF87864-1-6A) Photo by Margy McClain

lish National Alliance or the Polish Roman Catholic Union, which then contribute to the school's maintenance. Other schools feel that the resulting financial support also means giving up some decision-making powers to the larger organizations. Pulaski School has chosen to remain independent, maintaining full control over school affairs and assuming full financial responsibility.

Administration: The Polish Schools Network

The Polish Teachers Association in America addresses the shared concerns of the Polish schools in the Chicago area's fifteen-school network. One of the most pressing issues is the unique curriculum needs of ethnic schools. Language and other texts developed for use in the home country do not relate to the experience of children growing up in the United States, while books developed for students with no knowledge of the language are inappropriate for children who speak the language at home. Ethnic schools are forced, therefore, to adapt books which are not suited to their needs or to write new ones.

For many years individual teachers in the Polish Saturday schools had to resolve the problem of teaching materials on their own. Some were remarkably successful. Mrs. Maria Neumann, a seventeen-year veteran teacher at Pulaski High School, proudly opened a closet door to reveal five floor-to-ceiling bookcases holding an extensive library of Polish literature and reference books that she has accumulated for her students. In another classroom hand-drawn, wall-size maps of Poland illustrated historical changes in the nation's territory.

The PTAA began to develop its own textbooks and teaching materials in the mid-1960s. Its first project was *Polska Mowa* (*The Polish Language*), an introduction to the Polish language for older children and adults. Now in its eighth edition, *Polska Mowa* is used not only in Polish Saturday schools in the United States, Canada, England, and Australia, but in college and high school Polish language classes.

Later projects focused on developing literature and history readers for the elementary and junior high school grades, because high school classes can often use high school literature texts from Poland. History texts from Poland written since the Communist takeover are considered unacceptable, however. The PTAA has developed, therefore, a four-volume *History of Poland*. Texts are also exchanged with Polish schools in England and Canada, where similar curriculum-development efforts have taken place.

Like so many other activities in the Polish schools, creating the textbooks is a labor of love. Professional educators from the PTAA volunteer their time. It is an extensive commitment, since writing a text can take several years.

In the 1970s, as the Polish school network expanded rapidly, the PTAA began work on a standardized curriculum to aid teachers and allow students to move more easily between schools. The PTAA established guidelines for the types of classes to be offered: kindergarten, eight years of elementary school, and four years of high school for Polish-speaking children; introductory classes for children who do not speak Polish; and a singing, music, dance, and theater program. The association is developing detailed curriculum guidelines for each year.

The PTAA offers a variety of support services to its member schools. It sponsors activities, notably popular essay and poetry recitation contests, that promote Polish language teaching. A poetry recitation contest in 1982 attracted enthusiastic participation from eight hundred students from Polish Saturday schools, public and private high school Polish classes, and area colleges. The organization also maintains a small lending library of teaching aids, including pictures, slide-tape programs, and equipment.

Polish community organizations often work together, and the PTAA supports the activities of many other Chicago-area Polish institutions. One concrete manifestation of community solidarity is the Polish Constitution Day Parade in May. Among the floats decked out in Poland's red and white colors students march, bearing Polish language school standards. From each flag the school's namesake—Pulaski, Chopin, Paderewski— watches over its charges.

The PTAA was originally organized as a professional organization for all teachers of Polish descent, even those not teaching in Polish schools. The organization sponsors teacher in-service seminars, and has co-sponsored courses with the Chicago Board of Education to help new arrivals qualify for American teaching credentials.

The PTAA also serves as an accrediting body for teachers who apply to work in the Polish schools. The group is very concerned about upholding standards. It verifies the applicants' Polish credentials, then places their names on a waiting list. In spite of low pay and inconvenient hours, there is usually a waiting list for positions in the Polish schools. In Poland teaching is a highly respected, if poorly paid, profession. Many teachers newly arrived in Chicago are unable to learn English well enough to get recertified to teach in American schools. Being unable to work in the profession they often love is a blow to their self-esteem, so immigrant teachers seek out the Polish schools.

Pulaski's principal, Mr. Józef Żurczak, understands their motivations completely: "They say that they only feel like people on Saturdays.... They miss their profession, they miss working with children." Others feel very strongly that they should not waste specialized training and talents: "I can't ask an engineer or a mechanic to do it," says Helena Ziółkowska. "I'm the one with the training and it is my responsibility to use it." Some younger women at home with small children, often Polish school graduates, find Saturday school a convenient way to keep up with previous acquaintances.

Personal motivation must be high to keep teachers in the schools. Salaries often do not cover much more than the cost of gas and childcare. One teacher said that during the 1960s she worked for six dollars a day and paid her babysitter ten dollars. Salaries now range from eight to ten dollars per hour.

Ninety percent of the teachers in the Polish Saturday schools were born and educated in Poland. They range in age from twenty-five to seventy. Newly arrived teachers help to keep contemporary Polish language in the schools, while bilingual teachers raised in the United States teach the classes for children from English-speaking homes.

The PTAA provides a constellation of services that supports the educators and schools of the Polish schools network. Efforts in all areas—textbook development, curriculum standardization, and teacher accreditation and development—reflect the association's high standards as professionals and its determination to provide an educational experience through which students really master the language.

The Future of the Polish Saturday Schools

The Polish schools serve primarily their own ethnic community. In the 1980s, however, one of their major concerns is their relationship with the larger society. The schools would like to be recognized by the Illinois State Board of Education so that their students would receive credit for their achievements in a second language. State recognition would be a great help to Polish and other ethnic schools in attracting and keeping students.

Polish and other ethnic schools realize that they are helping to supply a resource—bilingual people—that is much in demand by government and business. These schools help to fill the gap left by declining foreign language education in American schools. Ethnic school officials, teachers, and parents are frustrated that recognition of their efforts is coming so slowly. Several proposals to the State Board of Education over the past ten years have been rejected. Yet the fact that the issue has arisen at all is an indication of the increasing willingness on the part of ethnic communities to make a public case for recognition of their contributions to the larger American society.

Will the Polish Saturday schools continue to serve the needs of Polonia? As the generation that founded the Polish Saturday schools graduates their youngest children from high school in the early 1980s, the future is uncertain. Third- and fourth-generation Polish-American families have not supported the Saturday schools strongly in the past. Although there are significant numbers of more recent immigrants, earlier immigrants perceive the attitudes toward Polish education of these recent arrivals to be different from their own. As past PTAA president Helena Ziółkowska noted:

> People who came to this country from Europe in the late '40s and '50s were survivors of World War II, and they were very patriotic. And to them survival meant to be Polish and to keep the Polish language, and faith, and traditions.... If these people were able to transfer their motivations and feelings to the next generation, then these children have children now, and they send them to Polish schools. But not all of them succeeded. Some of the children went to Polish schools because they had to, and once they got married, sometimes to people of different nationality, they didn't pay that much attention....
>
> But people who come from Poland right now are of different stock.... Many of them don't feel that they should keep up the Polish tradition. Not everybody, but quite a big percentage, assimilates very quickly. They don't talk Polish at home ... it's very sad.... I don't feel sorry for them, I feel sorry for their children, because they end up not knowing anything about themselves.
>
> I have a duty to give what I received to the next generation. Language, culture, history, tradition, national pride enrich your life. But more than that, if you know who you are and where you come from, you know what you're worth.

Conclusions

Perhaps the most important contribution of the Polish schools is that they help young people develop a positive sense of self-identity that includes being Polish-American. Being ethnic in the United States is a pervasive part of American society, one that does not disappear readily even over several generations. As this fact becomes more widely acknowledged, we need to seek ways to help people accept their ethnic identity and use it positively. Polish and other ethnic schools provide a useful skill—knowledge of a second language—which can, in itself, be a source of pride and achievement. We are also struggling with the problem of having thousands of Americans go through life coping with profound ambivalence and self-doubt because they have been told that "being ethnic" is not a positive part of "being American." Ethnic schools strengthen the fabric of American life as they help young people to accept, validate, and integrate their varying heritages into their concepts of being American.

Acknowledgments

I extend my deep appreciation to the Polish Teachers Association in America, Inc. and its staff, and to General Casimir Pulaski Polish School and its staff, students and parents, all of whom generously aided me in my efforts to understand the Polish schools. In particular, Wiktor Barczyk of the PTAA introduced me to the schools and accompanied me on several occasions. Helena Ziółkowska, PTAA president, not only gave generously of her time during the project but read subsequent drafts of my report with a critical eye. Polish-educator Edwin Cudecki first put me in touch with the PTAA and has shared many insights into Chicago Polonia. James Ylisela offered valuable suggestions in drafting the final version of my report.

Selected Bibliography

Bolek, Francis. *The Polish American School System.* New York: Columbia Press Corporation, 1948.

Franchine, Phillip. "Chicago Taps Language Wealth." *American Education,* vol. 16, no. 4 (May 1980), pp. 8–15.

Hoffmann, Wilma M. "Chicago Area Ethnic Weekend Schools: Goals and Achievements." Ph.D. dissertation. University of Chicago, 1978.

Kantowicz, Edward R. "Polish Chicago: Survival Through Solidarity." In *Ethnic Chicago,* rev. ed., Melvin Holli and Peter d'A. Jones, eds. Grand Rapids: William B. Eerdmans Publishing Company, 1984.

Krolikowski, Walter P. "Poles in America: Maintaining the Ties." *Theory Into Practice,* vol. 20, no. 1 (Winter 1981), pp. 52–57.

Parot, Joseph John. *Polish Catholics in Chicago, 1850–1920: A Religious History.* DeKalb, Illinois: Northern Illinois University Press, 1981.

Notes

1. On the struggle between ethnic religious orders and the Archdiocese for control of ethnic parishes, *see* Edward R. Kantowicz, "Polish Chicago: Survival Through Solidarity," in *Ethnic Chicago,* rev. ed., Melvin Holli and Peter d'A. Jones, eds. (Grand Rapids: William B. Eerdmans Publishing Company, 1984).

2. During World War II the Polish government in exile established itself in England. The Polish Army fought alongside the British Army and, when the war ended, the Polish Army demobilized in England.

The Senshin Gakuin and the Dharma School of the Senshin Buddhist Church of Los Angeles

Los Angeles, California

Amy E. Skillman

History of the Senshin Buddhist Church

The Senshin Buddhist Church is located about ten miles west of downtown Los Angeles. It was founded in 1928 for the express purpose of teaching the Japanese language and conveying the teaching of Shinran Shonin, a disciple of Buddha and the leader of the Jodo-Shinshu sect of Buddhism. There are two distinct and on-going school programs at Senshin: the Senshin Gakuin, a Japanese language school, and the Senshin Dharma School, a Japanese Buddhist study school.

Because the Hompa Hongwanji (main temple) was located downtown, Senshin grew quickly, offering as it did the convenience of proximity to the local Buddhist community. A critical need for additional facilities arose with the increased enrollment of students which resulted. The dedication of a new classroom building took place in March 1938. The Gakuin (language school) was formally incorporated as a non-profit corporation in the state of California the same year. The establishing families were able to clear the mortgage on the church in the closing years of the 1930s.

With the bombing of Pearl Harbor on December 7, 1941, a special cabinet meeting was called to consider emergency steps required for the continuance of the Gakuin; however, both schools were suspended indefinitely. The government assembled Senshin families, with the exception of those who had evacuated voluntarily, on May 1, 1942, at the Santa Anita Assembly Center in Arcadia, California, and sent them to the Granada Relocation Center in Amache, Colorado. Before leaving they straightened up the interior of the church building and boarded up the exterior for security. Rev. Julius A. Goldwater, a caucasian minister of the Jodo-Shinshu sect, assumed responsibility for the care of Senshin and the main temple.

Pre-school pupils at the Dharma School in Los Angeles drawing "me pictures." (ES82-041682-11) Photo by Amy E. Skillman

157

Following VJ Day—August 11, 1945—the Reverend Mr. Goldwater converted the Gakuin into a hostel for the returning families until they were able to find accommodations. The Dharma School reopened immediately; in response to many requests from church members, the Gakuin also reopened.

The Senshin Buddhist Church became independent from the Hompa Hongwanji on May 1, 1951. Because of the growing Japanese and Japanese-American population in the area, the *sangha* (congregation) felt that a community temple could better meet its needs. According to the terms of incorporation for the Senshin Gakuin, the church membership was divided into regular members who are second-generation Japanese-Americans (*nisei*) and associate members who are first-generation Japanese-Americans (*issei*). The corporate officers were nisei and the board members were issei.

On September 21, 1963, the church membership adopted a five-year plan to construct a $250,000 religious-education complex and a new minister's residence. Construction began on March 10, 1965, using architectural plans submitted by Shimosono-Tawa. On May 1, 1966, thirty-eight years after the founding of the Gakuin, Senshin's facilities were capable of meeting the needs of 500 Dharma School students and 150 Gakuin students, and of housing the many activities of their affiliated organizations. The church membership has paid all construction costs over the years.

A twenty-year, $250,000 trust fund (*zaidan*) was established in 1971 as a commemorative project, to insure the economic sustenance of the congregation. The principal is to remain untouched; the earnings will offset any operating deficit, underwrite extraordinary programs, establish scholarships, and fund projects for the well-being of the congregation. Due to the trust fund, the temple currently finds itself in a strong position to meet the needs of its congregation.

Church Leadership

There are currently two reverends at Senshin: the Reverend Hoshin Fujikado and the Reverend Maseo Kodani ("Reverend Mas" as he is called). The Reverend Mr. Fujikado, who is Japanese, is most directly involved with the Japanese-speaking members (issei) of the church. He is also principal of the Gakuin. Reverend Mas is Japanese-American and works more closely with the English-speaking members of the church. He is advisor to the Dharma School. The combination of Japanese and Japanese-American leadership appears to be a positive force at Senshin.

Reverend Mas explained that many Japanese-Americans carry with them a sense of being a "national embarrassment" to Japan. They look Japanese and, in many ways, act Japanese; but they no longer speak the language, nor do they always understand their cultural make-up. This has caused a barrier between the Japanese and Japanese-Americans in many communities. Senshin tries to accommodate the needs of both groups. On Sunday morning the service begins with both reverends present. Just after Reverend Mas's sermon, the Japanese-speaking members leave with the Reverend Mr. Fujikado to continue their service in a small chapel behind the auditorium. The other church members disperse to their various Dharma classes.

Reverend Mas's sermon is a very important part of the cultural enlightenment offered at Senshin. He begins talking about some physical aspect of Buddhism (bells, flowers, or batik), explaining not only how it relates to Buddhism, but also how it relates to everyday life. He also relays a story, either from his experiences in Japan or from the storehouse of traditional tales and myths surrounding Buddhism. He presents his sermons in a very story-like manner. In fact, "sermon" seems an inappropriate word. Reverend Mas has the ability and desire to transmit to the listeners an increased understanding of their own personalities. As a leader he has initiated many of the changes at Senshin which have enabled the members to explore their cultural identity.

The Senshin Gakuin

The Senshin Gakuin currently teaches Japanese to approximately 25 students, aged five through sixteen. At its peak enrollment ran as high as 150. Most of the Japanese and Japanese-Americans who lived in the area have moved away in the past ten years, however. They still return to the church for service on Sundays, but prefer to send their children to a language school closer to home. There are at least four other Japanese language schools in the Los Angeles area. That fact indicates that interest in maintaining the language is still high. Yet the area surrounding Senshin has changed from Japanese to Afro-American, causing a decrease in local interest in learning Japanese. In fact, the school has considered folding twice, due to low enrollment, but the members decided to continue.

The Senshin Gakuin does not pay rent or overhead, because the church donates the space to the school. Students pay a monthly fee of twelve dollars, which covers the books and the honoraria paid to the teachers. The church covers any unforeseen expenses.

Senshin Gakuin—School Administration

A cabinet made up of the principal, head instructor, chairperson, assistants, treasurer, and advisor governs the Gakuin. Members of the board fill these positions. The board has about ninety members, thirty to thirty-five of whom are very active. All major decisions come before the board for discussion and ruling. Most adult members of the church are members of the board.

The Senshin Gakuin is also a member of the American Japanese Language School Association (AJLSA), which is part of the Buddhist Churches of America and is headquartered at the Hompa Hongwanji in downtown Los Angeles.

Senshin Gakuin—Teachers

There are only two teachers, both of whom are from Japan: Sumiko Ono, who teaches first through third grade, and Henry Inouye, who teaches fourth through nineth. Ms. Ono began teaching Japanese in America in 1975 and has been teaching at Senshin for two years. In 1982 she had four students—three girls and one boy. Three of those students graduated to the upper level, so there is concern that the lower level class will not continue. Mr. Inouye has been teaching the upper level classes at Senshin for twenty-one years. Three students graduated from the class in June 1982, so his classes will remain about the same size.

The AJLSA sponsors conferences every three months for teachers in the Southern California area. The purpose is to discuss problems, ideas, and curriculum materials. The teachers determine what should be included in the curriculum materials and seek printing assistance from the Japanese Education Department. Even so, not all the teachers in Southern California follow the same format.

There is another organization, called the Kyoto System, which offers materials and conferences for Japanese language teachers. The system requires that teachers be trained in education. While Senshin does not require teachers to be trained in education, they can choose to go through a training program. Both the AJLSA and the Kyoto System offer seminars every year.

Senshin Gakuin—Classes and Curriculum

A key difference between AJLSA and the Kyoto System is the emphasis on the various written characters of the Japanese language. The Kyoto System first teaches *katakana* characters, used for translating other languages into Japanese. The system then goes on to teach *hirakana,* common Japanese writing, and *kanji,* the complex Chinese characters used in formal communications. The AJLSA teaches hirakana first and katakana next, interspersing a few kanji words from the beginning. One might infer that teaching katakana first emphasizes the use of Japanese as a second language—a major consideration among Japanese-language teachers.

The question of whether Japanese is taught as a first or second language is further reflected in the choice of curriculum materials. In the past the instructors used books that were printed and published in Japan. Now, however, they use books that are developed in the United States. Although these books are "much easier" than those developed in Japan, Mr. Inouye feels that they are useful because they reflect American ideals and "seem to fit these kids better." The newer books do not have much information about Japanese culture and tradition, a fact that Mr. Inouye seems to regret. He feels the students are better able to learn the language with these books, however.

Workbooks with exercises to complement each section of the textbook accompany the books. Ms. Ono only gives the students one-half hour of homework from the workbook. The Kyoto System requires much more homework and asks the parents to help their children. Ms. Ono feels this is not constructive, because the parents end up doing most of the homework and the children do not learn. Even so, both teachers feel the children forget all they have learned during the week.

Both teachers design their own tests and grade the students on an A, B, C scoring basis. Mr. Inouye also designs a test each year for the high school students who wish to receive their language credit in Japanese. Dr. Kumizuko at the University of Southern California approves the test.

While Mr. Inouye closely follows the format of the books, Ms. Ono prefers to combine the books from the United States with a book from Japan. The books from the United States are very basic, teaching how to count, tell time, order lunch, and so forth. They can get quite boring. The book from Japan has stories about Japan, folktales, more grammar, and more words. She explained that the book expresses more Japanese feelings. For instance, the Japanese have many ways of describing the beauty of a flower, each one expressing a different feeling. Ms. Ono wants to teach those feelings to the children.

The students at the Senshin Gakuin are divided according to proficiency. A student's grade level in the Gakuin many not always correspond to his or her grade level in the regular school. It is rare for a student to fail a Gakuin class.

The Gakuin classes meet every Saturday from 8:30 A.M. to 12:30 P.M. from September through the middle of June. The morning includes four fifty-minute periods, with a ten-minute recess between each period. The subjects taught are conversation, reading, writing, meaning, and composition.

Ms. Ono begins each day with conversation or a new subject, because she feels the children are more awake and alert at that hour. During the second period the focus is on reading, meaning, and translation. For the third period they concentrate on writing single characters and, occasionally, composition. Composition is very difficult for the children at this age, so she keeps it to a minimum. Because the children tend to be tired and hungry by the fourth period, Ms. Ono likes to involve them in some cultural traditions, such as origami, folktales, or painting, which are more enjoyable learning tools and will hold the children's attention. She tries to conduct such periods entirely in Japanese.

Mr. Inouye follows a similar pattern. He gives a test on a recent lesson in the second period. He devotes the third period to reading and the fourth to writing. In the past he included lessons about Japanese culture, especially folk dance, but Reverend Mas now includes so much of that in the

Dharma School that it is not essential to include it in the language school. This reflects the complementary nature of the two programs. Mr. Inouye occasionally tells stories and shows films about life in Japan; his focus, however, is conversation. Both teachers feel that, while reading and writing are valuable, the most important aspect of learning the language is conversation—to speak comfortably with proper pronunciation. They seem to feel that speaking is more important for students returning to Japan or speaking with first-generation immigrants. It is also important for continuing and maintaining the language in the United States. Ms. Ono expressed the feeling that, since the students are Japanese, they should speak Japanese. In general, the students read and understand Japanese better than they speak it.

The issue of Japanese as a first or second language is important with relation to the format of the classes as well. Years ago, when the nisei were learning Japanese to communicate with older family members, the classes focused on grammar and were entirely in Japanese. Mr. Inouye said he would get mad at the students for using English in the classroom. One former student could remember the smack of the ruler across the knuckles for such an offense. Today, however, the third- and fourth-generation students require a different method of teaching. As Ms. Ono explained, it is important that the teachers speak English to explain things to the students. "I strongly believe you have to communicate with the children first," she says. "Then you teach Japanese to them." (ES82-AS-C8) She also feels it is essential to build a positive relationship with the students in order to spark their interest. The use of both languages seems to create a more relaxed atmosphere in the classroom than was evident in the past.

The classrooms are very much like public school classrooms, with rows of desks, chairs, large blackboards on two walls, a bulletin board on the back wall, and cabinets of bookshelves under the windows on the fourth wall. Textbooks and students' records are kept in a small room adjacent to Mr. Inouye's classroom. Posters from Japan, lists of kanji, a small shrine with a drawing of the Buddha, and artwork created by the students decorate the walls. Japanese children's magazines, art supplies, and Japanese toys fill the bookshelves.

In Ms. Ono's class a few tables are pulled together and they all sit in a circle, giving the feeling of a school session one might experience in the home. There is a feeling of love and caring between the teacher and students. In fact, one of the students is Ms. Ono's child. The younger students seem sincerely interested in what they are learning. There is no pressure placed on the students to participate, yet they are all attentive.

Mr. Inouye's class is a bit different. The students practice among themselves while Mr. Inouye moves from one level to the other, working individually with the students in each level. All the students listen occasionally while each one recites from his or her reading book. The students seem to enjoy working together. Mr. Inouye is extremely helpful to the students, even while they are taking tests. He seems genuinely concerned about their success. The students call him *sensei,* which means teacher or wise one. Each class begins and ends with a traditional bow of respect.

Both teachers make a point of keeping any religious beliefs out of the lessons, so that anyone can take the classes. It is important to keep in mind, though, that almost all of the students are members of the Senshin Buddhist Church, as are both teachers.

The Senshin Gakuin culminates each year with the graduation ceremony held in the auditorium of the temple complex. In previous years they also held a speech contest, but the class has not been large enough recently to continue that tradition. Today the graduation ceremony combines the two.

With the exception of a few moments, the ceremony is entirely in Japanese. The program has two parts. During the first half the students sit in rows with the audience, while the president of the church, head instructor, Gakuin advisor, and principal sit on the stage. An American and Japanese flag hang on the wall behind them. The ceremony opens with the "Star Spangled Banner" (in English). Graduation diplomas and perfect-attendance awards are given out at this time. Each student walks up on the stage alone and receives the award and gift from the members of the cabinet. Next, advice and memories are exchanged between the graduates and the younger students. Their brief speeches are punctuated by traditional Japanese graduation songs. One song has the tune of "Auld Lang Syne," yet is considered traditionally Japanese. This year an award was also given to Mr. Inouye for his twenty-one years of dedication as a language teacher at Senshin.

During the second half of the ceremony the students take the stage and recite or read from their reading books one by one. It is interesting to note that a student's performance follows the award of diplomas, which suggests that the student's success is not contingent upon the performance at the ceremony. Instead, because every student performs in Japanese, every student is honored for his or her progress. This year Ms. Ono's class recited a Japanese folktale from memory. Each student recited one part of the tale, holding a drawing which depicted that particular aspect of the story. The upper-level students read various dialogues, such as a story, a proverbial tale, or an accounting of the geographical features of the earth.

Photographic session and feast followed the ceremony. With the exception of one traditional Japanese cake, the food was typically American. The ceremony is a positive combination of both American and Japanese traditions, reflecting a degree of comfortableness in the Japanese-American community's sense of identity.

Senshin Gakuin—Parents

On the whole the parents send their children to the language school because they feel it is important for them to have a sense of their cultural identity. They feel that language is one of the most important aspects of culture; understanding the language will help one understand the culture. The parents also feel that, while their children will grow up as Americans, an understanding of their Japanese heritage will help them deal with the fact that they are different from most of the people they will associate with throughout life. For many the Senshin Gakuin is the only opportunity for their children to interact with other Japanese-American children.

For some parents it is important that their children be able to communicate in Japanese, should they ever visit Japan. It is understandably difficult for someone who looks Japanese to feel comfortable in Japan without speaking the language. One parent explained the changes in parents' motivations over the years. Initially, Japanese was taught to children because parents thought they would be returning to Japan and wanted their children to maintain their proficiency. The next generation taught their children so they could communicate with the first- and second-generation immigrants. Now the children learn the language to assist the United States in maintaining good relations with Japan. Another reason expressed by both parents and children is that Japanese can satisfy the student's language requirement in college.

In many cases the parents do not speak Japanese. They grew up at a time when most Japanese-Americans were demonstrating their loyalty to the United States; consequently, parents emphasized few Japanese traditions in the home. For those who did go to a language school, the classes were very strict. Most parents and teachers agree that the looser format is more effective for today's children.

Despite the motivations for language instruction articulated by many parents and children, Mr. Inouye occasionally feels that he is babysitting. He feels the parents merely drop the children off, come back four hours later, and do not always express an interest in their child's progress. Obviously, this attitude, which can also be found in the public schools, is not the attitude of all parents.

Senshin Gakuin—Students

Mr. Inouye feels there are many things the children would rather be doing on Saturday morning. Ms. Ono also expressed her sorrow that the children, "hate to go to Japanese School. Even my kids, they always complaining. That hurting me a lot." (ES82-AS-C8) A student overhearing the conversation shook her head in disagreement.

The children do not appear to mind going to the language school, however. They may complain about it before they get there, but, once there, they seem to have a good time. Most of them are there because their parents want them to learn Japanese. They are not sure why and, when asked, they appear apathetic. "Since I'm Japanese, I guess they want me to learn Japanese so, if I go to Japan, I can talk to my relatives ...," says Yumi Yoshida. (ES82-AS-C1)

Harumi Saneto provides a variation on the theme of parental motivation:

Taiko Drum group practicing at the Dharma School in Los Angeles. (ES82-15311-32) Photo by Amy E. Skillman

Well, I don't know, I don't remember. I remember my mom said, like, when I was little, all I did was talk Japanese. But then, when I went to school, I forgot everything, 'cause everyone else was speaking English. She said if I remembered it, then I wouldn't have to come; but then, I didn't remember it, so I have to come.... (ES82-AS-C3)

Because the students attend both the Senshin Gakuin and the Dharma School, they know each other well. Some of the older students see each other at public school, but, because they are in different grades, they do not spend much time together. There are a few pairs who are best friends. The junior and senior high schools in the area are culturally integrated, so the Senshin students have friends from a variety of cultural backgrounds. In fact, several of them expressed interest in learning Spanish more than Japanese. A few have friends at other Japanese language schools, as well as friends who go to Hebrew school. They rarely share their language school experiences, however, except (according to a few students) to teach each other the usual four-letter words.

Senshin Gakuin—Future of the School

Given an opportunity to make any changes in the Senshin Gakuin, the first concern is to increase enrollment. There is a feeling that enrollment will increase as parents with young children renew their involvement with

Senshin. The church currently has affiliated organizations for all age groups except the twenty-five- to thirty-five-year-olds. Consequently, this age group is less involved with the church when their children are very young. As their children begin school, however, many of the parents rejoin the church, becoming active in the Adult Buddhist Association.

Another desired change, expressed particularly by Mr. Inouye, concerns the lack of conversational ease on the part of the students. He would like to add a language class that would be strictly Japanese conversation. Such a class might also be offered for adults.

A final concern, expressed by the students, is to update the books so they are not so corny and boring. This might make the classes more enjoyable and improve comprehension.

In summary, although the Senshin Gakuin has experienced major fluctuations in enrollment, the Japanese-American community still considers it an important means by which it can understand, maintain, and enhance its sense of identity.

Senshin Dharma School—School Administration

Like the Senshin Gakuin, the Senshin Dharma School has a cabinet responsible for making major decisions. It meets once a month with all the teachers to discuss the program for the upcoming two months. Although the teachers have quite a bit of freedom in planning their classes, these meetings help to maintain a meaningful and cohesive program. The students pay no tuition. Instead, the parents make an annual donation to the Dharma School. The Dharma School occasionally sponsors a fund-raising event within the church. The various affiliated groups also have fund-raisers to support their activities from time to time.

Senshin Dharma School—Teachers

The teachers at the Dharma School are all members of the church. They teach entirely on a volunteer basis. All of them have attended Dharma School, many at Senshin. There are currently fourteen teachers, ranging in age from seventeen to fifty, with between two and thirty years of experience. The teachers are not required to have any formal training, yet a knowledge of Buddhism and the desire to explore and share Buddhist philosophy with the children are preferred qualifications.

When the Dharma School first began, before World War II, the teachers all held jobs as public school teachers; that was one of the few jobs that Japanese women could hold at the time, and most of the Dharma School teachers were women. A woman, usually the reverend's wife, who was trained in these arts and was responsible for flower arranging and food preparation for all the services, also taught traditional arts classes at the church.

Senshin Dharma School—Classes and Curriculum

Previously, all classes, whether religious or artistic, were very structured. Students had to stand and repeat a moral code when the teacher entered the classroom. The classes themselves consisted of formal lectures about the various teachings of Buddhism. For the most part, the same teachings occurred each year, but with greater detail and depth as the students got older. The school directed little attention toward other aspects of Japanese life. This format continued until after World War II.

Today's Dharma School is quite different. The classes meet for about an hour and a half each Sunday in the classroom building of the temple complex. The students are divided according to age, with each level having a Japanese-Buddhist name, such as Sanghateen. There is also an adult study class that meets at the same time on Sunday and again on Wednesday evenings in members' homes. The classes are informal, with many of them focusing on specific projects.

All classes are in English. The Buddhist Churches of America (BCA) offers conferences and workshops for any interested teachers. Held throughout the year, they guide teachers in the presentation of materials and offer an opportunity to share ideas. There is also an annual conference for the Young Buddhist Association, during which high school and college students can interact with other Japanese-Americans. One teacher expressed the feeling that these conferences have taken on a predominantly social characteristic over the years. She is sorry that an opportunity to share religious ideas has become more of a social event, but agrees that it is, perhaps, just as important for students to interact comfortably with other Japanese-American Buddhists.

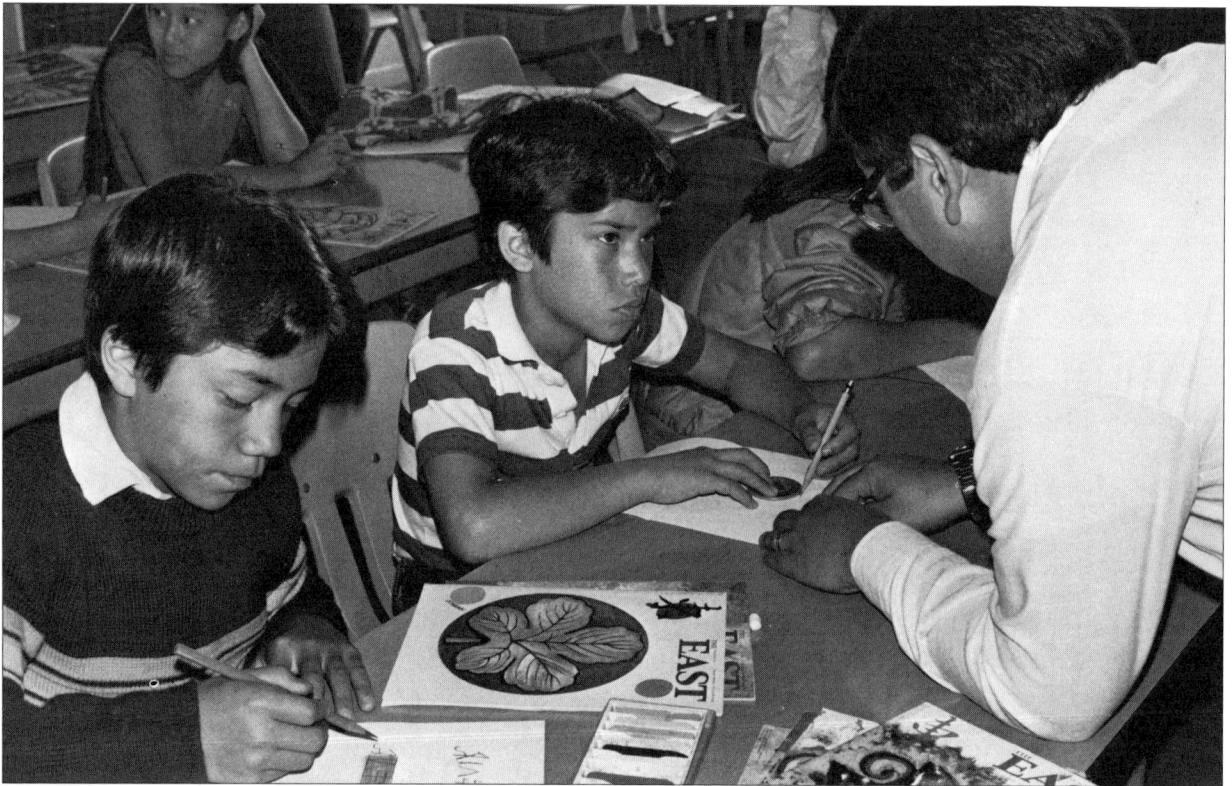

Students in batik class at the Dharma School look through copies of *East* magazine for designs. (ES82-17427-17) Photo by Amy E. Skillman

The BCA, headquartered in San Francisco, publishes a wide variety of educational materials for Buddhist organizations. As a member of the BCA, the Senshin Dharma School receives the materials free of charge. They, in turn, pass them along to the students. The Senshin Buddhist Church also publishes a variety of service books itself, and is currently working on a history of the altar in their temple. In fact, the church complex includes a large library and information center located in the building that houses the classrooms. The library has several shelves stacked with books about a wide variety of belief systems, photographs of all past reverends, a counter covered with several handmade objects, a glass case containing religious objects used in the service, and a counter for flyers and announcements of upcoming community events. The table in the middle of the room currently holds a high pile of research materials for the altar publication.

The curriculum materials from the BCA have been in pamphlet form in the past, focusing almost entirely on Buddhist teachings. Recently, however, the Dharma School received the new *Dharma School Teachers' Guide* from BCA. It is in notebook form and contains 433 pages of guidelines and classroom projects for teaching Buddhism. The subjects include traditional and non-traditional arts, ideas for conducting family histories and exploring oneself, and approaches to the many American and Buddhist holidays.

Many significant changes have occurred in the Dharma School over the past fourteen years. In fact, Reverend Mas feels that many of the changes would not have been possible at most other temples. Perhaps the most drastic change, and the one most difficult to accept, concerns the best point at which to teach the Buddhist doctrines to the children. There are two schools of thought on the subject. Some feel the doctrines should be taught from the beginning and that to wait until the children are older is a waste of valuable time. Reverend Mas, on the other hand, believes that children will understand the doctrines better if they can apply them to practical experiences. He explained that enlightenment can be quite brutal, because it is achieved through letting go of the ego. One must have a healthy ego in order to put it aside, however. For that reason, he has introduced several programs to help members, both young and old, develop a stronger sense of identity to prepare for the process of enlightenment. He feels it is important that Japanese-Americans understand their Japanese and their American background. Bicultural identity can be painful, especially for young adults. They need to be exposed to overt cultural traditions, as well as to less obvious traditions—such as relationships within the family unit—which contribute to one's personality. Reverend Mas's goal is to help Japanese-Americans feel comfortable with their bicultural identity.

The Dharma School programs reflect the goal of exploring bicultural identity. The students learn batik, research family crests, write haiku, videotape major church events, create self-portraits, and examine Buddhist doctrines. Each student is also a member of an affiliated social group within the church, which offers several opportunities for interaction. The adult study classes provide an opportunity for adults to learn about their heritage and become better able to encourage and explore it with their children. One particular class focused on the many differences between the Japanese and the Chinese, as found in their literature. The adults seemed very attentive and appeared to appreciate the cultural distinctions made. Once again Reverend Mas related things to everyday living. For example, to illustrate the Japanese preference for odd numbers versus the Chinese preference for even numbers, he asked how one might arrange four chrysanthemums. Most of the class agreed they would remove or add a flower before attempting to arrange them.

The Kinnara Taiko drum group and the Gagaku traditional court music group are also important activities for adults. Participants range in age from seventeen to fifty and include men and women. There is also a Taiko group for younger people. Members often bring their children to the Gagaku group classes to expose them to the tradition and its unfamiliar sounds. As Reverend Mas explains, if his daughter chooses not to hold on to her Japanese identity, that is her choice. "I want her to know what she is throwing away," he adds.

Because of the method of training for the Taiko and Gagaku group, it is often difficult for young people to maintain involvement for long. The philosophy of lack of ego involvement is predominant. Members are encouraged to learn all the instruments and all their parts, but little reinforcement, either positive or negative, is provided. The experience is viewed as a kind of microcosm of the Buddhist philosophy, as well as the realities of everyday life. The interrelationship between cultural traditions and beliefs is characteristic of Senshin, as is the method of teaching.

An important aspect of the two musical groups is the element of tradition. The oldest form of orchestral music in the world is being preserved by the Gagaku group; the newest piece of music in the style dates from 900

A.D. The Taiko group, on the other hand, combines the experiences of Japanese-Americans in Los Angeles with the Japanese musical tradition. The group combines African, Latino, and Native American rhythms with jazz, rhythm and blues, and traditional forms in each presentation. As Reverend Mas explains:

You preserve it, and then you have something else, so, each time, you add something. The Japanese never throw it away, they always just add to it. That's what we want to do—we want to say that if a new form comes it doesn't replace the old. (ES82-AS-C13)

A performance by the Sanghateens (the group affiliated with the junior high school), which they developed for their teacher as a bridal-shower present, expressed the ideal of combining traditional and modern elements beautifully. The dancers wore traditional kimonos and samurai dress. Executing many traditional steps, they danced to disco played through a cassette tape player.

The Senshin congregation seems to have responded enthusiastically to the new programming. As with all change, reactions were mixed initially. Some feel even now that the cultural traditions have taken precedent over the religious teachings. More balance may be necessary. Yet the need for balance may be more closely related to a need for order. The diverse programming lends an air of disorder. Dharma School no longer has the format of school. One student commented that they do not have regular classes—"It seems more like hobbies." A teacher also expressed frustration that she was not able to fit all of her religious lessons into this year's schedule because of the many cultural programs.

Reactions to the new *Dharma School Teachers' Guide* are also varied. While most of the teachers feel that the new guide is a welcome change, they also indicated that it probably will not be used much at Senshin.

Reverend Mas said he would probably refer to it occasionally for a good story to include in a sermon, but that it is too structured for the current Dharma School teaching staff and programs. Terry Nakawatase, a teacher who has been at Senshin for thirty years, said that the most productive way to utilize the guide would be to offer workshops to all the teachers to acquaint them with all its possibilities.

The guide has not yet been implemented in the classes, so it is difficult to know what the students' reactions will be. They do seem to be responsive to the increased cultural activities and are now getting involved in gathering oral histories from first-generation immigrants.

Perhaps the best assessment of the value of the Dharma School comes from one student who explained that she invited her girlfriend to church one day and her friend has been coming on her own ever since. She is only fourteen, but, because the atmosphere has something special to offer her, she has made the choice to continue attending.

Conclusions

Although unusual in Southern California in 1982, the Senshin Buddhist Church is not unique in the history of the migrations of people throughout the world. The church has always been a central meeting ground for immigrant groups as they arrived on foreign soil. Often it was the only tie with the homeland, culture, and language of the past. It brought people together and gave them a sense of identity and security in a strange environment. Over the years, however, as immigrant groups began to feel more comfortable in American society, the church often became less important as a cultural center. Senshin reinforces the bond between belief and culture once again. For many the bond gives strength and stability in a fast-paced, changing world.

Selected Bibliography

Boddy, E. Manchester. *Japanese in America*. Los Angeles: n.p., 1921.

Herman, Masako, ed. *The Japanese in America, 1843–1973*. Dobbs Ferry, N.Y.: Oceana Publications, 1974.

Horinouchi, Isao. "Educational Values and Preadaptation in the Acculturation of Japanese Americans." *Sacramento Anthropological Society* 7 (Fall 1967).

Hosokawa, Bill. *Nisei: The Quiet Americans*. New York: William Morrow and Company, Inc., 1969.

Kashima, Tetsuden. *Buddhism in America: The Social Organization of an Ethnic Religious Institution*. Westport, Conn.: Greenwood Press, 1977.

Levine, Gene N., and Colbert Rhodes. *The Japanese American Community: A Three-Generation Study*. New York: Praeger Publishers, 1981.

Thernstrom, Stephan, ed. *Harvard Encyclopedia of American Ethnic Groups*. Cambridge, Mass. and London: Harvard University Press, 1980.

German-Russian Ethnic Studies at Emmons Central High School
Strasburg, North Dakota

Timothy J. Kloberdanz

The German-Russians comprise one of the larger ethnic groups in the Great Plains region today. Descended from German colonists who first settled in Russia during the 1760s at the invitation of Czarina Catherine the Great, the German-Russians are particularly numerous in the Dakotas, Nebraska, Kansas, eastern Colorado, and the Canadian prairie provinces.

When they settled in Russia, the German-Russians lived in closely knit, agrarian villages that were established along religious lines of affiliation (i.e., Lutheran, Evangelical Reformed, Roman Catholic, Mennonite, or Hutterite). For more than a century in Russia the German-Russians avoided intensive contact, not only with their Russian and Ukrainian hosts but also with German colonists living in neighboring villages. The major German enclaves in Russia included those of the Volga Germans (Wolgadeutschen), established in 1764–67, and the Black Sea Germans (Schwarzmeerdeutschen), established in the late 1780s and early 1800s.[1]

The German colonists in Russia enjoyed decades of self-imposed isolation, until the reforms and Russification measures of Czar Alexander II took place in the 1870s. These reforms caused thousands of German-Russian colonist families to uproot themselves and emigrate to the New World. Having prospered as grain farmers on the treeless Russian steppes, the German-Russian emigrants were attracted to the plains of North America and to the pampas of South America. The German emigration from Russia began in the mid-1870s and continued until World War I. As in Russia, the German-Russians who came to the New World tended to maintain regional and religious affiliations in their settlement patterns. Thus one primarily finds Volga German Protestants in Nebraska, Volga German Catholics in western Kansas, and Black Sea Germans in the Dakotas.[2]

German-Russian studies teacher Les Kramer giving a lesson in genealogy at Emmons Central High School, Strasburg, North Dakota.
(ES82-12678-34A) Photo by Timothy Kloberdanz

177

There is no way of determining exactly how many Americans of German-Russian descent presently reside in the United States, due to recent census records that rarely distinguish German-Russians from other Americans of German ancestry. Yet, German-Russians have become a highly visible ethnic group in the Great Plains states, partially due to the success of two active, ethnic organizations that boast ever-increasing memberships: The American Historical Society of Germans from Russia (AHSGR), founded in Colorado in 1968, and the Germans from Russia Heritage Society (GRHS), established in North Dakota in 1971.

German emigration from the Black Sea region of South Russia coincided with the opening of United States homestead lands on the northern Great Plains. By 1920 some seventy thousand German-Russians of the first and second generation of immigration were living in the state of North Dakota alone.[3] Today North Dakota may have twice as many citizens who are descendents of German-Russians as any other state in the union.[4] When one considers that the entire state of North Dakota has a combined population of only 652,437 (1980 census), one can imagine how numerous the German-Russians seem in such a sparsely settled area.

While North Dakota attracted representative German groups from all of the major settlement areas in Russia, the vast majority came from the Black Sea region near the port city of Odessa. The first German-Russians immigrated to what was then "Dakota Territory" as homesteaders. Although they could not establish closed agrarian villages as they had done in Russia, German-Russians who shared the same religion and regional dialect did establish their homesteads in close proximity to one another. Since some of the better farmlands along the wooded river valleys already had been claimed by Scandinavian immigrants, the German-Russians settled in the southern, central, and north-central portions of the state. Their communities form what has been called the "German-Russian Triangle." Most of the state's German-Russians live within this triangular portion of the state in areas homesteaded by their immigrant forebears less than a century ago.

The town of Strasburg, North Dakota, lies seventy-five miles southeast of Bismarck, the state capital, and about a dozen miles north of the South Dakota line. German-Russian homesteaders established the community in the spring of 1889. They named the struggling pioneer settlement in honor of Strassburg, their home colony in South Russia. With the building of a nearby railroad in 1902, Strasburg gradually grew in size until its inhabitants numbered 700 people in 1930.[5] Yet, as in other small towns on the northern Great Plains, the paucity of farms and jobs prompted many of the local youth to find employment elsewhere. The population of Strasburg, North Dakota, is approximately 623 today (1980 census).

Located in the southern half of Emmons County, Strasburg is in an area densely populated by people of German-Russian ancestry. Neighboring communities, such as Hague and Linton, are well known to North Dakotans as towns where the "German brogue" remains a distinguishing characteristic. While the Strasburg area is primarily German-Russian and Roman Catholic, there is a small settlement of "Hollanders" (who belong to the Dutch Reformed Church) southwest of Strasburg. Large numbers of Protestant German-Russians are found only a few miles to the east, and the Standing Rock Sioux Indian Reservation is located due west, across Lake Oahe and the Missouri River.

As one approaches the prairie community of Strasburg by car, one immediately notices two things: the immense size of its Catholic church, the spire of which can be seen high above the trees and surrounding structures, and the signs off Route 83 that proudly call attention to the fact that Strasburg is the hometown of music maestro Lawrence Welk. Born in a clay-brick pioneer home near Strasburg, Welk grew up practicing an old accordion brought from Russia by his father. Eventually, Lawrence Welk's shy, reserved style, Emmons County "German brogue," and champagne music became well-known trademarks in the entertainment world.

Emmons Central High

On the northwest edge of Strasburg, well within sight of Saints Peter and Paul Catholic Church, stands Emmons Central High School. The pale brick building is one of two high schools in the small community which are within easy walking distance of each other. Emmons Central is a parochial school that serves the Catholic youth of Emmons County, while the local school district administers Strasburg Public School. The casual observer who attempts to see Strasburg as a homogeneous ethnic community—united by a common religious and cultural heritage—will be hard pressed to explain the existence of two high schools in such close proximity to one another.

Checking available published sources regarding the history of the two schools, I found that the first school in Strasburg was parochial, established in 1910 in the basement of the parish church by Ursuline nuns from Calvarienberg, Germany. In 1918 parishioners built St. Benedict's Catholic School, but there were no high school graduates until 1927. Due to financial problems, the parish turned over administration of St. Benedict's school to the Strasburg School District in 1931. The Catholic parish did not regain control of St. Benedict's school until 1960, the same year in which the Strasburg Public School was established. In 1966 St. Benedict's high school in Strasburg consolidated with St. Anthony's high school in Linton (a neighboring town to the north) and Emmons Central High School resulted. At the time of this consolidation Emmons Central High School was "subsidized by all Catholic parishes in the county and ... [provided] an opportunity for Catholic education to a student population from seven different parishes."[6]

The consolidation that occurred in 1966 has meant that Emmons Central High School is no longer a community-based parochial institution but a county-based religious school. Nonetheless, all of the students who attend are German-Russian. By comparison, the Strasburg Public School, while it serves many German-Russian students in the Strasburg area, also meets the needs of non-Catholic, non-German-Russian students. The 1982 graduating class at the Strasburg Public High School numbered twenty-five students. Several were of Hollander background (with family names such as Haan, Nieuwsma, and Van Beek). The 1982 graduating class at Emmons Central High School, on the other hand, numbered twenty-nine students, all of whom came from Catholic, German-Russian families (with surnames like Baumstarck, Silbernagel, and Wikenheiser). In light of the above facts it is perhaps not surprising that Emmons Central High School offers German-Russian Ethnic Studies as an integral part of its curriculum.

History of the German-Russian Ethnic Studies Class

Although I was able to observe the German-Russian studies class at Emmons Central High School on three separate occasions, I had to conduct extensive interviews with the instructor to obtain a better idea of the many topics covered. Mr. Les Kramer, principal of the high school and instructor of the German-Russian studies class, told me that he has been teaching the class since 1974. Before coming to Strasburg he taught high school in the neighboring prairie town of Hague, where he first offered the German-Russian studies class. Although the high school in Hague was extremely small (the 1982 graduating class numbered only seven students), Mr. Kramer considered it an "ideal school" because of the deep sense of community that existed there. He pointed out that all of the German-Russian students at the Hague High School "traced their heritage back to villages five, six miles from each other in Europe." (ES82-TK-C4, Side 1, 62–69)

In 1977 Mr. Kramer and several other high school teachers in North Dakota received small stipends to develop or expand ethnic curriculum materials at their institution. Officials at the University of North Dakota in Grand Forks administered the awards, made possible by special funding from the Office of Education. According to Mr. Kramer, there has been no follow-up study or even any contact from the granting office for the past three or four years.

Class Structure and Curriculum

The German-Russian studies class at Emmons Central High School follows a general sociology class offered by Mr. Kramer during the first semester. He has designed the sociology course to sensitize students to cultural differences and human diversity. The main text used in the class is James D. Calderwood's *The Developing World: Poverty, Growth and Rising Expectations.* The book is the subject of some controversy with other educators, says Mr. Kramer, since "the United States does not come out of that book smelling like roses." (ES82-TK-C3, Side 2, 331–344) In his mind the sociology class is a prerequisite to delving into German-Russian cultural studies. He often tells his students at the outset of his classes to ask themselves three basic questions:

"Who am I?" "Why am I?" "What do I intend to do about both?" Those are the questions we have to answer, in light of what others are doing around the world. Until you answer those three questions, I tell the kids, life is really not worth much. (ES82-TK-C3, Side 2, 390–398)

Mr. Kramer teaches German-Russian Ethnic Studies daily every second semester from 11:00 A.M. to 12:00 noon, under the official title "International Relations." He justifies the broader course title by noting that he continues to work basic sociological and anthropological concepts into the German-Russian material (e.g., examples of ethnocentrism, nuclear vs. extended family patterns, etc.). While Mr. Kramer makes use of a number of published works in the German-Russian studies class, he focuses on three volumes in particular: Karl Stumpp's *The German-Russians: Two Centuries of Pioneering,* the main text used by the students; Karl Stumpp's *The Emigration from Germany to Russia in the Years 1763 to 1862,* a large volume for genealogical research; and Joseph S. Height's *Paradise on the Steppe,* a cultural history of the Catholic Black Sea Germans in southern Russia. He also uses sometimes a slide-sound program entitled "At Home on the Prairies: The Germans from Russia," produced by the Germans from the Russia Heritage Society, depending on its availability from the public library in the neighboring town of Linton. In addition, Mr. Kramer distributes approximately seventy pages of mimeographed handouts to the students, including maps of German-Russian settlements in the Old World and the New, illustrated essays on German-Russian material folk culture, life histories, and booklists.[7]

The German-Russian studies class at Emmons Central High School has various areas of inquiry:

1. *German-Russian Surnames.* The course begins with an examination of the family names of German-Russian students in the class. Mr. Kramer attempts to show the students how their German names derived from ancestral occupations, places of origin, physical traits, etc. According to Mr. Kramer, "[Sioux Indian names like] Red Bull and Chasing Hawk aren't really any different than their names." (ES82-TK-C3, Side 2, 15–40).

2. *Map-making and Study.* The students study the areas in Central Europe where their forefathers originated; the migration route from Germany to Russia; major German settlement areas in Russia; German-Russian immigrant settlements in the New World; and the location of German-Russian settlements in North Dakota, specifically in Emmons County.

3. *Study of Living Conditions of German Colonists in Russia.* About this section Mr. Kramer explained: "We really try to bring home the living conditions ... [by considering the question] What was it like to be a European peasant?" (ES82-TK-C3, Side 2, 68–73).

4. *German Language and Traditional Songs.* Discusses German-Russian dialects and folksongs. Sometimes Mr. Kramer teaches the students a German song that is later sung at a German-Russian dinner prepared for the parents. A

typical song might include the German-Russian funeral hymn "Das Schicksal [wird keinen verschonen]" ("The Fate That Spares No One"). Mr. Kramer noted that since fewer and fewer students speak or even understand German, the language section is becoming increasingly difficult to teach.

5. *Material Folk Culture*. Studies German-Russian folk architecture and the making of *Brennmist* (a fuel made from dried animal manure, used by early German-Russian settlers in both Old Russia and the Dakotas). In the past the students have built models of a *Semelanka* (German-Russian earthen house), *Backofen* (bake oven), *Ulmer Schachtel* (boat used by the German emigrants who went to Russia via the Danube), and a horse-drawn wagon.

6. *Homesteading "Game"*. This is an exercise that Mr. Kramer adapted from a similar one used in some schools in Nebraska. It is basically a "farming game" set in North Dakota between 1885 and 1887. "Students attempt to run a farm at a profit over a three-year period." The object of the game is "to provide the students with some insight into the problems faced by homesteaders in the 1880s and to involve them in the decision-making process." Students receive a scoring sheet. They attempt to farm and invest successfully in the face of unpredictable factors, such as droughts, severe winters, grasshopper infestations, poor markets, and so on.

7. *Discussion of Cultural and Personality Traits of the German-Russians*. In this unit Mr. Kramer asks the students to identify some of the dominant attributes of the German-Russians. A discussion often follows regarding the contributed responses. The traits invariably include such descriptive characteristics as conservative, closed off or ethnocentric, religious, stubborn, and "crazy-clean" (an obsession with cleanliness). Mr. Kramer admits that he often plays the devil's advocate, regardless of whether the suggested trait is a positive or a negative one.

8. *The German-Russian Dinner*. Toward the end of the semester the students prepare a German-Russian dinner for parents and other invited guests from the surrounding communities. All the foods are homemade, including such table items as butter and ketchup. Students prepare most of the dishes in the home economics room of the high school on the day of the dinner.

For the dinner that I attended students prepared and served the following foods: *Kuchen* (cake), *Knepflesupp* (dumpling soup), *Fleischkiechla* (a deep-fried dough and meat dish), *Bratwurst* (homemade sausage), *Sauerkraut un' Nudla* (sauerkraut and noodles), and homemade ice cream. On the day of the dinner, maps and exhibits made by the students were placed on display in the room where the dinner was held. In years past German-Russian singers and musicians have provided entertainment at this event. Parents of the students donated all of the German-Russian food brought to and prepared at the school.

9. *Field Trip to German-Russian Sites in Emmons County*. After the students have examined the German-Russian history of their immediate area, Mr. Kramer takes them on a field trip to see some of the sites they have read about. The emphasis of the field trip is early German-Russian settlements in the southern half of Emmons County: Tiraspol, Elsass, Odessa, Katzbach, Krassna, and Rosental. At many of these locations nothing but a lonely cemetery remains. Mr.

Kramer invariably directs the students' attention to the wrought-iron cemetery crosses made by early German-Russian blacksmiths. The crosses are an important ethnic symbol and are readily identified as such even by non-German-Russians who travel through south-central North Dakota. Mr. Kramer and the students also visit the few remaining examples of German-Russian folk architecture in the area, including a number of clay-brick houses built by early German-Russian homesteaders.

10. *Genealogy and Family History Research.* Depending on the amount of time available and student interest, Mr. Kramer encourages the students to research their individual family backgrounds. He recommends books and other sources that can aid in the individual's search for German-Russian genealogical data. He also distributes a general reading list for those students who want to continue reading about the German-Russians at their own leisure.

The amount of time spent on these subjects depends primarily on the enthusiasm shown by students. Mr. Kramer explained that, since every group of students is different, each German-Russian studies class is somewhat different in its format and emphasis. In addition, he schedules events such as the German-Russian dinner and the field trip bearing in mind a number of other considerations, such as the agricultural cycle, weather, and student availability.

I was able to observe the German-Russian studies class at Emmons Central High on three separate occasions. On April 13 I observed the class while the students made maps and planned the menu for the upcoming German-Russian dinner, on April 28 I participated in the dinner, and on May 6 I accompanied Mr. Kramer and the students on their field trip. One of the things that I found most surprising about the class was the emphasis on active participation rather than mere listening or note-taking. When I questioned Mr. Kramer about this, he admitted: "I'm real big on 'doing,' if at all possible." (ES82-TK-C3, Side 2, 28–31).

A strong, cold wind was blowing across the prairie on the day of the field trip, sending tumbleweeds flying high above some distant rock piles erected by the early German-Russian settlers. While I thought such weather might force Mr. Kramer and his students to postpone the trip, I soon found out that nothing could be further from Mr. Kramer's line of thinking. Following the field trip, as we talked in the welcome warmth of his office back at the high school, Mr. Kramer explained to me that a basic purpose of the field trip was to give the students:

a feel for the wind, and the rocks, and the psychological barrier they [the early German-Russian pioneers] ran into when they got here. And on a day like today . . . we can get a feel for that . . . [when] there was nothing out there but prairie, rocks, and wind. (ES82-TK-C32, Side 1, 228–240)

Teacher

A description of German-Russian Ethnic Studies at Emmons Central High School would be inadequate without further discussion of the instructor, Mr. Les Kramer. A native son of Emmons County, Mr. Kramer is thirty-six years old. In addition to his responsibilities as principal of the Emmons County High School, he farms southwest of Strasburg in the Krassna settlement area. He and his wife, Colleen (née Schmaltz), have two small children. The fact that he and his family refurbished the old Strasburg train depot, transforming it into a comfortable rural home, suggests Mr. Kramer's appreciation for the past.

Both Mr. Kramer and his wife are former graduates of Emmons Central High School. Their oldest child, Nathan, is in grade school at St. Benedict's, which adjoins the Catholic high school in Strasburg.

In my interviews with Mr. Kramer I discovered that his thesis that one can appreciate an ethnic heritage only after one "steps away from it" reflects personal experience. Following military service and some long periods of inner reflection in Southeast Asia, he returned to North Dakota and attended the state university in Fargo. By the time he enrolled in college, he admits: "I had reassessed all my values . . . my thinking." (ES82-TK-C3, Side 2, 273–285). Since that time he has read and studied the history and culture of the German-Russians extensively. Despite his deep appreciation of his ethnic heritage, he has tried to maintain "balance" while instructing his students about their German-Russian culture. He indicated on several occasions that he wants his students to consider many different aspects of their heritage—both positive and negative—and how they continue to influence their lives today.

When we're through with this whole process, then the thinking process hopefully takes over with [the students], and they begin to realize that much of the tradition that we've just studied from the past is still very much a part of them. (ES82-TK-C3, Side 1, 388–393).

Students on a field trip to the Rosental German-Russian cemetery, north of Strasburg, North Dakota.
(ES82-196613-1-16) Photo by Timothy Kloberdanz

In regard to the feedback that he receives from his students concerning the German-Russian class, Mr. Kramer noted that there is seldom much immediate response. As one who has studied the cultural dynamics of his own ethnic group, he realizes that compliments among the German-Russians are rare, particularly for those of the teaching profession.

At the high school level the rewards aren't that great ... there aren't as many as you would like. But with teaching that's just the way it is. It's not like medicine; you don't get daily feedback on what a great job you're doing. You may never hear it for twenty years, and then only a comment in passing that you had some influence on a person's life. (ES82-TK-C3, Side 1, 262–268).

Students

There were ten students ranging in age from sixteen to eighteen in Mr. Kramer's most recent German-Russian Ethnic Studies class. They included Sam Gross, a senior from St. Michael's parish, northeast of Linton;

Gerald Holzer and Dale Horner, seniors from St. Anthony's parish in Linton; Sheila Nagel, a senior from Strasburg; Annette Roehrich, a junior from Strasburg; Josephine Vetter, a senior from St. Michael's parish; Rose Vetter a junior from St. Michael's parish; Mark Volk, a senior from Hague; and Katherine Wikenheiser, a junior from Strasburg.

As I mentioned previously, I was able to observe Mr. Kramer and the students interacting on three separate occasions. The first time was during the April 13 class session when the German-Russian dinner menu was being discussed and planned by the students. At one point in the class there was an interesting discussion about faithfulness to "German-Russian tradition." Mr. Kramer had encouraged the students to plan the German-Russian menu with authenticity in mind. Taking this as a cue, a female student asked in a serious tone of voice if "red-eye" (a homemade grain alcohol beverage popular among many German-Russians) could be served at the school during the ethnic dinner. When Mr. Kramer answered negatively, another student drew laughter when she stated, "If we'd stick to tradition, we'd all be getting drunk." (ES82-TK-C1, Side 2, 48–55).

On April 28, the day of the German-Russian dinner at Emmons Central High School, I watched and photographed the students as they prepared a four-course menu. There were no German-Russian cookbooks present. At times the students argued among themselves about how to prepare certain foods "the right way." It became obvious that the real problem was not the usual recipe variations found among German-Russian families, but some major differences arising from the fact that a number of the students came from outlying parishes many miles away. The preparation of Fleischkiechla, for example, met with mixed reactions, since this particular dish is not shared by all German-Russian families. Originally of Tatar origin, the deep-fried Fleischkiechla are most popular among those German-Russians who trace their ancestry to colonies in the Crimean portion of South Russia.

On May 6, the day of the field trip, a number of the students rode with me as we visited German-Russian sites in Emmons County. I was amazed that a few of the students indicated they were seeing the sites for the first time, even though they had spent their entire lives in the county. My amazement lessened as I realized that, for some students, the sites we were visiting were well outside of "their" settlement area.

While I was able to interview only two students from the German-Russian studies class, their impressions proved to be of interest. Both students (interviewed separately) indicated they were uncertain whether they had learned anything in the class that would be of value to them in later life. Both felt that the more satisfying segments of the class dealt with the study of German family names, the map work, the "homesteading game," and the discussion of German-Russian traits. They agreed with most of the traits listed in class, but felt it was an exaggeration to characterize German-Russians as being "crazy clean." One student even commented, "I didn't believe that too much.... I don't think we're cleaner than anybody else. I would think we're dirtier, really." (ES82-TK-C5, Side 1, 118–124). For both students the German-Russian studies class helped answer questions about their ancestors and their past, particularly as it related to the old country.

I knew beforehand that we [our ancestors] went to Russia, but I didn't know we were that far south. I thought we were in northern Russia. Then I learned that some of the climate [in south Russia] was like California. I didn't know that—thought it was cold [in southern Russia], just like North Dakota. (ES82-TK-C5, Side 1, 146–160)

Parents and Grandparents

I met the parents and grandparents of some of the students for the first time on the day of the German-Russian ethnic dinner at Emmons Central High. Following the meal and program we talked informally about the German-Russian studies class. The parents seemed pleased with the efforts of their sons and daughters in hosting the dinner, although this pride was never articulated. When I asked about the delicious foods we had just eaten, there was only discussion among those present regarding culinary differences among the German-Russians.

The most talkative and enthusiastic adult at the dinner proved to be none other than Wendelin Wikenheiser, the eighty-six-year-old grandfather of one of the students. Mr. Wikenheiser, whom I interviewed at length a few days later, was born in southern Russia and emigrated to North Dakota with his parents in 1903, when he was eight years old. Today he is one of the few surviving Russian-born elders in the Strasburg community. On the day of the German-Russian dinner Mr. Wikenheiser studied the maps and other materials that were on display at the high school with keen interest. Later, while interviewing him, he spoke of the German-Russian class at the Catholic high school as being "a pretty good idea." He lamented, however, that the students at the high school were not studying the German language more intensely. He confided that he felt it unfair to have to translate everything into English for his "educated" grandchildren. (ES82-TK-C6, Side 1, 123–146).

Talking with Mr. Wikenheiser further I found him to be somewhat ambivalent toward formal education, an attitude shared by many other German-Russians of his generation. Mr. Wikenheiser's pride in the success of his old friend, Lawrence Welk, was evident and he obviously enjoyed talking about the popular bandleaders's early days in Strasburg. As Mr. Wikenheiser was quick to point out, Strasburg's wealthiest and most famous native son "didn't have much education." (ES82-TK-C6, Side 1, 462–475).

Conclusions

Although I had done fieldwork among German-Russians prior to my research at Emmons Central High School, never before had I studied the actual process of conscious cultural transmission in so clearly delineated a setting. After years of observing German-Russian people interacting at informal gatherings, church services, wedding dances, funeral dinners, and agricultural tasks, it was exciting to actually watch a German-Russian adult instruct young members of his group about their ethnic heritage. Many of the cultural values, attitudes, and perceptions shared by German-Russians—which I had tried so hard and so long to pinpoint in my early observations—were being identified, discussed, and scrutinized by the percipients themselves!

An analysis of the data I collected during my fieldwork at Emmons Central High School is difficult since I only scratched the surface of what I quickly discovered was a complex and multi-faceted phenomenon. A score of related questions and lines of inquiry would emerge with each bit of information that I uncovered. While I realize that this is always the case in any scholarly endeavor, I did not think studying one ethnic school would pose the kind of challenge that it did.

In analyzing the format and the materials for German-Russian Ethnic Studies at Emmons Central High School, I found that the class was basically an honest, balanced attempt to convey some of the more prominent aspects of German-Russian ethnicity to the students. It was refreshing to see German-Russian culture being presented in the kind of down-to-earth, nuts-and-bolts fashion many Black Sea German Americans of the Dakotas pride themselves in exemplifying. There were no colorful posters of mist-covered castles in Germany in the school room where the German-Russian class was taught, no tall, Bavarian beer steins, or solemn-faced busts of Wagner. At the German-Russian dinner prepared and served by the students the foods were typically German-Russian and the music playing in the background was a tape recording of a group of local German-Russian farmers singing traditional old country favorites, like "Zu Strassburg" and "Wir sitzen so froehlich beisammen." Most reassuring of all was the fact that not one dirndl or even a pair of *lederhosen* was anywhere in sight.

The class directs a great deal of attention toward the making of models and artifacts that would mean little to most other Americans of German ancestry (e.g., the German-Russian Semelanka or earthen house, the Ulmer Schachtel–Ulm emigrant boat, and Brennmist or manure fuel). The production of such handcrafts underscores the fact that the instructor of the German-Russian studies class at Emmons Central is encouraging the students to focus on specific aspects of their Slavic-influenced heritage—rather than those of their "German" ancestry.

While Mr. Kramer and his students have chosen to focus on distinctive aspects of their German-Russian heritage, I believe something is gradually taking place in the class that may not be readily apparent to the participants. At times "German-Russian culture" is discussed and viewed as if it were a truly homogeneous phenomenon. Since Emmons Central High School is no longer a one-parish, community institution, it now draws German-Russian students from settlement areas well outside of Strasburg. While many of the Strasburg students trace their ancestry to the Kutschurgan Black Sea German colonies, a number of other students from the outlying parishes are descendents of emigrants who came from the Bessarabian and Crimean German-Russian colonies. Regional differences (as manifested in dialects, foodways, farming patterns, and so on) may lead to confusion on the part of those German-Russian students whose community or family traditions do not always run parallel to the material presented in the class. At any rate, one outcome of the German-Russian studies class at the high school may be a heightened awareness of German-Russian identity in its broadest sense, rather than a vague feeling for one's traditions at the purely local level.

In regard to the articulation of cultural values, the seventh unit covered in the class deals directly with German-Russian cultural and personality traits. This section of the course always provides a forum for much student discussion about German-Russian values and attitudes. In my interviews with two students, both pointed out that, while this subject was interesting, it posed some problems, since the students were unable to see themselves as compared to "outsiders." They admitted that their contacts with people who are not German-Russian were quite limited. Nonetheless, they agreed with most of the German-Russian values and attributes discussed in class: industriousness, a love of the land and of farming, religiosity, conservatism, frugality, and stubbornness. They disagreed with the instructor that German-Russians were "crazy clean," feeling it to be an exaggeration. They did not list other attributes, such as affability, generosity, and sobriety, as characteristic of the German-Russians.

A large circular poster with illustrations of a German-Russian earthen home, windmill, and plow graced the front of the room on the day of the German-Russian dinner at the high school. Two neatly lettered German expressions appeared on the poster *"Arbeit macht das Leben suess"* ("Work makes life sweet") and *"In Amerika durch Gottes Gnade!"* ("In America through the Grace of God!"). A smaller poster, bearing numerous pictures of agricultural scenes, bore the legend: "LANDSLEUTE—Part of our German-Russian Heritage as Farmers."

Another characteristic of the German-Russians, repeatedly pointed out by Mr. Kramer, is their ambivalence toward formal education. He explained this attitude as stemming from the past history of the German-Russians, since they viewed schools in Russia and later in the United States as threats to their cultural and religious integrity. This fear was compounded by the German-Russian belief that education was not essential for those engaged in agricultural pursuits. According to Mr. Kramer, such attitudes persist and are contributing factors to the unstable financial situation of the Catholic high school in Strasburg today. Mr. Kramer pointed out that many German-Russians tend to be tight fisted and, consequently, dislike making pledges; but at the same time they want to see Emmons Central—"their school"—remain open. Thus the future of the German-Russian studies class, and indeed that of the very high school which offers it, remains uncertain. (ES82-TK-C8, Side 2, 73–95).

Perhaps the most important thing that I learned while studying the German-Russian class at Emmons Central is that high school educators can offer both a well-balanced curriculum and an ethnic heritage component without sacrificing program quality.[8] The students at Emmons Central High School are free to choose whether to enroll in the German-Russian studies course. If they decide to do so, they are able to attend the class during regular school hours. Furthermore, since the course includes basic anthropological and sociological concepts, it serves the students in two important ways: by providing a formal opportunity to explore various facets of the German-Russian culture and by encouraging the students to view their heritage against the larger backdrop of human experience.

Acknowledgments

I am deeply indebted to the following individuals, all of whom helped make my ethnic heritage school research a truly enlightening experience: Mr. Les Kramer and his German-Russian Ethnic Studies class at Emmons Central High School in Strasburg; Mr. Alan Hummel of Hague; Mr. and Mrs. John Vetter of Kintyre; Mr. Wendelin Wikenheiser from Strasburg; and the Clarence Wikenheiser family of Strasburg. Appreciation also is due Michael M. Miller, Millie Nieuwsma-Buekea, and Rosalinda Appelhans Kloberdanz.

Postscript

On May 21, 1985, the doors of Emmons Central High School were locked following final commencement ceremonies. This time, however, a simple spring ritual symbolizing another school year's end had profound and deeply troubling significance to many German-Russian families—the doors of Emmons Central were to remain permanently closed.

Rising education costs and declining student enrollment were cited as two of the major reasons for the parochial school's shutdown. Newspaper reporter Lucille Hendrickson described the emotion-charged event in an article entitled "Goodbye, Emmons Central, Goodbye Forever" (*The Bismarck Tribune,* May 26, 1985). Hendrickson perhaps summed up the feelings of many people in the Strasburg, North Dakota, area with the words "the death of a school is a grievous thing for a small community."

Notes

1. An excellent background study on the German-Russians is Adam Giesinger's volume *From Catherine to Khrushchev: The Story of Russia's Germans* (Battleford, Sask., Canada: Marian Press, 1974).

2. See Richard Sallet, *Russian-German Settlements in the United States,* trans. Lavern J. Rippley and Armand Bauer (Fargo, N.D.: North Dakota Institute for Regional Studies, 1974).

3. Sallet, p. 112.

4. This estimate is based on a number of comparative sources, especially William C. Sherman, *Prairie Mosaic: An Ethnic Atlas of Rural North Dakota* (Fargo, N.D.: North Dakota Institute for Regional Studies, 1983).

5. Sallet, pp. 36–37.

6. See "History of Strasburg Schools," in *Moments to Remember,* Michael M. Miller, ed. (Strasburg, N.D.: The Strasburg Schools Alumni Association, 1976), pp. 62–63.

7. Copies of all available handouts used in Mr. Kramer's class are deposited at the American Folklife Center, Library of Congress.

8. Emmons Central High School has a level II accreditation, placing it among the top 25 percent of the schools in North Dakota.

Lebanese Arabic School at St. Elias Maronite Catholic Church and Greek School at Holy Trinity-Holy Cross Greek Orthodox Cathedral
Birmingham, Alabama

Brenda McCallum and Nancy Faires Conklin

Like most Greek and Lebanese communities in the United States, those in Birmingham were established in the years following 1890, up until the immigration restrictions in the 1920s.[1] Immigrants who came to Birmingham entered one of the fastest growing, most rapidly industrializing cities in the nation. Within this expanding economy, most Greeks and Lebanese established themselves in commercial enterprises, servicing the needs of the new, urbanized working population drawn from the rural areas of the region, as well as from Europe and the Mediterranean. Migrants from the surrounding countryside, both black and white, and immigrants from northern and eastern Europe primarily sought industrial jobs. The developing Greek, Lebanese, Russian Jewish, and Italian communities, however, sought out economic opportunities in businesses providing food, dry goods, and other necessities to the wage workers.

Within Birmingham's commercial economy the immigrant businessmen and businesswomen carved out highly specialized niches into which they could readily introduce newcomers to their communities. They were attracted to enterprises requiring little capital and limited knowledge of English and local custom. Jews became leading retailers of clothing and, eventually, owners of department stores. Italians opened small grocery stores in laborers' neighborhoods, selling staples and meats. Greeks became the primary purveyors of fruits and vegetables, starting with small carts and street stands and developing into produce store owners and food distributors, as well as owner-operators of restaurants, bakeries, and bottling companies. A 1908 city survey listed 125 food-related businesses owned by Greeks.[2] Most Lebanese worked first as peddlers, venturing out into the rural areas of Alabama and canvassing the city with dry goods and notions. By the 1920s most of these itinerant salespeople were able

Parish priest Father Richard Saad and fieldworker Nancy Conklin looking at the collection of books in the library at St. Elias Maronite Catholic Church, Birmingham, Alabama.
(ES82-195995-2-10A)
Photo by Brenda McCallum

to establish stores, wholesaling and retailing dry goods, fine linens and laces from Lebanon, and, in some cases, groceries and produce. The Southside neighborhood, center of the Lebanese community, had twenty Lebanese-owned stores in the 1920s.[3]

Unlike many native-born American business owners, who restricted their clienteles by race, the immigrant entrepreneurs sought out customers without regard to ethnic considerations. The economic advantage of their liberal business practices was tempered by animosity created among the area's powerful segregationists and nativists who were resentful of the immigrants' presence and success. Greek and Lebanese economic advancement took place within a social context that was aggressively racially bifurcated and overwhelmingly Protestant. Along with their fellow immigrant Jews and Italians, the Greeks and Lebanese were sometimes regarded as "colored," their very presence a challenge to the myth of a biracial, socially segregable South. Orthodox and Maronite alike, the Mediterranean peoples faced anti-Catholic religious hatred. It is within this context of economic opportunity and social structure that the development of the Birmingham Greek and Lebanese communities' autonomous institutions must be understood.

History of St. Elias Maronite Catholic Church

The Lebanese community in Birmingham was established in the years following 1890. Settlement continued until the immigration restrictions in 1924. Most Lebanese migrated first to cities in the Northeast or Great Lakes and thence to Alabama. The founding Lebanese families in Birmingham originated in farming villages in the area around Zahle in central Lebanon. They were attracted to Alabama by opportunities to enter into itinerant trade among rural residents or in urban areas amidst the growing numbers of mining, steel, and iron workers. They did not often choose farming or even industrial wage labor because they intended to return to the old country. Also, the tenant farmer and sharecropping agricultural system prevalent in this region was antithetical to their experience and ambitions as independent small farmers.

Most Lebanese immigrants became peddlers, traveling the back roads carrying notions, dry goods, and hand-crafted items on their backs. The profit was high, the investment low, and only minimal English was necessary. A route and stock could be obtained from more established Lebanese who owned shops and organized routes for newcomers. As they became permanent settlers they often moved from peddling into storekeeping and wholesale grocery and produce businesses. By 1915 sixty-five Lebanese families were settled in Birmingham and had established a Maronite Catholic church with an Arabic school in the afternoons.

St. Elias Maronite Catholic Church is the primary center of Lebanese community life in Birmingham. Together with a Melkite church and a secular ethnic club, it is one of three major institutions founded by immigrant Lebanese, all still active today and located near the center of the traditional Lebanese Southside neighborhood.[4] The pioneering immigrants established a social club, originally called the Phoenician Club and continuing today as the Cedars Club, the locus for parties, meetings, recreation, and a variety of secular activities. They founded two churches to continue the major Christian traditions of Lebanon in their new homeland. A minority of the ethnically Lebanese population of Birmingham are parishioners at St. George Melkite Greek Catholic Church, which also enrolls Catholics from other nations, including Palestine, Greece, and Russia. St. Elias is the religious home for the majority of the city's Lebanese. Its parishioners adhere to Maronite Catholicism, the majority Christian religion in Lebanon. This study focuses on ethnic education in the St. Elias parish, since it is the largest institution and, unlike St. George Melkite, specifically a Lebanese parish.

To understand the history of ethnic maintenance efforts at St. Elias, it is necessary to first consider the relationship between the Maronite faith and the Lebanese nationality. While the institution of Maronitism and concept of Lebanese nationality became closely tied during the period of Lebanon's struggle toward independence in the 1920s through 1940s, at the time of large-scale immigration to Birmingham the identification of Maronitism with Lebanese nationality was tenuous. The development of Lebanese national identity among the St. Elias parishioners played an important role in their efforts to establish an ethnic school at the church.

At the turn of the century the notion of ethnic identity among the Maronites, and the Melkites as well, was tied to their local region or village and their faith, rather than to a political entity.[5] The regions from which most American Maronites, including those to Birmingham, emigrated were not actually in the province of Lebanon, but rather in Syria; contemporary Lebanon was not created until after World War II. Yet the Maronites did not identify with Syria, for most Syrians were Muslim and most Syrian Christians were Orthodox. When pressed for their nationality, early immigrants would report Syrian because they carried Syrian papers, but among themselves they spoke of a Maronite community or of their native village. They developed a notion of Lebanese nationality in response to the American nationality-based definition of ethnicity and to distinguish themselves from other Syrians. Several of our Birmingham respondents commented that the early settlers "had to be taught" that they were Lebanese by the priest who came to them from the old country in 1930.

To make matters more difficult, the American Catholic Church regarded the Maronites, whether "Syrian" or "Lebanese," as just another ethnic group to assimilate into the "universal" Latin Rite. The Latin bishops, not understanding the Lebanese adherents' liturgical distinction from Latin Rite Catholicism, thwarted Maronite efforts to create autonomous churches and competing schools. They also discouraged them from practicing their rituals in the Antiochene style and the Aramaic, Syriac, and Arabic languages. It was not until the second Vatican Council in 1965 that acknowledging the integrity of the Eastern Rites became a policy of the Roman church. Catholics are now instructed to follow the rite of their fathers when a parish of that rite exists.

Thus the Lebanese Maronites found themselves in something of a double bind. On the one hand, they needed to respond affirmatively with a clear, nationality-based sense of ethnicity if they were to withstand the assimilation into the American cultural mainstream. On the other hand, they had to convince the American Catholic Church that their demands for separate institutions were based not on national, but on doctrinal differences.

In St. Elias today the debate continues. The priest identifies himself first as a Maronite Catholic and second, and only privately, as a Lebanese. His parishioners see the Maronite Church as the spiritual and cultural center of their own ethnic community, however. These distinctions—between ecclesiasticism and nationalism, between sacred and secular church functions—and the role of the lay community in controlling and sustaining the parish school are important determinants of the practice of ethnic heritage and Arabic language education in the parish.

St. Elias was founded in 1910 in a converted public school building at 20th Street and Sixth Avenue South. It was named after the church in Wadi-el-Arayeche, the home village of many Birmingham families. Until the 1960s St. Elias was one of only two Maronite churches in the Southeast.

The Antiochene patriarch, who supplied the parish with a series of priests from Lebanon, originally had authority over St. Elias. Once established, however, the parish became a responsibility of the Latin Rite Diocese in all other matters, and had financial obligations to the bishop and to the Latin parochial schools.

St. Elias experienced considerable attrition in its membership over the first thirty years, although it does not appear to have been as high as the estimated fifty percent reported for Maronite congregations reported nationally.[6] It remained in its original, temporary, and inadequate quarters as the community settled away from the church area into the neighborhoods of Glen Iris and Idlewild on the southwest side of Birmingham. Finally, the church closed in 1939 for lack of a priest; appeals to the patriarchate went unanswered for over six months. The community then directly contacted a priest who happened to be visiting his brother in Detroit and later obtained permission from the patriarch for Father Joseph Ferris Abi-Chedid to come to Birmingham rather than return to his monastery in Lebanon.

When Father Abi-Chedid arrived just sixty-one parishioners reassembled at St. Elias. The only remaining functioning church organization was the Ladies' Altar Society, which raised $311 to add to the church treasury of $7.87 so that Father Abi-Chedid could reopen the building and begin calling the Maronites together again. He quickly learned sufficient English to read the Gospel and to communicate with the Birmingham business and professional community. He then set about obtaining property in the Lebanese neighborhood and managed to have almost a full city block of land donated to the parish.

In 1949 construction began on the present church building at 836 Eighth Avenue South. At the time of Father Abi-Chedid's retirement and return to Lebanon in 1970 the complex consisted of the church, a parish house, an auditorium/cafeteria, and a four-classroom educational building. There were also plans for an additional four classrooms and a small convent. The congregation paid for each of the buildings in cash raised primarily through the Ladies' Altar Society weekly Lebanese dinners, which became a veritable institution for many Birmingham residents.

The church had a series of short term resident priests after Father Abi-Chedid. In 1972 the present priest was appointed to St. Elias. He was a member of one of the first classes to graduate from the American Maronite Seminary in Washington, D.C., and is the first American-born priest at St. Elias. Although of Lebanese descent, he is also the first priest not to speak Arabic fluently. Since his arrival he has concentrated his efforts on consolidating the parish membership, reaching out to Maronites who had turned to the Latin Rite, and restoring the teaching and celebration of the Maronite Rite. With the help of the Ladies' Altar Society, he has also begun converting one classroom into a library—one of only two or three such Maronite libraries in the United States.

In 1982 St. Elias' congregation numbered 260 active families, totaling eight hundred to a thousand people, most of whom are of Lebanese descent. These numbers reflect the post-1965 immigration, which has brought primarily educated, professional people, displaced by recent conflicts in the Middle East. St. Elias is now one of three Maronite churches in the Southeast, including churches in Atlanta and Miami, and one of fifty churches and five missions in the entire country. In 1962 the pope authorized an apostolic exarch to the United States with a mission to unify the American Maronites. The exarch of Detroit became bishop of the Eparchy (Diocese) of St. Maron of the United States in 1971, and the Maronites were removed from the authority of the Latin hierarchy. The eparchy is now administered from its seat in Brooklyn, New York. It oversees the churches and missions, the seminary in Washington, D.C., and a convent in Youngstown, Ohio. Nationally, Maronites number over thirty-six thousand.[7] The current priest has applied for an assistant at St. Elias so that he can extend his outreach to Maronites in the Nashville, Tennessee and Mobile, Alabama, areas who now worship at Latin Rite churches.

St. Elias maintains friendly relations with St. George Melkite Greek Catholic Church only three blocks away, and the ethnically Lebanese parishioners sponsor some joint activities. St. Elias is the meeting place for the American-Lebanese Alliance, though it occasionally meets at St. George to demonstrate its ethnic, non-denominational basis. The two major religious festivals celebrated at St. Elias and other Maronite churches are the Feast of St. Maron on February 9 (Gregorian calendar February 14), and the Feast of St. Elias on July 20 (Gregorian calendar July 25). The former is marked with a special mass followed by Arabic food, music, dances, and other entertainment, and the latter is celebrated with a religious observance and a church picnic.

History of St. Elias Arabic School

The parish organized the first Arabic language classes in 1915, just five years after the church founding. During the early years Khattar Wehby, one of the few well-educated immigrants, conducted the classes. At first they took place in a section of the old church and later at another location. Wehby taught as a volunteer, giving classes after school for several hours each day. Both the students and the teacher were bilingual in Arabic and English and used the two languages in class. The classes were to make the children literate in Arabic, familiarize them with Arabic/Lebanese literature, and supplement the cultural education they were receiving in Latin parochial schools.

The classes were not successful for very long. Wehby persevered, starting classes each fall until the 1920s, but the consistent attrition discouraged him. Wehby's daughter, an active St. Elias parishioner, describes her father's efforts:

He didn't receive any cooperation. And, you know, he didn't want anything from them. He'd say, "Give me your children. I don't want anything, just let me teach them." ... Well, it just wasn't supported, I mean, in that they didn't cooperate with Papa. Maybe the parents kind of just drifted away. And then my father just got disgusted and he just quit. (ES82-Mc/C-C3)[8]

As textbooks Wehby used grammars, dictionaries, histories, and poetry and essay volumes that he had brought with him from Lebanon. Although trained in classical Arabic, he taught the vernacular language. "We learned

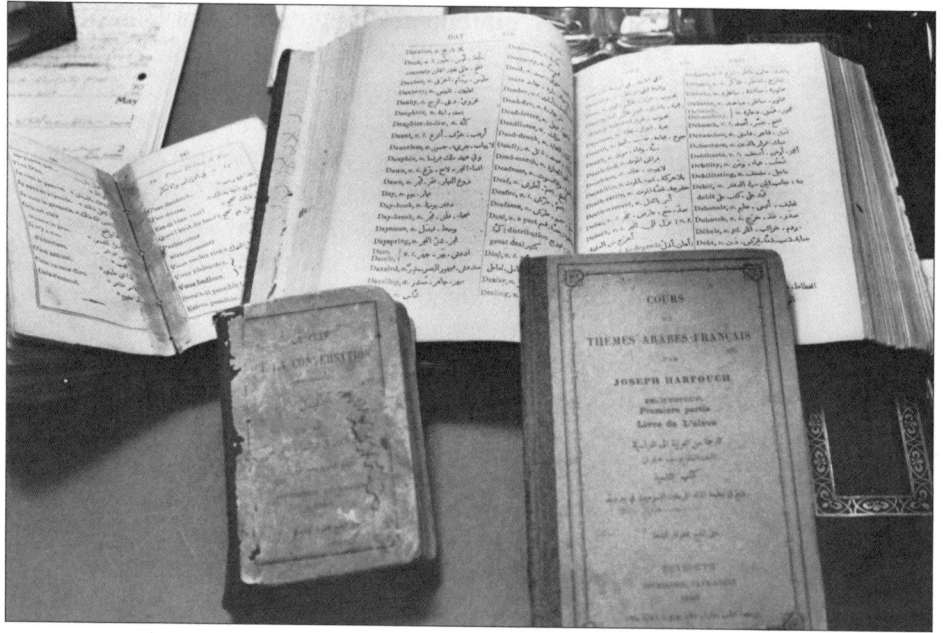

Collection of early Arabic dictionaries and grammar books used at St. Elias School. (ES82-195995-3-20) Photo by Brenda McCallum

the alphabet. We learned to read, to spell. We learned poetry and songs," says his daughter. Except for the songs, the efforts were directed toward refining the children's language skills. She also recalls that the instruction was:

More or less, I would say, conversational. . . . And the spelling and things like that, but barely writing. 'Cause I don't think we ever got to the point where we were doing too much writing, especially not the [script]. I think we were printing more or less. (ES82-Mc/C-C3)

Another parishioner who attended the Wehby classes for Arabic-speaking children reports a similar experience:

And the reason we learned—we took part in the choir at the church and we sang in Arabic. And we took the books and would start reading out of the books, the Arabic language print. Now, script [handwriting], I can't read, but I can read print. (ES82-Mc/C-C4)

The next serious efforts at language education did not take place until Father Abi-Chedid became priest of St. Elias in 1940. He came to Birmingham intending to open a full-day Maronite parochial school, but his parishioners had a different priority.

The people were hungry for a new church. In fact, he didn't want to build a new church first; he wanted to open a school first. He says—which is true—"without the school you have no parish." The children are going to disperse, they're going to go to other places, they're going to learn other cultures, and you just won't have your parish. (ES82-Mc/C-C4)

The school building was not immediately forthcoming, so Father Abi-Chedid introduced Arabic classes for the young people after school and on Saturdays. One of his pupils recalls the instructional style:

He tried to teach us Arabic, but his bedside manners were very rough and the children were very scared of him. We'd just shake. He was just very stern and strict, and, I don't know, we just couldn't learn from him. (ES82-Mc/C-C16)

Father Abi-Chedid's students were no longer Arabic-speaking or bilingual in Arabic and English; they were second- and third-generation Birmingham Lebanese, with, at best, passive knowledge of the language. A second-generation Lebanese-American in Birmingham describes his own skills as typical: he can understand a considerable amount, but he cannot respond nor can he read or write Arabic. "Even though they [his generation's parents] knew Arabic, and we were spoken to by them in Arabic, and I understood it, we were never taught to speak it fluently," he explains. (ES82-Mc/C-C16)

Father Abi-Chedid emphasized conversation, pronunciation-drill (in some cases, physically trying to force laryngeals out of his pupils), and the alphabet. The classes would start up again and again and stop because the children dropped out after a month or so. "I guess that's why I know the alphabet so well," says one student, "we went through it so many times." (ES82-Mc/C-C16) Although these experiences were not promising, Father Abi-Chedid did not waver from his determination to have a school at St. Elias to replace the Latin parochial education of the parish children.

At his parish's wish Father Abi-Chedid built first the new church and then the rectory. Working with the Ladies' Altar Society and the Knights of St. Maron, a special parish lay organization established for the purpose, Father Abi-Chedid raised the money necessary for the first half of the school building. Finally, in 1958 the prospective school's auditorium/cafeteria was completed and in 1960 the first four of the eight planned classrooms. The completed complex would be in the shape of a cross. The school was to have eight grades and teach all subjects required by the state. In addition, the school would offer instruction in Lebanese heritage and the Maronite Rite.

To ensure the realization of his dream of a school, Father Abi-Chedid established a designated Maronite education trust fund. The proceeds from the Lebanese lunches and dinners that became so popular in Birmingham in the 1950s and 1960s contributed substantially to the fund. After Father Abi-Chedid's retirement, however, his "school money" was restored to the diocesian and parish general funds, to be used for support of existing programs. The final four of the planned eight classrooms were not built. No teachers were hired.

The disposition of the "school money" continued as a live issue at St. Elias. School advocates in the congregation saw their opportunity to establish a full day school that would be responsive to their ethnic and cultural needs to have been lost to other priorities and, some argue, failure to recognize the imperative to have a Maronite Rite-based curriculum for Lebanese-American children.

The parish today owns a substantial school complex of which it makes very little use. The land adjacent, designated for the remainder of the school, stands vacant. In such a situation it is unlikely that the school issue would easily disappear from memory. Indeed, parishioners and priest report that, over ten years later, it remains a subject of debate within the congregation.

Advocates of the school foresee a full curriculum of public and parochial school subjects, as well as supplementary classes, including Lebanese history and culture, the Maronite Rite, and the Arabic language. One believes that Arabic should be begun "at an early age—two or three. I think it would be great for the younger, because it's easier for them to speak at that time." (ES82-Mc/C-C16) Another describes the school she envisions this way:

Well, they would teach them who they are and where they came from. Teach them the history of Lebanon from the time of the Phoenicians to the time of our present-day situation. Teach them their religion, which is the oldest rite in the church. Teach them the family life.... And besides, they would get this basic education that is necessary for college or high school.... We were going to have nuns who would teach them in English, except the Arabic language, and the rite, and the church—the hymns, the prayers, and everything that they would learn in church.... Probably they would have included in their classes the Arabic language, as a course. That would be in addition to their regular studies. (ES82-Mc/C-C4)

Pupils would be drawn from the 250 or 300 (respondents' estimates vary) children in the parish. Others might come from Latin Catholic families who feel their children "miss all that tradition and heritage" in the Latin church, suggests a church council member. Financial arguments are made in addition to the cultural and religious justifications for the school: between 50 and 75 percent of St. Elias' children attend Latin Rite parochial schools, where they pay out-of-parish tuition. School advocates would redirect the supplements provided by St. Elias to families who cannot meet the cost of Latin Rite schools, an amount they report to be at least $15,000 per year.

The most outspoken advocates of the Maronite/Arabic school argue that capital remaining from revenue generated in the 1950s and 1960s that was earmarked for the building fund established by Father Abi-Chedid should also be dedicated to the proposed education project, and that these monies would go a long way toward supporting the school, were it staffed by nuns.

Even the teaching staff of the projected school is a much discussed issue. Father Abi-Chedid had first planned to bring eight nuns directly from Lebanon. Later the parish contacted nuns at the Maronite National Shrine in Youngstown, Ohio. We had Maronite nuns "waiting to teach, and the bishop did not encourage them," recalls a parishioner who was very active at the time. "We have a bishop who is not very aggressive. He did not encourage them. They finally got disgusted and went back to Lebanon." (ES82-Mc/C-C4) A pro-school group within the congregation has recently discussed the question with four Latin Rite nuns of St. Rose of Lima in Birmingham who attend St. Elias and who declared themselves willing to learn the Maronite Rite and take on the jobs. Another pro-school spokesman prefers to look to Lebanese nuns; they are European-educated, he says, and multilingual. His group's plan would be to send them to Sacred

Heart College in Cullman, Alabama until they pass the state teacher's certification examination. If established, the St. Elias school would be the only Maronite school in the United States.

Along with the controversy about a Maronite parochial school, Arabic language classes have continued to take place at irregular intervals. In the 1970s a Lebanese priest from St. George Melkite offered classes at St. Elias. One adult versed in Arabic attended and enjoyed the classes, but says the parish children could not keep up.

We had one priest of the Melkite church. He was very learned. He taught a higher grade, where the young ones could not [keep up]—you have to start from the beginning. . . . I went when the priest was teaching, because I knew a little bit higher Arabic and I could appreciate it and learn it. (ES82-Mc/C-C3)

In recent years there have been classes given by seminarians from Lebanon interning at the parish. One man, who was at St. Elias for three summers between 1978 and 1980, offered Arabic classes twice, as part of the Summer Enrichment Program. This program for families includes Lebanese cooking, movies, crafts, and other "enriching activities," notes the parish priest. A respondent who attended with his wife and older children recalls that the classrooms were filled. "We went there very energetic. There's no textbook. You bring your own pencil and paper, and you get there, and you write. You try to write it down and pronounce it, and it's very hard to pronounce." While the Summer Enrichment Program itself lasted only four weeks, the weekly Arabic classes continued throughout the summer. The parish priest observes that attrition was high: perhaps eighty started the class in 1980 and ten remained at the end.

In the summer of 1982 the interning seminarian was a Lebanese-American who did not meet the minimum Arabic speaking and reading skills guidelines established by the bishop. To expose his intern to the language and renew Arabic teaching at the school, the parish priest arranged that an immigrant Lebanese who is a professional elementary teacher offer a children's class. Unlike most of the post-1965 immigrants, her family is highly language retentive, a fact that the priest attributes to their plans to return to Lebanon. This woman, who teaches her own daughter Arabic at home, agreed to take on other children in the six to ten age group. An announcement in the Sunday bulletin drew children and also a number of adults. An additional teacher was then found from among the recent immigrants, and an adult class has also begun.

Both classes met for just one hour each week during the Sunday school period between early and late mass. This time was usually devoted to religious instruction. The children's class had just over ten children. The teacher was introducing the alphabet, reading and writing, counting, and rhymes for word memorization, using photocopies of elementary school books she used in Lebanon. She assigned homework tasks of rewriting, copying, and translating, which the pupils completed diligently. The seven or eight adults in the other class requested conversational Arabic. They devoted their time to speaking, not reading and writing, with the exception of learning the characters associated with the sounds that have no parallel in English. Practical conversational phrases were the main emphasis. This appears to have been the first course at St. Elias following a conversational approach. Attendance was good and enthusiasm high. Most of the adult students had minor passive knowledge of Arabic, but could not speak it. The parish priest expected the classes to go on into fall, if the interest continued at the present level. The adults had hoped for a longer session or a weekday evening class, but their teacher was not available except on Sunday mornings. If the adult classes continue, they may have to be scheduled for another time.

Future of the St. Elias Parochial School

Under Father Abi-Chedid the parishioners worked together to raise the building funds, first for the church and rectory and then for the school. Now, with no plans for further expansion of the school, the church, or the rectory, there are fewer activities at the church, because money-making projects are not as necessary.

The parish priest argues that the idea of a school at St. Elias runs counter to the American Catholic Church's general movement away from parochial education, brought about, in part, by the loss of nuns and the high cost of lay teachers. More importantly, however, he sees Maronitism as a rite, a special tradition of Catholicism, and resists the equation of Maronitism with Lebanese ethnicity. In part it is a question of making clear the doctrinal and ritual integrity upon which the church is based. As he explains:

People associated the rites [Maronite and Melkite] with ethnic communities which wanted their own parishes. And that is a misnomer, because a rite is a distinct entity in the Catholic Church, and that includes us. We're a Maronite church and they're [St. George Melkite] a Greek Catholic church. And so those will stand, you know. The ethnic thing, if we depended only on ethnicity, I think it would die out. (ES82-Mc/C-C1)

The confusion of religious and ethnic identification is peculiar to American Maronites and other Maronites living overseas, since there is no competition from the Latin Rite or misunderstanding of the diversity within the Catholic faith in Lebanon itself. As an American, the current priest is more sensitive to the issue than priests from Lebanon might be, or, indeed, than other priests at St. Elias have been. While he is cautious about too close an identity between Maronitism and Lebanese ethnicity, he does not try to entirely disassociate the two. Examined closely over several interviews, his caution appears to stem from a concern that the emphasis will tip away from the internal Maronite faith to external cultural manifestations of a non-religious nature, rather than that the association of Maronite with Lebanese is incorrect. As a priest, his primary concern must be with spiritual affairs and the maintenance of the faith. He does not wish to see himself in a dual role as the leader of the ethnic community. No doubt this, too, is partly the response of an urban American socially far removed from the village-leader role of priests in traditional, rural Lebanon. Yet St. Elias is a Lebanese Maronite parish in the Deep South, long isolated and self dependent; its congregation may have broader expectations of the roles its priest should assume than might a parish in a more densely Maronite and Lebanese area, such as the Northeast.

The parishioners do not attempt to make the delicate distinctions between faith and nationality upon which their priest insists. As one put it, "Well, that sort of goes together, being Maronite and being Lebanese. If you're Lebanese, you're Maronite. Because the Maronite is the majority in Lebanon." And, further, "Well, the church, really, is the real foundation of the [Lebanese] community. Everyone gathers here. If you don't see them at all, you see them at church." (ES82-Mc/C-C4) Others directly connect religious and cultural life as well:

I love it. I love the music, the food, the dancing—it's all the religion. To me it's a great culture ... we [i.e., American-Lebanese generally] keep the food and lose all the other [elements of culture], and we're so fortunate that we [in Birmingham] have the church and our whole life. ... Right now the church is the center of everybody's life; that's what's holding us all together. If we didn't have the church, we'd be like all the other Lebanese communities. I think we're very fortunate in this area to have two churches. (ES82-Mc/C-C16)

For these parishioners, maintaining the Maronite faith and Maronite religious education are identical with maintaining Lebanese ethnic and cultural awareness; they are simply inseparable.

The struggle surrounding the St. Elias school must be understood in light of the above sentiments. The priest and his parishioners share deep concerns about the education Maronite children receive in the Latin schools and the effects that Latin school attendance appears to have on the level of participation at St. Elias. Families are drawn to do volunteer work for the school's parish instead of their own, and the children make friends among their Latin Rite schoolmates. In addition, part of the Latin school curriculum is Catholic liturgy, catechism, and custom, and Maronite children learn that this is the universal Catholicism. Until Father Abi-Chedid started to grant first communion to St. Elias youngsters early—at six instead of seven years of age—the Maronite children were even studying for and taking their communion at school in the Latin Rite with their Latin classmates.

Because the majority of the children attend parochial school and thus receive extensive religious instruction during the week, the Sunday school hour at St. Elias has been devoted largely to "remedial" education in the principles of Catholicism for the minority who go to public school. Most parochial school children do not even attend. The priest introduced a quarter hour specifically on Maronitism in 1981, based on materials he and parish teachers had developed. In the fall of 1982, for the first time, Maronite curriculum materials from the exarchate education department were to be available for children's religious instruction. The priest hopes to expand the Sunday school into a full hour of Maronite Catholic study, using the exarchate materials to supplement the standard books and catechism based on the Latin Rite.

In tribute to his eminent predecessor, Father Abi-Chedid, and his educational ambitions, the current priest has had the church library named after him. For two years the Ladies' Altar Society has been developing the library's collection, which consists of books and pamphlets on Maronitism and Catholicism; a section of books and pamphlets on travel, archaeology, history, and art in Lebanon and the Middle East; a few Arabic and Syriac grammars and dictionaries; yearbooks and convention books from St. Elias and other American Maronite churches; and issues of *The Challenge*, the American exarchate newspaper. The library has already acquired a few Arabic language texts. Parishioners have donated a considerable number of old Arabic books. For the priest the "real special" section is the one on the Maronite Rite and the history of the Maronite people:

> We wanted the library to specialize in things of our rite, and of our history, and of our culture.... Books are very hard to get and expensive to find—in English.... Any Arabic books we've gotten, people donated them from their homes and things. We're trying to classify them, identify them, and put them out.... You'd be surprised. A young person comes by doing a paper in school, and is trying to do it about the Maronite Rite, and the history of Lebanon, or something, and they would have a source here. We want to have things here they can't find anywhere else.... We want to have regular hours, but we're not at that point yet. (ES82-Mc/C-C1)

The library committee of the Ladies' Altar Society will help plan a summer literature and film series to help advertise the library, during which there will be readings from the books, or films and tapes about the rite and Lebanese culture.

If this approach—centering more on Maronite Catholicism and making clear the specific ritual, dogma, and history of the church, supplemented with certain cultural activities—is sufficient for the parish priest, it certainly is not for many lay advocates of the St. Elias school. They argue for the necessity of a school from various perspectives. One family of early immigrants to Birmingham, for example, represents the faction of parishioners oriented toward the old country. They are conservative, socially, religiously, and ethnically. One of their concerns about the Latin schools is that they are no longer strict enough with the children. Of the Latin nuns the family would hope to retain as teachers in a school at St. Elias one family member says:

> But these nuns are still real nuns. They are full habits. And that's what we want. We don't want these nuns who look like me and you, and they call themselves nun. They're no more nun than I am. (ES82-Mc/C-C4)

They fear that St. Elias is, increasingly, "mainly social," not religious. This family has been central to all fund-raising activities in the past, but "I told them, 'You want our family back here, you're going to have to start that school going, because the church doesn't need anything else!'" (ES82-Mc/C-C4) Deeply religious, this family, like its priest, fears the dissolution of the Maronite parish, but espouses a different strategy for maintenance efforts, i.e., closer alignment of ethnicity and religion via parochial schooling that integrates secular and sacred needs.

Another parishioner who shares a concern over the integrity of the family and abhors marriage outside of the ethnic and religious community arrives at his support of the school in a somewhat different fashion. A third-generation American in his mid-thirties, he has no strong ties to the old country. Whereas two young men of the family discussed above were to return to Lebanon to marry village girls during 1982, this parishioner and his family, and even his parents, have never visited the old country. He is not trying to preserve old country ways in the United States but to create a sense of place and self for his Lebanese-American family. While others in his age group opted for assimilation as an escape from "foreign-ness," he has overcome his ethnic, minority-child experience by integrating and promoting his Lebanese heritage. He speaks of the privileges he had in the Birmingham community in comparison to his wife, who grew up Lebanese in a Mississippi town with no ethnic or ethno-religious institutions. A school at St. Elias would be a means for passing on to his children a fuller cultural experience and sense of place than he and his wife have had.

I'm not that old country, and I'm not that modern. But I think we should know who we are, and about our background, and be proud of it.... A lot of people my age wish we could speak it [Arabic], and that's how come we want the school. You know, there are a lot of young married couples with children.... We'd just have a fit to have a school down there ... I would just love for my kids to go to their own church, to their own school, and to participate and be around their heritage more and be around their own people more. (ES82-Mc/C-C16)

He envisions the school as a bulwark against external social change, as a positive affirmation of the immigrant experience, and as a cultural link between grandparent, parent, and child.

Interestingly, it is the latter parishioner who is most emphatic about Arabic language retention or renewal. The elders in the first family cited above grew up in an Arabic-speaking home and some of the younger adults also speak the language. Their homes are basically English-speaking today, however. The new Lebanese brides will be multilingual, although their Lebanese-American grooms are not, and their homes, too, will be English speaking. In contrast, the adults in the second family, without old-country ties and essentially monolingual in English, try to use the few Arabic words and phrases they still remember in daily conversation at home. While many innovations at St. Elias distressed the first Lebanese-oriented family, they did not mention the increasing use of English in the liturgy. The latter family, on the other hand, wants to see the entire mass returned to Arabic.

At St. Elias in 1982, 95 percent of the mass was in English. The Holy Consecration was recited in Aramaic and the choir sang "a couple of hymns" in Arabic. This is a radical shift from 1940, when Father Abi-Chedid was coached so that he could recite his first reading of the Gospel in English; he memorized the sounds, not understanding a single word. One parishioner, who speaks Arabic and is a professional musician, has transcribed numerous Arabic hymns into phonetics for the use of monolingual choir members. Prayer books have bilingual texts and a phonetic rendering of the Arabic, so that parishioners can read along. In the parish priest's view the switch to English has been positive for the congregation:

I'm satisfied with just keeping the flavor of it. . . . Aramaic is more important [than Arabic], because it was the liturgical language. Like Latin, it was preserved just for the liturgy. And Aramaic was closer to our people, because they spoke it at one time. And also, Christ spoke Aramaic. So I think there will always be a closeness to that language, because of those associations. . . . You know, I have a flavor, a flavor for it, too, and I can read Syriac 'cause that's how we're trained. . . . My idea was that, if the rite was going to thrive, people had to know what they were doing, especially the young. I think these things are, can be, transmitted with a flavor, but in English—what they never knew, what it was before. And the thing about these churches—the Maronite and the Melkite churches, this old way of thinking—was that they were old-country churches, you know, for the old people, or those that didn't speak English. I think we've had to change that, if there was going to be any hope for the young people to come, to understand what they were going. . . . And it's successful; it can't help but be successful if you approach it like that. We have more young coming to our church now than ever before. (ES82-Mc/C-C1)

He articulates quite eloquently the linguistic-assimilationist position. Yet the priest speaks often of this notion of "flavor." It arises in his description of the Arabic language classes. Although he maintains that the language learning efforts are largely fruitless in terms of actual linguistic skills, he thinks it is good for parishioners to have the experience of studying the alphabet and learning a bit about the language. He especially approves of their learning vocabulary sets, such as greetings, household items, foods—"you know, table-talk kind of stuff"—since it puts them in touch with the culture they have in their homes.

I don't think it is really going to mean a lot, except to give you a flavor of the identity, which is all right.... Now there's more than an awareness and a real desire for identity.... [It would not be good if] you didn't know what to call the food your grandfathers ate and that you eat every Sunday. And they're pretty good. There's nothing else like them. (ES82-Mc/C-C1)

The priest and his intern, both Lebanese-Americans, cite the Arabic kinship terms as a specific example of how exposure to the old-country language helps the people conceive of and internalize their own cultural world view. As a child, the priest marvelled at the wealth of kinship terms that enabled his parents to denote each member of the extended family in a single expression of relationship. "I don't know them all myself, but it's fantastic. There is no way we can do it [express this concept of kinship] in English."

Arabic language advocates remain confident that the young people in the parish could become effective bilinguals, and that is one of the outcomes they would expect from the school. One notes that his five-year-old son can recite the non-English sections of the mass already.

Left to me, the whole mass could be in Arabic. I feel like we have a prayer book, we can read it, and then we can learn the words in Arabic also. You repeat it so many times, and you hear it and can pick it up. (ES82-Mc/C-C16)

He would send preschoolers to Arabic classes before they ever started regular day school.

I would give anything if they would open it up. If the Father would think the way some of us think; but he doesn't.... I don't know, I hope we get a school. I really feel that, if we don't, that we'll lose it all. (ES82-Mc/C-C16)

History of Greek Immigration to Birmingham

Local legend has it that three seafaring brothers were the first Greek immigrants to Alabama. The first settled in Mobile in 1873, the second in Montgomery in 1878, the third—George Cassimus—in Birmingham in 1884. Cassimus is described as a British merchant seaman, who hired out with his two brothers on a Confederate gunrunner. He arrived in Birmingham from the port city of Mobile, first working for the fire department and later opening up a lunch stand.[9] Despite the legends surrounding the origins of Alabama's first Greek settlers, most Greek immigrants to Birmingham entered the United States through Ellis Island, settling in this country under less dramatic circumstances.[10]

Most Greek immigrants to the United States until after World War II were unskilled single males. They often planned to return with their savings from America to their Peloponnesian villages to establish a farm or business, or to support their kin or dower their daughter or sister, both strong Greek traditions. Many of the Greek immigrants to Birmingham, however, as well as those who settled elsewhere in the country after 1900, were already married, or later returned to Greece to find a bride, intending from the outset to establish permanent residency in America.[11]

The majority of the early Greek immigrants to Birmingham came from the Peloponnesian area and the islands of Corfu, Samos, and Rhodes. They settled in metropolitan Birmingham, as well as in many of the satellite communities—Ensley, Bessemer, Wylam, and Pratt City in particular—oriented toward Jefferson County's coal mines and iron and steel mills. In the city of Birmingham proper Greeks settled on the Southside, especially on Cullom Street, and in Norwood.

Reports conflict on the number of early Greek residents in the city, and the official federal immigration and census statistics are inconsistent. Growing from the 100 enumerated in the 1900 Census, Greek residents in Birmingham numbered between 900 and 1,200 in Ensley by 1913.[12] Census data from 1920, however, reported only 485 Greeks in Birmingham.

Before World War I, but especially after 1920, Greeks in Birmingham, as elsewhere, began leaving their jobs as common laborers to go into retail businesses. A Greek-American middle class emerged fairly early in the community's history in this country.[13] The majority of the Greeks soon

Christine Grammas showing fieldworker Nancy Conklin the Holy Trinity-Holy Cross 50th anniversary commemorative book. (ES82-197517-1-28) Photo by Brenda McCallum

made opportunities for themselves in wholesaling and retailing.[14] By the early 1900s Greeks had such a monopoly on street vending that a 1902 petition to the city council unsuccessfully tried to revoke their retail licenses.[15] Many emerged as restaurateurs in the 1920s. Other early Greek-owned businesses included hotels, barbershops, shoeshine stands, laundries, and billiard parlors.

The most recent wave of Greek immigrants to Birmingham followed the 1965 Immigration and Nationality Act. Some 142,000 Greeks emigrated to the United States during the late 1960s and early 1970s. These later immigrants included both men and women with professional and technical training. Many came from Athens or central Greece and had no intention of returning to their homeland.[16] The Birmingham Greek community, however, also includes a sizeable number of recent immigrants who have been educated only through grammar school.

History of Holy Trinity-Holy Cross Greek Orthodox Cathedral

The seventh Greek Orthodox congregation in the United States, Holy Trinity Church, was founded in 1902 with the organization of a lay committee, the Lord Byron Society (named in honor of the British poet who championed Greek independence). The committee's purpose was "to establish a Greek Orthodox Church, also to assemble the members of the community in one place for order and social improvement."[17] Rev. Callinicos Kanellos, an ethnic Greek from Constantinople, Turkey was its priest. He celebrated the first mass in 1907. After a three-year fund-raising drive, during which the small parish met in rented halls, the Society purchased a former Methodist-Episcopal church building on 19th Street and Avenue C South (now 3rd Avenue South).

In 1906 the parish of one hundred members was officially named the Greek Orthodox Community of Holy Trinity, Birmingham, Alabama, and received a state charter. Daily afternoon Greek school classes began shortly after the organization of the church in the "little run-down building" next door, that was also used as a general meeting place.[18] When Father Kanellos left in 1912 he was replaced by Father Germanos Smirnakis, described as "a most learned man, a good linguist, and the author of several books ... [who also] lectures every Sunday evening to his people on various subjects—religious, historical, hygienic, etc."[19] A succession of, presumably, Greek-born priests appointed to the Holy Trinity parish by the Archdiocese followed Father Smirnakis.

On the eve of the Depression the Greek-American community in Birmingham numbered over fifteen hundred. "With this expansion came inter-community [sic] tension," between factions of parishioners with differing values relating to ethnic heritage, language, and education.[20] Dissent within the community began developing in 1926 over the selection and hiring process of an additional teacher. At the base of the argument was a long-standing controversy within the Greek-American community between ecclesiastical and lay community authority in church affairs. The argument continued through 1932. After unsuccessful efforts at reconciliation the Birmingham Greek community formally split over the school issue in 1933. Approximately one-third of the Holy Trinity parishioners "withdrew their membership and formed another parish, that of Holy Cross [with] aims and purposes being, of course, the same, but in a manner more to their liking."[21]

Not formally recognized by the Archdiocese, a small group of male parishioners led the group. The group advertised in the New York Greek newspaper *Atlantis* for a priest and hired Father Dionysios Dimitsanos from Corfu in 1933. Services had previously been held in the Fraternal Hall belonging to Holy Trinity, but within three months the dissident parish had 150 members and began extensive fund-raising efforts to build its own church. They reached their goal in 1934, with the aid of the American Hellenic Educational Progressive Association (AHEPA) and other community organizations. They built the first Holy Cross Church at North 25th Street between Seventh and Eighth Avenues in Birmingham. From the outset Mr. Anagnostou, one of the two teachers involved in the confrontation at Holy Trinity, taught Greek school classes in the church building.

Competition between the two parishes continued. In 1931 Holy Trinity ("the original church") bought the properties next door and erected a new educational building. In 1935 the Archdiocese officially recognized the dissident parish, Holy Cross. In 1938 Holy Cross built a new church next door to its old one, again with AHEPA's aid, and began using the former church as an educational building. A Youth Center was completed in 1951. In 1949, after some disagreement about relocation to an area nearer the homes of one community group, Holy Trinity built the present church (dedicated and consecrated in 1956) on its old site.

Reconciliation efforts between the churches began in 1947. It was the social activities of the youth groups of both parishes that finally reunited the Greek-American community in Birmingham. The factionalism between the two churches had divided the entire community for thirty years, during which time the community's mutual aid and church-affiliated organizations, including the church youth groups, began opening their social and recreational functions to one another.[22] The Greek Orthodox Youth of America (GOYA), a national organization aimed at the unification of independent Greek-American youth groups across the country, chose Birmingham to host the third annual GOYA conference in 1953. Members of both churches' chapters joined in its planning. The occasion resulted in the reunification of Birmingham's two Greek Orthodox parishes. The chairman of the event recalls the final gathering of the successful convention:

Nobody that came could forget the enthusiasm. I think one night they raised $45,000, just off the floor from the kids. There were old gold coins. People were crying. We realized all the great things that needed to be done for the community could not be done without the communities pulling together.[23]

A binding legal contract named the reconciled fifteen-hundred-member parish the United Greek Orthodox Community, Holy Trinity-Holy Cross, Birmingham, Alabama. It specified that a new priest would be brought in to serve the new community and outlined the usages of both parishes' new buildings. The Holy Trinity educational building would be used for joint Sunday school and Greek school classes; the Holy Cross Youth Center would be used for all parish social functions. The mutual use of each parish's former property appears to have continued until the 1970s, when the unified parish sold the property of the old Holy Cross Church after it had been damaged in a fire. To "satisfy the newer generation," Holy Trinity-Holy Cross replaced the old educational building with a modern one—the current Hellenic Orthodox Christian Center—dedicated in 1973. It contains Sunday school classrooms, the Greek language school classroom, a parish library, social halls, a gymnasium/auditorium, meeting rooms, and offices.

Most of the Greek-Americans in Birmingham interviewed about the split caused by educational differences agreed that it was unfortunate, but rationalized the community factionalism by drawing on Greek proverbial lore. An elder whose oral history is in the parish library said, "I know division is no good and all that, but, on the other side, it bring you progress, too. You have to fight for existence, you know...."[24] And as one of the elders interviewed in this study put it, "Everybody wanted to be chiefs. Nobody wanted to be an Indian. That's the trouble. That's the trouble with Greeks." (ES82-Mc/C-C14)

In 1982 Holy Trinity-Holy Cross was the third largest Greek Orthodox parish in the South, ranking behind Atlanta and Houston. It boasted the largest congregation and the only cathedral in the state of Alabama. Other smaller Greek Orthodox parishes exist in Montgomery, Huntsville, and Mobile. There is a "mission parish" as well in Daphne, Alabama. Since the 1953 reunification the Holy Trinity-Holy Cross parish has had five priests. A variety of church-affiliated groups continue to fulfill important aspects of the parish's religious, educational, and social missions. The 1982 Holy Trinity-Holy Cross roster listed 650 members, about 75 percent of whom, according to the current priest, are "ethnic Greek."

The issue of liturgical language is still controversial among parishioners. Some want to further increase the percentage of the liturgy that is in English (which has increased from 50 percent Greek and 50 percent English to 35 percent Greek and 65 percent English in the year and a half since the current priest, a Greek-American, took office) and others would return to services that are entirely in Byzantine Greek.

History of Holy Trinity, Holy Cross, and Holy Trinity-Holy Cross Greek Schools

The first language classes in Birmingham's Greek Orthodox community were offered shortly after the founding of Holy Trinity Church. As early as 1907, Mrs. Stamatina taught daily afternoon Greek school classes in a "shack" behind the church. She was followed by Andreas Kopoulos (also known as Mr. Andriakopoulos), who lived above the Greek school. A cantor at Holy Trinity, early parish records indicate that his salary was higher than that of the priest.[25]

The Hellenic focus of the school was made clear in its stated purpose: so "Americanized children [would be] secure in Greek thought, legend, and tradition."[26] The fledgling Greek Orthodox parish in Birmingham recognized the value of both Greek language maintenance and English language acquisition, and its lay organizations were instrumental in organizing and fund-raising for language education. In 1910 the Young Greeks Progressive Society was conducting English language classes for its membership of 150 young businessmen. A group of Greek women attended weekly sessions at a school on Highland Avenue,[27] and in 1911 a local chapter of the Pan Hellenic Union was organized in Birmingham with the objective "to plan and fund the Greek school."[28]

The earliest Greek school classes were held from June to September for three hours daily, Monday through Saturday. One room accommodated all elementary grades and teachers divided their time among students of various grade levels. As many as ninety students at one time—their desks arranged according to age and ability—studied Greek grammar, history, geography, literature, mythology, folksongs, drama, and dialogue. Exercise drills occurred on Saturdays, when students learned about religion and practiced athletics. The only available curricular materials were those imported from Greece by the teacher; the teacher often had the only books and students copied lessons from the blackboard. Rote learning, memorization, and recitation were the standard learning methods. Strict disciplinary measures were the rule.

One parish elder who attended Greek school classes from 1917 to 1922 describes the curricular materials and pedagogical methods used by Father Nicholas Lambrinides, the revered, multilingual teacher who had been trained in Constantinople before coming to America. He is widely remembered, even though he only spent six years in Birmingham.

We had only one book—the reader. All the rest of the subjects he would write on the board, like for history, for instance, and we would copy it, start on scrap paper. He demanded that we would put it in a composition book in calligraphy—and I mean without smudges, without misspellings . . . and that way we had pretty handwriting, and that way we would memorize what we wrote and we'd remember our history and religion topics and geography. He stressed geography, oh yeah! He would have the islands made in poetic form and we would point them out as we recited them. We would point them out, and if we made one little mistake we'd get a whack on the hand. He was very strict, but we learned; he made us learn. I knew the Greek geography as if I did, better than I knew the U.S. map. And I enjoyed it. I enjoyed the Greek School. . . . (ES82-Mc/C-C9)

Another second-generation Greek from Birmingham recalls her early experience in the "Hellenic" classes from around 1922 to 1928:

It was just a little, a house actually to start with, that they had bought and converted into the Greek school. And my mother happened to be on the Board of Education for the Greek school, so I had to be at school on time. . . . Actually, the curriculum was reading, grammar, writing, of course, and not penmanship writing but what they used to call *orthographia*, which was the correct spelling. . . . And correct grammar.

It started from the six-year-old and went on up to seventeen at least. . . . You know, I don't know how long I went to Greek school; it seemed like forever. . . . And our written examination we would write for weeks ahead of time, and then all our papers would be hung on a line so that our parents could view them. . . . If you were very unruly or did something very bad, we were sent out to cut the switches off the trees and we were switched on our hands—for doing something really bad, you know. It all depended on the teacher, what he thought was so terrible. (ES82-Mc/C-C8)

Both women also recall that the production of Greek patriotic plays, accompanied by Greek songs, was an important focus of the school year under Father Lambrinides and subsequent teachers. Such presentations were often a major feature of the annual graduation exercises, held at the Fraternal Hall next to the church or at Birmingham's Bijou Theatre.

A succession of Greek-born schoolteachers followed Father Lambrinides's tenure at the Greek school. Many teachers during this period also traveled on certain weeknights to the steel mill towns of Ensley and Fairfield to hold Greek school classes for the parishioners in those communities.[29]

In 1926 controversy began to develop in the Birmingham Greek Orthodox community over the hiring of teachers for the Greek school, its site, and policy-making decisions. This argument culminated in 1933 with the split of the community and the formation of the separate Holy Cross parish. Birmingham then had a second Greek school, supported, in part, by the fund-raising efforts of Holy Cross' Chapter of AHEPA, a community advancement group.[30] Holy Cross offered its own "parochial afternoon school of Greek," taught first by Mr. Anagnostou, and then, beginning around 1942, by the church's rector, the Reverend D. N. Sakellarides. After 1949 Christine Sepsas taught the classes, first taking pupils into her home and later affiliating with the new Holy Cross parish. Mrs. Sepsas's mother had also been a Greek school teacher. According to a former student Christine Sepsas is a "self-taught, natural-born teacher," who was prevented from attending college because Greek custom and family finances would only allow her brother to receive a higher education. No longer at the Greek school, she continues to offer classes in her home, teaching English to new immigrants in Birmingham. (ES82-Mc/C-C14)

Another teacher from Holy Trinity parish, Irene Kampakis, who graduated from a teachers' school in Athens, is also widely remembered today in the Greek community in Birmingham. Her former students describe her as being "very learned." A third-generation Greek-American who attended Greek school at Holy Trinity in the late 1930s and early 1940s recalls:

The class was divided—each row was a different grade. And, you know, that's surprising, because *every* Greek child was going to Greek school, every day, right after school. We'd get on the bus, get the tickets from the Birmingham Electric Company, because that's what used to be a streetcar.... We had to run and get the bus at six 'cause they wouldn't take your ticket after six o'clock on. It was packed. The streetcars were packed. We had to stand up and everything.... I wouldn't take a thing for those years. In fact, we sit around the table and talk about Greek school.... My kids have heard these stories a hundred and fifty times. (ES82-Mc/C-C9)

It seems that there were no formal Greek school classes in Birmingham during the war years, and by 1953 the two Birmingham Greek Orthodox parishes had reunited. By the mid-1960s and through the early 1970s

Greek school classes at the united Holy Trinity-Holy Cross Church had decreased to once-a-week evening classes, with a very high attrition rate by the end of the school year.

Although not directly cited by any of our American-born respondents, part of the problem during this period appears to have been staffing difficulties. In the late 1960s the one teacher at the Holy Trinity-Holy Cross Greek School was an elderly woman from Greece whose teaching style was not well received by her students, accustomed to the ways of American schools. One student called her a "strict-discipline, classic Greek schoolteacher" in the old country fashion. She was followed in the early to mid-1970s by an immigrant from Cyprus. A current teacher, an immigrant Greek herself, describes his pedagogical methods:

He was not for children. He [should have] taught adults. . . . He was really tough on the children, you know. He thought he was back in Greece, in the old school in Greece, and children would resent it. . . . Well, I'll tell you how it started. There was these three little girls—intermarriage, you know—so they were going to this Greek school. Well, one day he made a mistake. In Greek [he said], "Look at all these American kids come to Greek school." Well naturally . . . they didn't want to go back. And [my daughter] says, "If they're not going to go, then I'm not going to go." So I said, "If you're going to sit at home, then I'm going to teach you." . . . And the little girls say, "Well, can we come too?" And I say, "Yeah." And that was good, because that was one time [my daughter] really learned her Greek because, see, the four of them together, I had them two days a week, and I make them do things. I make them learn, and they [learned], like, "I want to go outside and play" and "Here's a beautiful tree," children's conversation. (ES82-Mc/C-C12)

This respondent has taught Greek language classes at Holy Trinity-Holy Cross on one or two weekday evenings since 1979. In 1982 she taught a two-hour Tuesday evening class to a mixed group of students, but their attendance was irregular and attrition rates were high. In her class of older students last semester, in which everyone knew the Greek alphabet, she used *Methods of English*, which her father employed when he taught her brother Greek. It is printed in Greek, English "phonetics," and English translation and focuses on exercises for social and business conversation as well as story and letter writing. Her students included fourth-generation Greek-American children and spouses converted to Greek orthodoxy through intermarriage. She describes their mixed attitudes toward language acquisition as follows:

Now I *do* have students in that class that would rather not use the English phonetics but read it in Greek, and they do. But I did find one thing—the non-Greeks that [are] within marriage, that [are] within the Greek faith [through intermarriage], they're more receptive to *learn* than the ones that actually are Greek, because they *apply* themselves because that's what they're there for. They have an *aim* within themselves to do something, so they are the ones that are really my best students. They are *learning* because that's what they are applying themselves to do.... No, we don't have history, all we're doing is strictly conversation, but, like I said, they do know the alphabet. They do know how to read in Greek if they do want to read it in Greek, but most of them will read in English. (ES82-Mc/C-C9)

During the same period two other native Greeks were teaching classes. One gave afternoon and evening sessions, primarily to adults, and experienced high attrition. A second teacher, raised in Greece as a member of a trilingual Greek-French-English speaking home, started teaching upon arrival in Birmingham in the late 1970s and attracts a somewhat more advanced level student group whose retention rate appears to be higher. In 1982 he taught a Saturday morning Greek school class at Holy Trinity-Holy Cross for adults only. He had six students in this class, including a recent convert married to a second-generation Greek-American and the couple's two daughters. The mother describes her daughters' ethnic identification and their attitudes toward Greek school:

[They] are very close to their background. The Greek is definitely prevalent. My children are so Greek-oriented that when they filled out applications for school [a special public school, gifted-child program]—they're twelve and fourteen—they put down *Greek*.... And I was in a state of shock. It didn't occur to me that they would even consider anything but American, but, you know, the Greek is really ingrained in them.... [But] one of them is rebelling against it [Greek school class] ... the younger one. Where the older one comes and enjoys it. She has more of a knack for languages than the other one. (ES82-Mc/C-C6)

This teacher describes the books he uses in the Saturday class:

I went through a lot of books from there [Greece] and found ones that, in my opinion, are good books, so I ... take the history of the 1821 revolution, *Iliad* and *Odyssey,* and some history of that era also. And since I know what they know, what I do is, I read a chapter and rewrite in a way that would be understood by the people.... I was writing little things, little essays I guess, in English or in Greek, and they would have to translate it to the other language. And I teach them some grammar and syntax—syntax is very important. It's very simple. There were very few rules.... What we do is, basically, my plan was to try to teach the people every time we meet a number of new words, and that's how we started out. And then after some time enough words, presumably, have been learned from both phrases, and [they] make little essays using those words. (ES82-Mc/C-C9)

His classes, which were to resume after a hiatus for his students' and his own vacations, were expected to continue in the fall of 1982 with many of the same students, some beginning their third and fourth years. The other teachers also plan to offer classes again in the fall. There is no reason to believe that the level of language education activity will diminish in the foreseeable future.

The factionalism over the Greek school that split the parish for thirty years no longer dominates this community; it is now thought of as a re-mote event. Vestigial factors underlying the controversy are manifested in parishioners' rationales for ethnic heritage and language education pro-grams and their ideas about how they can best be sustained. Community opinions about the Greek school, its past history, present status, and pros-pects for the future, often correlate with factors such as time of immigra-tion, age group, occupation, education, neighborhood of residence, native and home language, and ethnic and religious traditionalism or assimila-tionism, all of which were important elements in the controversy.

A newcomer to the community through intermarriage characterizes her fellow parishioners as "Greek Greeks" and "American Greeks," the former tending to be older immigrant Greeks with orientations toward the old country, the latter younger, native-born, professional young people. There do appear to be two groups, differing on questions of language used in the liturgy and approach to Greek language classes. But, interestingly, they do not contrast on the issue of the importance of Greek school at-tendance. The students in the Greek classes are made up of parishioners from both the more traditional and the more American-oriented groups; however, they tend to enroll in different classes.

For example, an "American Greek" family attends a class led by a youn-ger, well-educated professional man who immigrated from Greece and who uses contemporary second-language teaching strategies and simpli-fied Greek myths as texts. The rationale for this family to attend Greek school is not only to instill family heritage, but to offer their children the general educational advantages of a second language. The "Greek Greeks" articulate an ethnic identity that is less a complementary of cultures than an amalgam. Two elders from one of the Birmingham Greek community's founding families explain:

See, it's what you learn at home. You've got to go [with] what you learn at home. You see, when my daddy used to see, when we used to see the Greek flag—well, we marched and we see that Greek flag waving and the American flag right next to it. Why, you know, you'd just have all that patriotism in you for both countries. Because they're right there, side by side. (ES82-Mc/C-C14)

Her sister agrees, "Papa always said, 'You're an American. Don't ever forget you're an American, but never forget your Greek heritage.' He instilled that in us." (ES82-Mc/C-C9) This integration of "Greek-ness" with Americanism is the motivating factor for other parish Greek teachers and their students. Their classes tend to be more personally constructed, conversational rather than literary, and may include older teaching materials that they themselves used as schoolchildren. There may be Greek-American as well as Greek cultural content.

Community members commented on the group's sense of cultural necessity for preservation and perpetuation of the Greek heritage:

To me, without traditions it's nothing; that's the way I feel. And I hope I can instill this to my children. Without traditions we are nothing. You are *blank*. Well, really, that's the key. And traditions have got to be maintained, not only within the church but at least within the home, the family. And, OK, so we change and we look the other way, you know, when we start raping our various other traditions in the name of liberalism, and modification, and understanding. But certain traditions, if we eliminate that, why, we're back to nothing, we're nobody. (ES82-Mc/C-C10)

The current status and future direction of the Greek language school in Birmingham must be examined in relationship to its effectiveness in maintaining this cultural imperative and in reinforcing shared community values. But there is a considerable range of opinion among the parishioners we interviewed about their own ethnic identification and how it has changed over time, as well as about the importance and function of the language and cultural components in this maintenance effort. The future of the Greek school must be assessed in terms of how effectively it continues to be responsive to the church members' varied and changing needs, interests, and expectations for it. The Greek respondents expressed a variety of opinions about the history and degrees of commitment to the continuation of Greek school classes. Since the first generation of Greek immigrants in Birmingham are now deceased, the city's second generation of founding family elders (mostly women) can be used as the baseline from which to examine generational changes in attitudes toward ethnic and language education. This generation is perhaps the most ethnically retentive, although those cultural elements they choose to preserve are often archaic relics and survivals from Greece as it was at the time of their parents' immigration to this country at the turn of the century. Other Greek-Americans see them as having a "fantasy notion" about their Hellenistic roots. They received a grammar school education. Since they grew up during the post-World War I period, rampant with nativism and racism (particularly in the Deep South), their memories of experiences outside the Greek Orthodox community and of "American [public] school" are often unpleasant. On the other hand, their memories of attending ten years or so of mandatory Greek school classes on a daily basis are, on the whole, most pleasant. Greek school attendance reinforced cultural values and customs learned in the home and instructed them in standard Greek pronunciation and grammar. It also taught them to read and write the Greek colloquial language spoken within the rapidly growing Greek Orthodox community in Birmingham. Each stressed that learning to read and write standardized Greek was emphasized in the Greek school, because:

We already had [Greek] conversation at home.... All the children at that time did, because the parents couldn't speak English at all. And if they did, they wouldn't speak to us because they wanted us to learn the Greek. (ES82-Mc/C-C13)

On the whole, this group of second-generation Greek-Americans were upwardly mobile. These women's husbands, many of whom began working in Birmingham as street vendors, became wholesalers, retailers, and restaurant owners, and their children received a better education than they themselves had had. They are proud of and secure in their cultural preservation and transmission activities. This is manifested in their unself-conscious continuation of home and external ethnic customs, their children's attendance at the Greek school, their own activities as members and officers of the Greek school board and its parent-teacher organization, as well as their activity throughout the years in Greek community social organizations and their parish work as Sunday school teachers, choir teachers, and library volunteers.

They describe their own sense of ethnic identity as "Americans born of Greek descent." Their faith in Orthodoxy is so strong and their knowledge of its ritual so long-standing that they tend to be rather liberal on the issue of the choice of language for the liturgy. One respondent analyzes the historical relationship between the liturgical language and institutionalized language efforts:

Now to my parents [first-generation immigrants] it was important that I know the Greek language. And then there came a period of time where the parents [second generation] wanted their children to be a part, more a part, of the [American] community.... And, I think, because the parents worked so hard and seeked the better education for their children that it was uppermost in their mind that their schooling in the public school, or in the American school, or that they go to college, or whatever, were more important than going to Greek school. And I think this is why this change [in community attitudes toward the school] came about. The only thing that made them hold on to the Greek school, I think, was the fact that the church is, our religion is in the Greek language.... Because of this they try to hold on to the Greek language. (ES82-Mc/C-C8)

Their children were raised in Birmingham during the 1930s and 1940s, coming of age in the early 1950s. This generation, now the mainstay of the congregation, was better educated as a group than its parents, and is socially very upwardly mobile. During the post-war years there was little or no new immigration from Greece into the Orthodox community in Birmingham. Greek Orthodox spouses came into the Birmingham community from elsewhere in the country. Non-ethnically Greek wives also converted to the Greek Orthodox faith during this time and joined in local community activities. Greek-American communities all across the country were undergoing a period of homogenization and assimilation into the American mainstream. These third-generation immigrants, and their peers by extra-community and interfaith marriage, appear to be the least ethnically retentive and most ethnically ambivalent of the Greeks studied in Birmingham. They have been highly selective about the elements of their ethnic heritage they chose to preserve, have felt the most guilt about their passivity in transmitting their heritage to their children, and have rejected many of the traditions their parents saw as essential components of their own ethnic education, both at home and in more institutionalized and public settings. Not surprisingly, however, it is this group that has been the most active in public display events like the annual Greek Festival, which exhibits external ethnic customs, such as foodways, dance, music, and drama, to the public at large. They identify themselves as Americans, albeit of the Greek Orthodox faith. One second-generation American-born woman describes her personal and familial ties to Greece:

I really don't [have them]. The ties I have are because my children [adopted as infants] were born there, and of course, my mother and father. I think I'm just a real American. I, I love my heritage. I'm very, very proud of it. But I really don't have it [a Greek identity], and I don't think my children have either. (ES82-Mc/C-C8)

Many Greek-American women from this generation did not push their children either to learn the language or to go to Greek school, and their lack of assertion with regard to ethnic heritage and language maintenance is a sore spot with them even today. Their move to the suburbs, increasing interaction with their children's American public or Roman Catholic parochial school peers, and conflicts with extra-curricular activities are most often used as rationales for their leniency regarding cultural transmission, as this extract from conversation between two respondents illustrates:

A: Well, why do you not send your children to Greek school? Or have they ever gone?

B: They didn't want to go.

A: Have your children ever gone to Greek school?

B: Never gone to Greek school. I'll tell you why not. I would have to do all the transporting. They had so many other things to do and *I* would have to take them. And I guess it was just, their interest wasn't that big for me to sacrifice that time at that time. Now, oh yeah, *now* they want it.... Now they're learning it. Now they want to know Greek. But I couldn't tell them that, you know, ten years ago.

A: They blame the parents for not making them.

B: And then they would have blamed you for making them go. I used to blame my mother....

A: When he [my son] went to college, I never will forget, when he came home, on his first trip back home ... he turns around to me and he says, "I'll *never* forgive you for not making me go to Greek school."...

B: I feel I've failed my kids, 'cause when they were little, if I had spoken Greek to them as they grew up, they would know something, and I didn't. And I thought just bringing them down here [from the suburbs] for one hour a day, for once a week, what are they going to learn in that short little time? . . . But, I thought, well gosh, they don't even know how to count to ten, they're going to have to learn all that, and one hour a week is nothing. (ES82-Mc/C-C9)

These women, too, like their mothers before them, draw a strong correlation between native home language and the effectiveness of Greek school classes. They cite a decreasing incidence of conversational Greek at home:

The only difference in the kids that go to school today and us, I mean, I learned Greek because my grandmother, my grandfather were living. They were from Greece. My father was from Greece, but he spoke English. I mean, not well, but he spoke English and we could communicate. Of course I had to learn Greek because of my grandparents; we *spoke* in Greek. When we went to Greek school we knew what the teacher was telling us. I mean, you know, if she told us to shut the door, we could go close the door. These kids going to Greek school today don't, don't even know how to count to ten most of them. It's cold, they're cold. It'd be like you walking into Greek school class and learning Greek. . . . And I think that's the greatest thing about having a grandmother and grandfather that were born in Greece. . . . It's gotten worse, I mean, I can't speak Greek like I spoke it before—it's got an accent, an American accent to it. (ES82-Mc/C-C9)

Conversation during our group interview session at Holy Trinity-Holy Cross also stressed the interrelationships between language education at home and its institutionalized component in the parish language classes. Those interviewed agreed that the mother's role in language at home was as central as that of the extended family elders, and lamented their capitulation to their children's resistance to attending the Greek school.

C: They've lost a lot by not doing that. Like [another female respondent] and I were saying, when our children say, "I don't want to do that," we tend to say, "Well, that's OK." Whenever maybe we should say, "That's not OK, you *got to* do it."

A: Now, as a mother—my children are grown—my tendency and my husband's is to go where *we* want to be, you know, with *our* friends. Whereas then it was more of a togetherness. The mothers were in charge. The mothers came with us, and, not all the mothers, but mothers were appointed almost like what became the PTA in [public] grammar school.

C: I think that the mother's role in the Greek home is very, very important. (ES82-Mc/C-C8)

The Birmingham Greek Orthodox community's fourth generation, children who grew up in the late 1960s and early 1970s, during an era of increased ethnic awareness and ethnic revivalism, clearly define themselves as Greek-American. While they perceive their ethnic identity as dualistic, they recognize that this is not necessarily negative. They are in no sense ambivalent about or unwilling to use elements of both cultures and transform them into a synthesized whole that can revitalize their community's sense of self-identity. These women are ethnically self-conscious and aware. They care a great deal about the revival, renewal, and transmission of Greek ethnic heritage and language traditions. Ethnic Greeks and "married-ins" alike are learning about the community's foodways, family customs, and traditional dress from the older women by participating in parish social organizations, and are making every effort to reinterpret them in a meaningful way within their own homes. This self-conscious effort at ethnic education in the private domain carries over into the community arena; their children are active members of JOY (Junior Orthodox Youth) and participants in the parish's semi-institutionalized dance classes, as well as students at the Greek school.

These young women's efforts at ethnic education have further correspondences with the activities regarding institutionalized language education. They tend to be strong advocates of the Greek school:

It was not even publicized at that time [c. 1977, when she moved to Birmingham] that there was a Greek school. We felt it was necessary for the kids to learn Greek. We still do. It's helped them a great deal at [public] school. And they'll continue taking it as long as it's offered, no matter how proficient they get. My husband speaks two other languages and English and we feel it's important to speak different languages. (ES82-Mc/C-C7)

Crucial to the success of the Greek school at Holy Trinity-Holy Cross are differences of opinion within the community over the nature of institutionalized language education in the parish. The future prospects for such education must be assessed both in the light of the perceptions of the parishioners and of the parish priest, as well as in view of the centralization efforts of the Greek Orthodox Diocese of North and South America by the Department of Education.

There is considerable discussion of the proper role of Greek school education in the life of the parish. How closely should it be tied to ecclesiastical concerns, i.e., is Greek instruction important for reasons of cultural heritage, or as preparation to participate in and appreciate the (increasingly English language) liturgy? What should be the qualifications of Greek school teachers: need they be trained in pedagogy, educated in classics, holders of college degrees? This is a community and cultural tradition in which learning and intellectualism are highly valued. Are there approaches that are more appropriate for children and others for adults and, if so, how would the now all-age classes be restructured without discouraging those whose attendance is a family activity?

Although he is a newcomer, the parish priest's analysis of some of the school's problems generally concurs with that of his parishioners. The geographic spread of the parish members and their difficulties in transporting their children to the school, which is in downtown Birmingham, have already been noted. In a meeting in 1982 over this problem the Parish Council considered "satellites"—smaller language schools out in the suburban communities. The problem for students of choosing between their Greek Orthodox friends and activities and those at the American public/parochial schools is cited by priest and parishioners alike. Furthermore, the priest points out, some of the textbooks are outdated and the curriculum is seriously lacking, a conclusion with which we must agree.

In 1980 the Archdiocese announced a long-range plan to centralize and standardize the operation of Greek schools throughout the United States. The plan calls for an eight-year, afternoon program of Greek language and cultural study and for the publication of a complete series of Greek language texts to supplement those currently available. The Archdiocese and schools must resolve issues of teacher training and school financing if this national program of language education is to be successfully implemented, however. Additionally, Holy Trinity-Holy Cross, like the Archdiocese at large, must address a variety of special needs, e.g., non-Greek converts to Orthodoxy and new immigrants, in developing Greek school curricula that will serve all the varying constituencies which now comprise the parish.

Other Forms of Ethnic Education at St. Elias and Holy Trinity-Holy Cross

The St. Elias Arabic School and the Holy Trinity-Holy Cross Greek School are the most public and formalized expressions of cultural transmission undertaken by their communities. Although they are community based and quasi-institutionalized, they rest upon educational traditions which are integrated into the ordinary lives of Birmingham's Lebanese and Greek communities. The schools are a supplement to the informal learning that takes place in the home and community on a daily basis. Parish and community organizations represent a middle ground between institutionalized education and unself-conscious enculturation of children by family and community. Planned and casual community social events are one and two steps further removed from explicit teaching/learning situations in the language school setting. At the least formal level, even in family life, the element of self-conscious teaching of cultural heritage is very strong. Many of the activities, and sometimes the actual physical environments of Birmingham Greek and Lebanese homes, are calculated demonstrations of ethnic culture.

The following dialogue between two Greek respondents illustrates a common view of community education. The Greeks, they say are:

A: Very traditional people, who [have] ... church, religion, and family traditions [that are] carried out in the different ages. I think that's one of the main reasons [for Greek cultural retention], because our family traditions are so intertwined with our religious traditions, even though, within our church, we have holy traditions, which is altogether different from family traditions, and sometimes people mistake our family traditions for holy traditions.

C: I think it begins with the family, really. And then from there it sort of branches out to the Greek school, and then the church and organizations, and things like this. But it all begins with the parents, with the mother and the father. It did with us.

A: I think now it kind of works more through organizations a little more than it did in our first years [as a community]. And when I was a little girl, of course, the Greek school was very important. (ES82-Mc/C-C8)

Both women experience an inseparable relationship between the various settings in which community life and learning take place. The religious and secular cultures are "intertwined." The activities of home, Greek school, and parish organizations are seen as "branches" of the same effort.

While the components remain the same as in their childhoods, the emphasis has shifted—the social organizations bear more of the burden now, and the Greek school less. The learning continuum is unaltered, but the aspects of culture that are most important change as a community of immigrant Greeks becomes a community of Americans of Greek descent.

The high points of the Greek and Lebanese years are ethno-religious holidays. It is during the high holidays, such as Easter and saint's days, that the mother tongue is employed most extensively in the liturgy. In addition, secular songs are revived and members of the congregation otherwise monolingual use a host of expressions relating to the festivals. The holidays bring forth feasts of ethnic food, native costumes, banks of flowers, home decorations, and ritual objects, such as Greek Easter eggs, Catholic and Orthodox Lenten palms, and the Epiphany holy water for the Greek home altars. Special rituals are performed, both in the church and within nuclear and extended families and social networks.

These holidays are celebrations and simultaneously intra-group exhibitions of ethnic culture. Our respondents report an intense level of activity preceding the important holidays. Women cook, prepare the family home, and decorate the church. Greek men set up lamb pits. Lebanese men prepare their backyard grilling areas. The choirs rehearse. Children practice their dance routines and pageant speeches, and are fitted in their ethnic costumes.

Both the Maronite and Greek Orthodox communities also put on ethnocultural events for the general public. The annual Greek Festival attracts participants from the entire Birmingham area. In 1981, seven thousand meals were served and uncounted pastries sold. Trained young people led tours of the cathedral, for which they memorized the Greek terms for all the parts of the building and furnishings. While this event is calculated to raise money for the church and to introduce the Greek community to greater Birmingham, it is also an important expression of the Greek community's ethnic customs, as well as its deeper values. The president of the Philoptochos Society, the women's organization that works three days a week for six months to prepare the food for the festival, says:

I think that is one way we keep the Greek customs alive, through that, even though we don't like to admit that people kind of know us for our food.... Why fight it anymore? It's really something to be proud of. And our customs, our dances, too, because our children always do dances.... They [non-Greeks] tell us that they like to come because it's a family-oriented festival. And it really is—the kids are all working, the grandmothers, the mothers, some grandfathers are there, fathers, everybody. It's a community project really, but it's sponsored by the ladies' group. (ES82-Mc/C-C8)

The centrality of family and community life is made visible to outsiders, which in turn reaffirms the community's sense of ethnic integrity.

For the Lebanese the weekly public dinners which took place from the 1930s through the 1970s served a similar purpose. They put money in the building-fund coffers, created an ethno-cultural activity in which the parish members could become highly involved, presented a wholesome view of Lebanese life to the external world, and reinforced the value of the culture for the community itself. Birmingham's Lebanese also maintain a private social club, the Cedars Club, where organizations hold meetings, Lebanese young people and adults swim and play tennis, and a variety of more or less ethnically related activities take place. We visited the Cedars Club during their weekly bingo luncheon. It is open to the public and at least three hundred people of all ages—mostly women, some Lebanese, and many non-Lebanese—played bingo and consumed a lunch of Lebanese meat pies, *tabouli* salad (made from bulgur wheat and vegetables), Lebanese spice cookies, coffee, and iced tea. The Women's Auxiliary of the Cedars Club prepared the lunch and hosted the affair.

Greek and Lebanese community members also participate in a variety of casual and social activities that are culturally related. There are ethnic dance clubs at Holy Trinity-Holy Cross, and both Greeks and Lebanese regularly enjoy ethnic music and dance at weddings, festivals, and private parties. Until recently there was a Greek music band of young boys from Holy Trinity-Holy Cross who played for all sorts of events. The St. Elias parishioners hire Arabic musicians from New York or elsewhere for major parish events, sometimes even for weddings. One of the Greek Orthodox men's organizations sponsored a tour to New Orleans in the summer of 1982 to see a traveling art exhibit *In Search of Alexander*, a collection of Hellenic artifacts from the period of Alexander the Great. In 1981 a women's group visited the first Greek school in the United States in St. Augustine, Florida. The parish is participating in a national fund-raising drive to restore the historic school building to its original state and to erect a memorial chapel.

All such quasi-organized activities reinforce the cultural heritage that these ethnic communities wish to maintain and transmit. They form the background to parish members' aspirations for Greek and Arabic school courses, and indicate a continuing curiosity about and awareness of their ethnic heritage.

All of our respondents can readily provide a long list of examples of family practices stemming from their ethnic background. Not only are they conscious of the many aspects of their cultures which they are passing down through family life, but they also can describe the ways in which they are teaching them. Every respondent mentions ethnic music and dancing. All the women mention cooking instruction. One tells of teaching the Lebanese national anthem and other Arabic songs to her children and grandchildren. Another explains how he employs all the Arabic terms at his command with his children, and a non-Greek convert describes the strategies her husband uses to get their daughters to use their rudimentary Greek. Many respondents utilize proverbs in their mother tongue and eagerly relate stories about the old country, the early days in the United States, and Greek or Arabic school, which they often find themselves retelling at their children's request. One Greek-American tells how he repeats the bedtime stories his grandmother told him to his own children—stories he was surprised and delighted to discover were the great Greek "classics" when he studied ancient Greek in college.

To visit Greek- and Lebanese-American homes is to enter environments designed to express ethnic identity. Our hosts, Orthodox and Maronite, showed us their home altars decorated with icons or figures of saints, palm-frond crosses, and vials of holy water and incense. In one home the daughter's bedroom displays a collection of Greek dolls, including the mother's own dolls, the grandmother's dolls, and new dolls brought back from Greece. The mother also showed us a mounted display case containing artifacts from her wedding, explaining why it hangs over the marriage bed. Paintings and photos of family members, small brass, porcelain, and wooden objects distinctly Arabic in design, and Oriental rugs decorate a St. Elias elder's living room. Even in casual settings Maronite women wear gold jewelry, especially hoop bracelets. Lebanese homes contain Oriental rugs, Lebanese lace tablecloths, and photos of Lebanon. Some homes display photos of family in Zahle, their village of origin. In one basement we were shown a special griddle for Lebanese bread and a permanently installed, triple, gas-fueled grill over ten feet long in the backyard. Jars of clarified butter and cultured *laban* cheese are staples in Lebanese kitchens.

Every surface and every wall in one Greek-American home holds a display of Greek artifacts. They range from replicas of ancient vases to postcards of costumed Greek dancers, Aegean seascapes rendered in oil, and homeland statuary. The living room and dining room walls are blue, and even the furniture is upholstered in the Greek national colors. These hosts provided a Greek dinner for us—all traditional dishes with fresh Greek herbs from their garden and Greek wine. The apartments of the elderly are repositories for family and Greek memorabilia. Every home we visited had a large album of photos from trips to Greece conveniently at hand, which was quickly brought forth for our examination.

All of these practices reflect conscious statements of ethnic identity and strategies for its maintenance. In the more middle-class homes the objects are carefully chosen, consisting largely of artistic artifacts of old country, high culture. In the more working-class homes fine art and crafts are intermixed with mass-produced replicas designed for tourist consumption.

Looking beyond material artifacts to less obvious forms of ethnic expression, it is important to analyze the range of ways of "being" Greek or Lebanese, beyond exhibiting ethnic identifiers. One facet of deeper cultural identity is home language use. In all the homes we visited Greek or Arabic was in regular use, at least among the residents themselves. One couple share Greek as their first language, though they make use of English augmented with Greek when speaking to their daughters. Several elders use Arabic with family and friends of their generation, but increasingly make use of English with the younger generation, practically to the exclusion of Arabic.

In addition to language choice, we were aware of conversational strategies that were derived from the mother-tongue culture. The Greeks we interviewed tend to speak rapidly, respond quickly to queries, and to interrupt and overlap each other and even the fieldworkers. There are scattered remarks about the contentious "nature" of the Greeks, e.g., "Everybody wanted to be chiefs.... That's the trouble with the Greeks;" "There will always be a lot of conflict;" "If Greeks don't have an enemy outside to fight, they just fight with each other." (ES82-Mc/C-C12) The relatively loud, quick, and assertive style of discourse we encountered indicates that Greek-language conversational norms unconsciously pervade the community's English as well.[31]

By contrast, our talks with Lebanese-Americans were far slower in pace. There were long pauses between our questions and their responses. Answers appeared to be careful and deliberate, often clarified with illustrative stories. There was almost never an interruption either of the fieldworkers or of each other. While the discourse styles typical of Arabic conversation among Lebanese have not been researched, the differences from our own Anglo-English and, markedly, from Greek-American speech style were pronounced. The Lebanese appear to maintain a sense of careful timing and deliberation, even in English.

Perhaps the clearest indicator of family life as an expression of culturally appropriate behavior and cultural values is the extreme hospitality with which we were met in these two communities. The Greek Orthodox priest took it upon himself to carefully question us about the nature and goals of the research project, selecting those we would interview based on our initial interview with him. His secretary called one day and informed us that a series of interviews had been arranged and we were to come to Holy Trinity-Holy Cross, where the parish members would report to meet us. Thus our Greek interviews were clearly conducted under the auspices of the parish priest. The interviewees were prompt, interested, and open. Subsequently some interviewees took it upon themselves to introduce us to "real" Greek life by inviting us to their homes for food, music, and conversation, so that they could share their photo albums, artifacts, and stories and demonstrate Greek hospitality.

Our first and primary contact at St. Elias was also the parish priest, but he simply provided names of potential contacts. Significantly, these suggestions included those who disagree most strongly with him on the issue of opening an all-day school. In the Lebanese homes, too, we were plied with ethnic specialties. Our most serious interview problem was bringing the meetings to an end. The parish priest, ever careful in distinguishing faith from culture, concluded one interview by remarking that, while he does not like St. Elias to be thought of as an ethnic community, he does see certain aspects of Lebanese life as part of Maronitism and intrinsic to parish life. "Well, the way of life, and the feeling that we have for each other, and the hospitality. There's always been Lebanese hospitality, always been. Always proud of that, and family life." (ES82-Mc/C-C1; ES82-Mc/C-C2)

The Southern Experience

Birmingham's Lebanese and Greek communities have several commonalities. Both are practitioners of Eastern rites of Christianity, faiths that are very ritualistic and "high church" by American Christian standards, especially from the Deep South, where Protestant fundamentalists and Pentecostals are the overwhelming majority.

The Greek Orthodox cathedral, like the Maronite church, functions as something of an out post for the faith. Holy Trinity-Holy Cross is the oldest, largest Greek Orthodox community in Alabama, and still the third largest in the South. St. Elias remains one of only three Maronite communities in the entire Southeast. The two parishes were founded within three years of one another.

Immigration began for both communities in the 1880s, typical for populations from countries in the Eastern Mediterranean. Both the Lebanese and the Greeks emigrated because of declining income from their tiny farms. They were uneducated, with the exception of a few individuals who became key leaders in the parishes and the parish schools. Because of the history of federal immigration law, the communities also grew in parallel ways.

Both communities derive their attitude toward education from a great sense of pride in their long literary traditions. Lebanese and Greeks alike value "the learned man" as teacher and leader. Both Nicholas Lambrinides, the most admired Greek schoolteacher, and Father Abi-Chedid of St. Elias were characterized by this term. The Lebanese described themselves as direct descendents of the Phoenicians and the great Arabic cultures preceding Turkish domination. The Greeks look back to the Hellenistic classical tradition.

These traditions have implications for language, ethnic school curricula, and pedagogy, as well as for the imperative for cultural preservation and transmission felt by many community members. An elder explains why the St. Elias parish supported Father Abi-Chedid's plan for a Maronite parochial school:

They were very interested in helping the pastor get the school started because that's the only way you're going to preserve anything. You'll preserve your heritage and teach your children who they are. And of course we have the proudest heritage there is. We started civilization. We started learning. We started navigation. We started accounting. Just name it and it was started by the Phoenicians. (ES82-Mc/C-C4)

While each of our Lebanese respondents asserted their forefathers' contributions to world culture with at least some brief informational remarks, the Greeks appeared completely confident that their culture would be well known and respected, at least by such educated Americans as the fieldworkers. Their remarks were intended to show how the classical culture taught as a scholarly subject in America is part of everyday life for Greeks.

The Birmingham Greeks and Lebanese have also shared a long struggle against overt racism. Greeks and Lebanese were sometimes considered non-white in the segregated South. Our interviews contain frequent references to discrimination in employment, housing, and schools. Here are some representative remarks on the early years:

In the South, there weren't too many ethnic groups. The only [ones were] Italians, Greeks—very few Greeks, very few Italians—and the Jewish people. And we were looked down, in fact, they called us "dagos" in those days [group laughter]. They did! They called the Italians and Greeks "dagos." And everybody would murmur if they wanted to speak to somebody in their native tongue; they would go secretly to speak so they wouldn't be ridiculed. (ES82-Mc/C-C10)
[For the first Lebanese peddlers] it was a very hazardous life because they went out into [the] country and sold to these people who, back in those days aliens were nil, you know. They were persecuted. They didn't know the language and might say the wrong word.... [The St. Elias community remained strongly committed to each other because] well, I think in the northern cities there was not that much discrimination. See, people here were even afraid to say they were Catholic at one time. Down South, you know, that is Baptist country. If you said you were Catholic, why you got it.
My father had to go to court one time. We had a cow in the yard and somehow the cow ... I don't think it bothered that woman, or anything; she just made a big suit out of it. Well he ... see that cross he's wearing on his lapel

[pointing to his portrait]? The lawyer told him to put that cross away because they, they're going to, it might make him lose the case. He said, "Well, let me tell you buddy, this is going to help me win the case, don't worry about it. I ain't putting away no cross. It's going to stay right here." Sure enough, he won the case. (ES82-Mc/C-C4)

Racial discrimination eased after World War II:

It made a lot of our American boys aware, especially here in the South, because we have a lot of what you would call "redneck" people that didn't know anything beyond their little area. . . . And when they were exposed to the farmlands of Italy, England, Belgium, and so forth and so on, they realized, "Hey, this is what I do. These are people, too." I think it exposed them to a lot. . . . (ES82-Mc/C-C13)

But vestiges remain:

[The Greek community at first tried to maintain its own separate culture and education because] I think at first it was because of this anti-immigrant. I felt this way when I was in grammar school. And I think the war [World War II] changed everything. . . . Now let me say this. You know my younger son, because of the prejudices and because it seemed at a certain time, even after the war, that high school children of different nationalities were not helped into getting into, not better positions, and to hold office in some of the clubs and these areas in the high school life. And they were discriminated against. Not the Greek people only, but, like I said before, the different groups. And he would always say when they'd ask him, or he'd say to me, "Well, I'm an American." Or if anybody asked him he'd say, "Well, I'm an American. My mother was born in America." You know, he was kind of defensive. (ES82-Mc/C-C9)

A Lebanese-American father of young children attributes his assertive stance toward ethnic heritage and language education to discrimination he and his wife suffered as children, and which he does not want his children to endure:

And I'm sure they [his wife's family] had a rough time in Mississippi growing up [apart from an organized Lebanese community]. . . . I know my mother and father did, in this area . . . I think they got so tired of defending, having people not understand. Me, I consider it ignorance if they do not understand. I just feel like they should look at their own background, you know, who are they to judge me? . . . And that's what I tell my children. And I tell them if anyone calls you anything bad—and I tell them what words I think are bad—you have my permission to pick up a brick and hit them. I don't like violence, but they do [have permission]. And we're in 1982 now and those days are gone, you know, where you have to defend your religion, and your heritage, and your background. (ES82-Mc/C-C16)

The Birmingham Greeks responded to nativism and segregation both by turning inward, i.e., creating employment in their own businesses and supporting each other in various mutual-aid associations, and by turning outward, trying to enhance the image of the Greeks to the larger public and actively combating discrimination. In 1922 several men from Holy Trinity travelled to Atlanta to meet with other southern Greeks and decide on a response to discriminatory practices and attacks by the Ku Klux Klan. They returned to found the third American Hellenic Educational Progressive Association chapter in the United States, following the lead of the communities in Atlanta and Charlotte, North Carolina.

The Lebanese also took care of their own under adverse conditions and struggled to alter the racist attitudes and behaviors of those they lived among. Dr. H. A. El-Kourie responded to Alabama Congressman and nativist John Burnett's proposal made at a Birmingham civic club that "non-whites" be excluded from immigration. In articles written to local newspapers and a volume of privately published essays, this Lebanese physician argued that not only was Burnett wrong in stating that Mediterranean peoples are "non-white," but that "Syrians" had been quick to adopt American ways and to advance themselves educationally and economically, making a substantial contribution to their city and nation.[32] The Syrians [Lebanese] are, El-Kourie stated, "law-abiding, 'thoroughly Americanized' members of the white race." Dr. El-Kourie became a national spokesperson in opposition to immigration restrictions and English language and literacy tests for immigrants, traveling to Washington, D.C., to testify before Congress.

Ethnic and religious discrimination did not cease with the nativists' success in passing immigration restrictions in the 1920s. The following decades were rife with attacks on blacks, "coloreds," the non-native-born, Catholics and other non-Protestant Christians, and Jews. Birmingham became one of the strongholds for the Ku Klux Klan, one KKK faction alone numbering ten thousand members in the city. Up until the Civil Rights Movement forced an end to *de jure* segregation in the 1960s, Greek- and Lebanese-Americans had to face possible challenges when using "white-only" facilities and services. Religious bigotry was a fact of life. Even today the communities endure insults grounded in ignorance and, from some elements, continued resentment. It is in this adverse context that the parishes of Holy Trinity-Holy Cross and St. Elias persevered in their efforts of religious and ethnic continuance. Their parish schools were instruments for community survival.

The Birmingham Greek and Lebanese communities have been remarkably culturally retentive and continue to express strong ethnic identity despite their small numbers. Immigrants to the Birmingham communities have observed this as well and, like us, believe that this may be due in part to the unusual social and cultural context in which they make their homes.

I think [an important reason] was this community being isolated from other Greek communities. Because when you go into the Carolinas, Virginia, start moving up North, you can go five miles and meet another Greek community, ten or fifteen miles, you're in another Greek community. So you're not an isolated person. You're really not isolated in those areas. Here in Birmingham it's very isolated. And I can see that within the people—becoming more clannish, I guess—and it's because of your different groups. I think [that elsewhere] it became a lot more cosmopolitan, and also more social, and not so much clannish. (ES82-Mc/C-C12)

I think the Birmingham [Lebanese/Maronite] community has always been very aware of itself. I really believe that. And I've heard compliments about them, nationally, you know, throughout my time as priest.... They've always stayed close to their traditions, and their identity, and their church; haven't gone too far away and had to pull them back. I mean, they know, they have had that awareness. And I think that's due to the churches which promote that and to the [Cedars] Club. (ES82-Mc/C-C1)

Conclusions

Brief fieldwork on ethnic language and heritage schools in these two parishes clearly suggests that the study of community-based education offers a valuable perspective on cultural maintenance and adaptation. By analyzing the "fit" between school organizations, content, and pedagogies and the cultures of the communities which create them, and, especially, through study of community-based schools in relation to other culturally supportive community and family activities, we can come to understand the world view that a community shares and is attempting to transmit.

Further work in this area would benefit from expansion and refinement in several directions. First, study of institutionalized education and other, less formalized, contexts for cultural transmission should be integrated to provide a fuller view of the ethnic maintenance process. Some components of culture, for example, religious ritual and ethnic language and literacy, lend themselves to teaching on an institutionalized basis, while others, such as ethnic cooking and family customs, are easily taught in the home. Formal and informal education cannot be ranked as more or less important; they are points in an array of cultural transmission processes that occur in a wide range of contexts, within the domains of the church, the lay ethnic community, and the family. Community members look to their institutions to provide support for (1) aspects of their heritage which require liturgical knowledge and ecclesiastical authority; (2) aspects that are difficult for them to transmit themselves; and (3) aspects which may require larger group participation. Further, understanding of traditional community values may be expanded by analysis of what the community thinks is best taught in an institutional context and what it leaves to informal learning.

Second, the question of language maintenance has rarely been treated to the careful and thoughtful analysis with which scholars have approached other forms of cultural expression. Whereas folklorists are very much aware of all forms and levels of cultural transmission, most linguistic analysis has been one dimensional: a community practices language maintenance if its young people grow up bilingual and it does not if they become monolingual in the mainstream tongue. Language, however, should be seen, as are other components of culture, as an elusive, complex, and situational phenomenon, expressed in both direct and indirect ways, and evoking various responses to, strategies for, and modes of retention and transmission. We should ask, for example, how the demands of particular situations in both public and private sectors affect the processes of cultural and linguistic change. What occasions demand "Greek Greek-ness?" What situations demand "American Greek-ness?" What situations call for "American-ness?" How do individual responses to such situations vary within each ethnic culture? What does it mean, for example, when St. Elias' priest states that it is important to keep the "flavor" of the Arabic language alive? What would the necessary "flavor" of Greek be to parishioners at Holy Trinity-Holy Cross? How is this metaphor of cultural distillation used when Greek-American respondents speak of "instilling" not only the mother tongue, but other aspects of their ethnic heritage, to their children?

Third, the study of ethnic heritage and language education can inform, and should be informed by, contemporary understanding of the dynamic nature of ethnicity.[33] Different aspects of culture demonstrate differing rates of change and degrees of assimilation, and the relationships among these rates are not constant across cultures. What is the place of community-based education in the evolution of ethnic identity? Why and at what points in a community's history is institutionalization of ethnic maintenance chosen as a strategy? What are the roles of the Greek Orthodox and Maronite Catholic churches as culture-preserving institutions? What are the roles of voluntary and mutual aid associations? In what respects does the family, or extended family, dominate as a force for cultural conservatism? How does the larger society impinge on these conservative forces, in both public and private realms? And, finally, how does ethnic education serve as a response to social, political, and economic factors in the community's environment? For example, what are the implications of the relationships between different socioeconomic classes and immigration status within the ethnic communities for maintenance of language and culture? What are the implications of various religious or political factions within ethnic communities?

The histories of Birmingham's Lebanese and Greek communities suggest that separate institutionalization was a positive response to a sometimes hostile environment, insulating the young in the community from negative encounters with racial and religious prejudice and reinforcing a sense of pride in a heritage not appreciated by the larger community. As the Birmingham profiles demonstrate, study of ethnic education promises to inform us about the practice of cultural maintenance as an affirmative, creative process.

Notes

1. For its discussion of historical background and socioeconomic context of migration and immigration to Birmingham, Alabama, this paper relies, in part, upon the work of Nora Faires, especially her contributions to a paper coauthored with Nancy Faires Conklin, "'Colored' and Catholic: The Lebanese Community in Birmingham, Alabama," in *Crossing the Waters: Arab-Speaking Immigrants to the United States Before 1940*, Eric S. Hooglund, ed. (Washington: Smithsonian Institution Press, 1987). We thank Nora Faires for permission to incorporate that material here. In comparing experiences of Lebanese and Greek immigrants to urban-industrial Birmingham with those of in-migrating rural southern blacks, we draw on fieldwork by Brenda McCallum, especially the "Working Lives" Collection of historical documents and tape-recorded interviews, which are deposited at the Archive of American Minority Cultures, Special Collections Library, The University of Alabama, University, Alabama. We also wish to acknowledge the cooperation of Jeff Norrell, director of the BirmingFind public history project, based at Birmingham-Southern College, for his assistance. Most especially, we wish to express our gratitude for the cooperation of the priests and parishioners of St. Elias Maronite Catholic Church and Holy Trinity-Holy Cross Greek Orthodox Cathedral throughout this project.

2. "The New Patrida: The Story of Birmingham's Greeks," a BirmingFind pamphlet (Birmingham: [Birmingham-Southern College], n.d.).

3. "Birmingham's Lebanese: 'The Earth Turned to Gold,'" a BirmingFind pamphlet (Birmingham: [Birmingham-Southern College], n.d.).

4. Among the founding families in the Birmingham community were adherents of the two primary Christian faiths in the Lebanese homeland. Both Maronites and Melkites are Eastern Catholics, giving allegiance to the pope at Rome, but worshipping in accordance with ancient liturgical rites distinct from the Latin, i.e., Roman, Rite practiced by the majority of the world's Catholics and by the American Catholic Church hierarchy. The mountains of Lebanon were, over many centuries, refuge to minority religious groups, including the fourth-century visionary and ascetic, St. Maron and his followers.

The Maronites, a uniquely Lebanese/Syrian faith under the domain of the patriarch at Antioch, have maintained their union with the Catholic Church throughout the centuries. Their Antiochene or, more specifically, Maronite Rite is characterized, among other things, by the use of Aramaic or Syriac in the liturgy. The first Lebanese to Birmingham were Maronites and they founded St. Elias. Other early Lebanese settlers were Melkites, followers of the Byzantine patriarch, and they with Greek Catholics of non-Lebanese nationality worship at St. George.

The Melkites are one of three major traditions among Catholicism's Byzantine Rite adherents; they are known collectively as Greek Catholics. Like Byzantine Rite adherents in southern, central, and eastern Europe, the Melkites split from Rome in the eleventh century. In the eighteenth century the Arab Orthodox reunited with the pope at Rome, as other Byzantine Rite practitioners had done in the intervening years. Their distinct rite they retained, however. Thus Melkite Greek Catholic churches, including St. George in Birmingham, may be multi-national, attracting not only their founding Melkites but coreligionist Byzantine Rite Catholics of European descent.

5. Phillip M. Kayal, "Religion in the Christian 'Syrian-American Community,'" in *Arabic-Speaking Communities in American Cities*, Barbara C. Aswad, ed. (Staten Island: Center for Migration Studies of New York, 1974), p. 111.

6. Kayal, p. 125.

7. *1979 Official Catholic Directory*

8. Interview by Brenda McCallum and Nancy Faires Conklin, April 28, 1982. This and all subsequent interview tapes cited were recorded by the authors from April to June 1982. Original tape recordings, transcripts, and other project data are deposited in the Archive of Folk Culture, American Folklife Center, Library of Congress, Washington, D.C. Duplicate copies of data collected during the course of this research are deposited in the Archive of American Minority Cultures, Special Collections Library, The University of Alabama, University, Alabama.

9. Sofia Lafakis Petrou, *A History of the Greeks in Birmingham, Alabama* (Birmingham: n.p., 1979), pp. 2–3.

10. Nicholas Christu interview by Sofia Petrou, February 3, 1977, transcript, Oral History Research Office, Department of History, University of Alabama in Birmingham, pp. 1–2.

11. James G. Patterson. *The Greeks of Vancouver: A Study in the Preservation of Ethnicity* (Ottawa: National Museums of Canada, 1976), p. 8.

12. Petrou, 1979, p. 19; "The New Patrida: The Story of Birmingham's Greeks," n.d.

13. Charles C. Moskos, Jr., *Greek Americans: Struggle and Success* (Englewood Cliffs, N.J.: Prentice-Hall, Inc., 1980), p. 17.

14. Christu transcript 1977, p. 12.

15. Petrou 1979, p. 9.

16. Moskos, p. 9.

17. The United Greek Orthodox Community, *Holy Trinity-Holy Cross* (Birmingham: n.p., 1956) n. pag.; Petrou 1979, p. 7.

18. Christu transcript 1977, p. 12.

19. Thomas Burgess, *Greeks in America*, reprint (San Francisco: R and E Research Associates, 1970), pp. 173–74.

20. Petrou 1979, pp. 29–30.

21. *Holy Trinity-Holy Cross*, 1956, n. pag. On the role of the church in American ethnic communities, the community-based nature of parish schools, and conflicts between sacred and secular functions of parish churches and schools, see Timothy L. Smith, "Lay Initiative in the Religious Life of American Immigrants, 1880–1950," in *Anonymous Americans: Explorations in Nineteenth-Century Social History,* Tamara K. Hareven, ed. (Englewood Cliffs, N.J.: Prentice-Hall, Inc., 1971), pp. 214–49; and Raymond A. Mohl, "The Immigrant Church in Gary, Indiana: Religious Adjustment and Cultural Defense," *Ethnicity,* vol. 8, no. 1 (1981), pp. 1–17.

22. Petrou 1979, p. 35.

23. Petrou 1979, p. 36.

24. Christu transcript 1977, p. 34.

25. Petrou 1979, p. 25.

26. Holy Trinity-Holy Cross Hellenic Orthodox Christian Center, *Dedication Book* (Birmingham: n.p., 1972–1973), n. pag.

27. Petrou 1979, p. 23.

28. Petrou 1979, pp. 26–27.

29. Petrou 1979, p. 25.

30. The United Greek Orthodox Community "Holy Trinity-Holy Cross," *50th Anniversary: 1906–1956: Holy Trinity Dedication* (Birmingham: n.p., ca. 1956), n. pag.

31. This conversational style has been documented among Greeks and Greek-Americans in the work of Deborah Tannen, e.g., "Oral and Literate Strategies in Spoken and Written Narratives," *Language,* vol. 58 (1982), pp. 1–21.

32. The articles appeared in the *Birmingham Ledger,* September 20, 1907, and the *Birmingham Age-Herald,* October 20, 1907. The essay collection is entitled "In Defense of the Semitic and the Syrian Especially" and was made available by Jeff Norrell.

33. See, for example, Mary C. Sengstock, "Differential Rates of Assimilation in an Ethnic Group: In Ritual, Social Interaction, and Normative Cultures," *International Migration Review,* vol. 3, no. 2 (1969), pp. 18–31; Judith A. Nagata, "Adaption and Integration of Greek Working Class Immigrants in the City of Toronto, Canada: A Situational Approach," *International Migration Review,* vol. 4, no. 1 (1969), pp. 44–70; and Nora Faires, "The Evolution of Ethnicity: The German Community in Pittsburgh and Allegheny City, Pennsylvania, 1845–1885," Ph.D. dissertation, University of Pittsburgh, 1981.

The Greek School at the Hellenic Orthodox Church of the Annunciation

Buffalo, New York

Lydia Fish

How shall we sing the Lord's songs
upon an alien soil?
PSALM 137

The first Greek settlers in Buffalo arrived in 1894.[1] By 1910 about ten families and approximately two hundred single men were living in the area. The first church, Evangelismos (Annunciation), was incorporated in 1911, and the first Greek school was established in 1916.

The school met at the church, on Oak Street. From the first it was a weekday afternoon rather than an all-day school. Subjects in these early years seem to have been limited to the reading and writing of Greek and the study of the Orthodox faith. Early teachers were the priest and an occasional layman; religious instruction and language instruction obviously went hand in hand. Unmarried girls and married women of the community begin to be mentioned as teachers in the 1920s.

A.P. Theodorides took over as school principal in 1933 and added history, geography, and penmanship to the curriculum. In the late 1930s, 250 children were enrolled in the school. At first classes met after regular school every day, and later on two or three afternoons a week. Some religious instruction seems also to have been given on Saturdays.

In 1937 the parish purchased a cultural center several miles away on Delaware Avenue, close to the site of the present church. Classes were held there for a while and then moved back downtown to an annex school close to the Oak Street church. In 1952 the church moved to its present building, which is still more or less downtown but in a much more elegant neighborhood. The new church, a beautiful stone building in a style best

Children from fourth and fifth grade Sunday school classes cracking Easter eggs, Buffalo, New York. (ES82-4-526392-10) Photo by Lydia Fish described as parish Gothic, was originally North Presbyterian Church, built between 1904 and 1906. For twenty years the Greek school and Sunday school classes met in a handsome stone parish house attached to the church. In 1972 a community center was completed in the same location, with a gymnasium for games and dancing and classrooms on the first floor. There are 756 families that are dues-paying members of the parish at present and approximately 200 more that do not support the church, although they may show up from time to time at services, social events, or the Greek festival held there.

In 1945 Father John Pallas became pastor of the church. The Greek school and Sunday school as they are presently constituted began after Father Pallas's arrival. Before that time it is virtually impossible to distinguish between the Greek school and the Sunday school, which seem to have had overlapping personnel and curricula. The reason for the separation of the two schools was probably that it was no longer possible to conduct religious instruction entirely in Greek and assume that all the children understood it. At about the same time the Archdiocese stopped printing Sunday school books in Greek, so it was obviously a national trend.

Teachers

The first teachers in the Greek school were the priest and an occasional highly educated layman, who often also acted as choir director. Although educated teachers were sought, the memories of some of the youngsters who attended the school in the 1950s and 1960s indicate that some teachers were recruited who had no more qualifications than an ability to speak the language and a strong sense of dedication to the preservation of Greek language and culture among the younger generation.

Today there are six teachers employed by the school: Mrs. Pullman, a trained teacher, Mrs. Serkizes, who has taught at the school for five or six years, and four Greek students who attend the University of Buffalo. Mrs. Pullman is paid $45 per week, Mrs. Serkizes receives $30 per week, and the Greek students receive $25 per week. The teachers are not specially trained, unless they are certified teachers. There are occasional workshops such as one conducted by the author of the texts presently in use and another recently presented in Rochester. There are many more workshops and seminars offered in the New York City area, where there are, of course, many more Greek schools.

School Administration

The school is financed by tuition payments and some fund-raising activities. For some years there was a Greek school board; more recently the school has been run by a Parent-Teacher Association (PTA), which conducts raffles, candy sales, and bake sales and puts on an annual dance to raise money for the school. In 1982 the parish council took over the responsibility for the school, which George Pappas, the principal, feels was a mistake. Since the council instituted a raise in tuition, the parents feel that they no longer need to donate their time. At present the students pay $50 tuition per year, with an additional $25 fee for books and supplies. The Philoptochos Women's Society usually contributes a few hundred dollars each year.

George Pappas is the only administrator of the school; he makes decisions about curriculum and so forth, in consultation with the teachers and the "greatly weakened" PTA. If the school had more money, he would like to purchase more teachers' aids (some good tape recorders, for example) and hire more qualified teachers.

Classes and Curriculum

Formerly, the classes were grouped only by age—the children started Greek school in the first grade at six and finished the sixth grade when they were twelve. This year, however, tests were given and the students were placed according to their level of proficiency.

The textbooks used are published by Theodore C. Papaloizos Publications in Maryland, which offers a complete curriculum, including workbooks. The Archdiocese is currently working on their own series of language books and George Pappas is using their first-grade reader this year. The main emphasis of the school is on language teaching; there are no special classes in history, geography, literature, or art. Little bits of all of these are sandwiched into the language lessons, along with some classical mythology and a fair amount of material on Greek calendar customs.

Several holidays are marked by special school programs. The last Sunday in January is Greek Letters Sunday, which is dedicated to Greek language schools and celebrated in North and South America. The most important holiday, however, is Greek Independence Day, which is celebrated on March 25, the Feast of the Annunciation. This celebration is an example of the identification of Greek ethnicity with the Orthodox faith; March 25, the date of the beginning of the Greek revolution of 1821 against the Ottoman Empire, was deliberately selected because it celebrates the bringing of the good news to the Virgin by the Archangel Gabriel.

Since the Feast of the Annunciation is also the name day of the parish, it is a very important day in the life of the parish community. After the Divine Liturgy there is a procession of officers of all the parish organizations and a program in the community center, followed by a dinner for the entire community. Speeches are given, some of them in Greek, by adult members of the parish. They usually have patriotic themes or extol the glories of Greek culture. All the children in the Greek school participate in the program, reciting little religious or patriotic poems, singing religious songs or Greek folksongs, and presenting a play about the beginning of the revolution in 1821. The teachers of the Greek school carefully coach the children for this occasion. Andreas Zapatinas, a Greek university student who taught at the school, says they are the same songs and poems he remembers performing as a child in Greece.

Changes in curriculum and attitude over the years are, of course, inevitable. When the Greek school in Buffalo was established, it provided essentially religious instruction to children to whom Greek was a functional language. As the Greek immigrants became more assimilated into American mainstream culture, less and less Greek was spoken in the home. Even though they might speak only Greek until they entered kindergarten, the children quickly learned to speak English and used it to communicate in most of their daily activities. Many Greeks married members of other ethnic groups, so children often grew up in homes where one parent spoke no Greek at all. The Greek school is now attempting to teach children to read and speak a language they may not hear at all outside of the Liturgy (which is koine, rather than demotic Greek anyway) or their social contacts in the parish. Religious instruction has been taken over by the Sunday school, and there really is no time to do more than give very basic language instruction in two hours a week. Greek language classes meet from 10:00 A.M. until 12:00 noon on Saturdays and are followed by dance classes.

Some of the changes in attitudes over the years are purely a result of demographic changes. When Buffalo Greeks began to move out of the old neighborhood near the church on Oak Street, it was no longer possible for the children to walk to Greek school every day, or even several days a week. Although the Greek school in Buffalo is located about as centrally as possible, it is still very inconvenient to transport children to it more than twice a week. (Most children who attend the Greek school also attend Sunday school.) Children who were attending suburban schools spent most of their social life with non-Greeks and were involved in many activities outside of the parish. There were some attempts to cope with the inconvenience of the school's location, however. In the late 1950s and 1960s satellite schools were opened (usually in Episcopal churches) in the Highgate area, in Depew, Lockport, and Niagara Falls.

Parents

Most parents interviewed said that they wanted their children to attend Greek school so they would understand better who they were, would learn about their heritage, or would be able to communicate with their Greek relatives. The Greek idea of family includes a huge network of people related either by blood or by spiritual ties, and being a *kuombaro* (godparent) establishes a real family relationship as well. Many relatives remain in Greece, and there is a great deal of visiting back and forth.

Having children attend Greek school does not require a huge financial commitment, but it does involve a tremendous commitment in time and effort. Suburban parents have to sacrifice an entire Saturday morning to drive the children to Greek school and dance classes, since Buffalo public transportation virtually does not function on weekends. Most parents help the children with their homework, which can be very difficult if the parent does not speak Greek himself. One of the parents I interviewed, Theo Pappas, described struggling through her son's first and second grade homework with the aid of a dictionary. The only parent I talked to who had been to Greek school herself was Victoria Pantelis, who went every afternoon after school as a child in Brooklyn. Most of the parents seem fairly satisfied with their children's progress, although there were quite a few complaints about lack of discipline.

Students

The students, for the most part, complain bitterly about the Saturday classes, the homework, and the tests. In short, they would much rather be watching cartoons. Everyone I talked to agreed that learning to speak Greek was a good thing, however, and the graduates felt, in retrospect, that it was worth all the suffering. The only regrets I ran across were from students who dropped out, or felt that they had not made the effort to really learn the language. Graduates of the school have the chance to take the New York Regents' Examinations in Greek and receive three high school credits if they pass. Since these tests are taken at the ninth or tenth grade level, several years after they have finished classes, special review sessions are held each year in June before the exams. Not many students take these exams, but the ones that do usually do well. Most of the students agree that they would send their own children to Greek school.

The comparisons made by the children between Greek school and mainstream education depend on which teachers the child has had. Almost all of them prefer the other teachers to the Greek university students. This is rather ironic, since the school makes such an effort to recruit them. The principal says that he much prefers to hire teachers who have finished high school in Greece. The young men know Greek very well, and some of them are very conscientious teachers, but I suspect the problem is that they do not relate very well to the Greek-American experience.

Most of the children I talked to have two more or less distinct social lives, although there is some overlap at festivities like birthday parties, and children invite American friends to the parish festival. While some of the suburban schools now have a dozen or so Greek children in them at any given time, most of the socialization with other Greeks is on weekends or at church-related activities such as Jr. GOYA (Greek Orthodox Youth Association) functions or dance rehearsals during the week.

Another outcome of the move to the suburbs is the growth of private classes in the homes of teachers or students. Private tutoring in Greek has gone on from the beginning, but in the past ten years private classes have grown to the point that there are probably more children taking private lessons than attending Greek school. There were two teachers in Buffalo giving private classes in 1982, one of whom also teaches in the Greek school. There is, naturally, a little ill feeling about these classes on the part of the Greek school and, until recently, it was a matter of policy never to hire a teacher who conducted private classes. Each teacher has four classes, which meet for an hour on a weeknight. Estimates of class size range from six to twelve students; the teacher receives $2.50 per hour per student. Since there are currently only forty-five students in the Greek school, private classes constitute a serious threat to its existence.

Several reasons are given for sending students to private classes. They are more convenient and parents do not have to make the long trek from the suburbs every week. The children have their Saturday mornings free for other activities. They also receive more individual attention, and discipline is better.

Sunday School at the Hellenic Orthodox Church

Probably no ethnic group in America indentifies itself so much in terms of religion; to a great extent, to be Greek-American is to be Greek Orthodox, however loose the ties with the church may become.[2] Native Greeks, largely because of their history, tend to see themselves as "Orthodox Christians" (as opposed to the Ottoman Moslems), rather than as Greek by ethnicity. They began to think of themselves as "Greeks" only after the formation of the Greek state around 1825. The immigrants who came to this country quickly established churches around which all the community activities, including the schools, coalesced. Therefore, Sunday school is a very real part of a second-generation Greek-American child's ethnic education.

The first teachers of the Greek Sunday school in Buffalo were the priest and some laymen who had been educated in Greece. Trained teachers were used whenever possible. Later mothers were brought in to assist the teachers. The Archdiocese provided a curriculum after the late 1940s, which first consisted of little pamphlets printed in Greek. Before that time Mrs. Olympia Pappas, the present principal of the Sunday school, had to find her own books (often in Greece), and write synopses for her teachers. In the early 1950s the Archdiocese started providing textbooks in English, but, until a few years ago, there was not one for every grade.

Over the years Mrs. Pappas has built up an excellent reference library for the use of her teachers. The subjects taught have not changed much; as she points out, the Orthodox faith has not changed. I have looked over most of the textbooks used in the school and have been quite impressed. In some grades the subject is the relationship of Christianity to everyday

Eighth grade Sunday school class with teacher Betty Pavlakis. (ES82-197823-5-36) Photo by Lydia Fish

life, and I think the Archdiocese has done a commendable job of tackling such very modern problems as sex and drugs. The books on the church holy days and saints' days, the sacraments, and the Creed are excellent. Filmstrips and films are also available from the Archdiocese.

The children do not pay for their Sunday school books, nor are the teachers paid: "They are paid by the smiles of the children." For about fifteen years the Sunday school was supported by the fund-raising activities of the PTA and the Mother's Club. More recently the parish council has taken over financial responsibility for the school. Unless the teachers are certified, they serve an apprenticeship with an experienced teacher; girls often help their mothers. There are some local and regional workshops and seminars for Sunday school teachers, but basically each parish is on its own. Father John Artemas, the current pastor of the parish, feels that some national coordination might be helpful.

Mrs. Pappas, the Sunday school principal, is an indefatigable recruiter. Every year she enlists future teachers from the Sunday school graduating class. She discovered, for example, that Nick Kadounas, a university student from Greece who was serving as a cantor, was also a formidable Biblical scholar. He is now very ably assisting Theo Pappas in teaching the senior class.

As is the case with Greek school, having a child attend Sunday school requires a commitment on the part of the parent. The family has to be at church by 10:00 A.M., often having driven in from the suburbs through the really unspeakable Buffalo winter weather. Since most of the children who attend Sunday school also attend Greek school, they have probably done this on the preceding day as well. Father John Artemas and the Sunday school teachers agree that it takes a spiritual commitment too; it is not much help dropping the children off at Sunday school if the parents do not attend the Divine Liturgy. Parents ideally should take time to discuss the Sunday school lessons with their children and pray with them. Intermarriage is very common in the Buffalo Greek community; Father Artemas estimates that 80 to 90 percent of all marriages he performs are mixed marriages. Usually the children are baptized into the Orthodox faith and often the non-Orthodox parent converts; but if this does not happen, the Orthodox parent must make a special effort to see that the children are brought to Sunday school.

Religious holidays are observed in the Sunday school, often with essentially non-religious customs, such as the cutting of the *vasilopita* (the New Year's bread) and Easter bread, or the cracking of red-dyed Easter eggs. Children take part in the preparation for the great feasts at the church, helping the women of the parish decorate the *epitaphion* (the flower-decked bier on which the cloth icon of the entombment of Christ is placed on Holy Friday), dye the Easter eggs and tie them up in tulle for distribution after the Divine Liturgy on Holy Saturday night, and make the palm crosses which are distributed on Palm Sunday. At one time the young girls were given lessons in preparing the *prosphoron* (communion bread), which is traditionally baked at home by Greek Orthodox women.

The liturgical year is a superb teaching device; with the passing of the seasons the child sees acted out the great drama of the redemption. The ceremonies of Orthodoxy are very literal; the flower-decked cross is carried in procession on Holy Cross Day, and the children are reminded that St. Helena found the cross in a bed of basil, because on that day great tubs of basil are placed on the *solea*, the raised platform at the front of the church in front of the icon screen. The church is filled with the fragrance of basil, and after the service each parishioner is given a handful of the herb to take home.

The climax of the yearly ritual comes in Holy Week. During the matins of Holy Monday, called the Bridegroom Matins, the priest carries an icon of Christ through the darkened church to remind the faithful that "The bridegroom comes at midnight." During the matins of Holy Thursday they are anointed with oil in memory of the woman who anointed Christ's feet. The reading of the Passion Gospels on the evening of Holy Thursday is interrupted by a procession with a cross, which is then set up on the solea for veneration. On Holy Friday the icon of the crucified Christ is taken down from the cross, wrapped in a white cloth, and placed on the altar by the priest. The icon of the entombment is then placed on the epitaphion and the people come forward to venerate the icon. At the Church of the Annunciation there is a very pretty local custom—little girls bring baskets of rose petals and scatter them over the icon. They are called *myro-phores* (myrrh-bearers) and represent the women who brought spices to the tomb of Christ. (Mrs. Pappas initiated this custom with Father Pallas. She remembered that her mother had always decorated the epitaphion in the little chapel in her family home in Greece, and she and her sisters gathered flowers to lay on the icon.) Afterwards the children crawl under the epitaphion, a symbol of dying with Christ. The same symbolism is continued in the evening service when the entire parish, carrying lighted candles and singing, carries the epitaphion in procession around the block. As they reenter the church, the epitaphion is held high, so that everyone can walk under it. They are sprinkled with rose water by the altar boys as they enter the brightly lighted church. Before the Divine Liturgy on Holy Saturday night the lighted Paschal candle (the light of Christ) is carried into the darkened church and everyone lights candles from it.

The altar boys are the most active participants in the Divine Liturgy, since they actually assist in the service. They are about forty of them at present, divided into teams of eight. They get a little formal instruction by the priest, but mostly learn from "on the job training," as one says. They start with undemanding jobs like carrying candles and work up to assisting the priest. Girls traditionally take no part in the services, but there is no canonical reason why they cannot be lay readers, and Father Artemas often asks girls to read the Old Testament lesson or the Epistle.

Dance Classes at the Hellenic Orthodox Church of the Annunciation

The third set of classes associated with the Church of the Annunciation is the dance classes. There has always been some sort of dance instruction associated with the church; one of the Greek school graduates I talked to remembered being taught dancing by his Sunday school teacher, and Mrs. Pappas told me about arranging some Greek dancing at a formal ball at the Albright-Knox Art Museum. Classes were always more or less informal, however, until Tina Kalen started her Greek Ethnic Society nineteen years ago. She arrived in Buffalo from Constantinople in 1957 and was looking for some way to "carry her flag" in America. Talking to children dancing at weddings and parties, she finally got a class together. She now has about thirty-five students, divided into juniors, seniors, and young adults. Tina and her troupe are a familiar sight at ethnic festivals in the Buffalo area, and the costumed dancers are one of the main attractions of the parish's Hellenic Festival every year. They are not particularly professional, since she takes anyone who wants to dance, regardless of talent. They dance with great verve and enthusiasm, however, and are obviously having a wonderful time.

Tina teaches her students the familiar Greek dances for weddings, parties at the church, and family gatherings: the *syrtaki*, the *tzamiko*, the *kalamatianos*, the *syrtos* and the *hasapiko*. Her technique is unusual, since she more or less talks them through the steps of a dance. If there are little ones who do not know the steps at all, she turns them over to an older child for instruction. She uses recorded music for class and rehearsals and live music for the festival. The dance classes are held in the gymnasium of the community center right after Greek school on Saturday afternoons. Like the Greek school and Sunday school, a child's attendance at the dance classes involves real commitment on the part of the parents. Not only do the parents have to drive their children to the church for classes and rehearsals, but they have to get them to performances as well. Most of the costumes worn by the children are made by their mothers, since the purchase of a *foustanella*, the short, full, white skirt worn by the soldiers of the palace guard and male members of Greek-American dance troupes, is a major expense.

The children enjoy the dance classes, and most of them have a marvelous time representing the Greek community at local festivals. Learning to dance has immediate and obvious value for the children, since they use the dances at parties. Like most of the ethnic learning experiences of young Greek-Americans, this one has religious ramifications. The Greek Ethnic Society is involved in more than ethnic display events—it also has charitable functions. Very few immigrants are now arriving in Buffalo, but quite a few Greeks come for medical treatment at Buffalo's many hospitals. Many of them have little money, do not speak English, and have no way of getting around the city. Tina visits these patients and their families (who often accompany them), translates for them, drives them to and from the airport, and raises money for their expenses. The children from her dance group and their mothers help her with these activities, visiting the sick and running little errands for them.

The Greek school classes, the Sunday School classes, and the dance classes are clearly defined, formal means of transmission of Greek culture to the children of the community. They also function as a means of letting the children work out their particular third-generation form of ethnicity as they wrestle with questions such as "Why do we celebrate Independence Day on March 25 as well as on July 4?" and "Why are services in our church different from those in Roman Catholic and Protestant churches?"

Conclusions

I think Joshua Fishman is right in pointing out that attending a mother tongue school is an almost obligatory second-generation ethnic experience; that it is the non-immigrant ethnic child's unique way of being an American, whether or not he is of non-English-language background.[3] This would explain something that puzzled Andreas Zapatinas, the young Greek university student who taught in the Greek school for several years. He says it was never made clear to him what the school was trying to accomplish—if they were really trying to teach the children to read, write, and speak Greek, it was clearly impossible to do so in two hours a week. On the other hand, if they were trying to teach them their Greek heritage, why was there not more emphasis on Greek literature, art, and history? He especially could not understand why modern Greek history was not taught at all.

His questions make a good deal of sense. If the purpose of the school is to establish language proficiency it is not succeeding particularly well. If it is to teach the children about contemporary Greek culture, it is not doing very well at that either. But Andreas is comparing this school to Greek education in Greece. If the purpose of the school is to help the children work out their identity as ethnic Americans it is doing a superb job.

The ethnic schools in the United States raise many questions for scholars in the fields of education, linguistics, sociology, and anthropology. For the folklorist, however, perhaps the most interesting aspect of these schools is that they challenge some of our most fondly cherished notions about folklore—that it is spontaneous, unselfconscious, and that it passes from one group or generation to another without formal instruction. Probably the greater part of ethnic tradition in this country is transmitted in a domestic context, although even this is not necessarily an unconscious process; carrying out the decision to say grace at the table every night in Greek, for example, will involve a certain amount of time and effort. The parents in the Greek-American community in Buffalo, like those of many ethnic communities around the country, however, have very consciously chosen to pass on many of their most cherished traditions in a formal educational context. No one who knows these children can doubt that the process has been, to a considerable degree, successful. Perhaps it is time for folklorists to take a long look at the process by which a group decides how and to what degree it will integrate with the American mainstream. I think we shall find that the folk, as usual, know quite well what they are doing!

Acknowledgments

I first came to the Hellenic Orthodox Church of the Annunciation in the spring of 1978. At that time I was working on a project to document ethnically based liturgical parishes in Buffalo. Father George Pantelis was extremely interested in what I was doing and suggested that if I really wanted to understand the Orthodox traditions I should record the entire liturgical year. For a year I taped and photographed the great feasts, spent an enormous amount of time at the church, and came to know the Greek community in Buffalo. The patience, tolerance, generosity and friendship displayed towards me by these wonderful people are impossible even to describe. Thanks to them, and especially to Father Pantelis, I have come to know and love the glories of the Orthodox Liturgy and the warmth and individuality of Greek character. When, after Father Pantelis's tragic death, Father John Artemas came to the parish, he made me as welcome as his predecessor had, and has been of enormous help in this project. To him, and to all the parishioners of the Church of the Annunciation, especially the ones who gave me interviews, I owe my deepest thanks. Special thanks are due to my friend Priscilla Carcales, secretary of the parish, who has answered endless questions over the years, translated, spelled words in Greek, and kept me supplied with coffee and pastry.

Finally, I would like to thank Tom and Jenny Putnam, who served as research assistants on this project and without whom it would never have been completed, and Pat Warner, who typed the entire report. Tom and Jenny logged the tapes, proofread the manuscript, recorded many of the interviews, took photographs, drove me all over the Niagara Frontier and provided endless encouragement. Pat Warner not only did her usual magnificent job of typing, but also kept track of all the various components of the manuscript.

Notes

1. For the reader who is unfamiliar with the history of Greeks in this country the best general introduction will be found in the article on Greeks in the *Harvard Encyclopedia of Ethnic Groups* (Cambridge, Mass.: Harvard University Press, 1980). It includes a short bibliography. George A. Kourvetaris has written an excellent description of the Greek-American family and has compiled a superb bibliography on the subject. *See* "The Greek-American Family," in *Ethnic Families in America*, second edition, ed. Charles H. Mindel and Robert W. Haber (New York: Elsevier, 1981).

2. The best short introduction to the Orthodox churches in this country can be found in the article on the Eastern Orthodox faith in the *Harvard Encyclopedia of Ethnic Groups*.

3. Joshua A. Fishman, "Ethnic Community Mother Tongue Schools in the U.S.A.: Dynamics and Distribution," *International Migration Review,* vol. 14, no. 2 (Summer 1980), p. 243.

OK, there is a flying
saucer flying above
the torah. There is a
force field around the torah.
Josh B.—

Its
Sund

St

West End Synagogue School
Nashville, Tennessee
Burt Feintuch

Although Jews make up a tiny percentage of the total population of the South, Nashville, like many other Southern cities, does have a lively, tightly knit Jewish community. An estimated thirty-six hundred Jews live in Nashville. Even after very preliminary fieldwork, it is clearly accurate to use the term *community* to describe the complex social relationships which bind those thirty-six hundred people together. Jewish education is one of the major components of the cement in which those bonds are set.

Jewish communities are typically well organized, with synagogues and a network of lay organizations serving as the significant ethnic institutions or organizations. Education is usually the province of the synagogues; at times the lay organizations include support groups for education. In Nashville there are three congregations, each with its house of worship and its associated school, and three of American Judaism's four movements are represented. Sherith Israel, the Orthodox synagogue, is on West End Avenue. An Orthodox Hebrew day school—a parochial school which combines the Orthodox tradition with instruction in secular subjects—shares the building with Sherith Israel, although the school is administratively separate from the synagogue. A few blocks west is West End Synagogue, the community's Conservative institution. That synagogue sponsors a religious school which convenes after school on Tuesday and Thursday afternoons, as well as Sunday mornings. The Temple, representing the Reform movement, is on Harding Road, in an area called Belle Meade, a mile or two west of the Conservative and Orthodox synagogues. Religious school at the Temple meets on the weekend.

Childrens' art in Sharon Beck's pre-school class at the West End Synagogue. (ES82-196112-1-37) Photo by Bob Gates

I chose to focus on Jewish education at West End Synagogue for several reasons. The Conservative movement in Judaism is generally thought of as occupying the middle ground between the strict devotion of Orthodoxy

265

and the more assimilationist stance of the Reform movement. The Conservative movement is seen as maintaining the traditions of Judaism, while adjusting to the demands made by life in contemporary American society. A textbook written for secondary students in Conservative schools describes the movement as follows:

Conservative Judaism stresses the element of historical continuity. Conservatism stresses that traditions have helped hold the Jews together. It believes that strict following of old customs is not good, but it believes in a living tradition which changes according to the needs of the time. Therefore Conservative Judaism has concentrated on keeping alive much of the Jewish religious tradition, including its customs, ceremonies and folklore.[1]

One reason for my choice, then, was an intellectual one—the question of the relationship between ethnic education and a sense of tradition which is promulgated on a notion of process rather than stasis, a viewpoint which accepts the fact of acculturation but not at the price of assimilation or the de-emphasis of tradition. A second reason was both personal and pragmatic. Until the age of thirteen I spent six hours a week in a Conservative school in the suburbs of Philadelphia. Although no longer involved in any institutional aspect of Judaism, I wondered whether what remained of my insider's cultural knowledge could be of use, particularly in consideration of the brief time available for the field research.[2] A third reason was purely pragmatic. After telephone conversations with people active in Nashville's Jewish community it seemed likely that West End Synagogue—its school administation, rabbi, and congregants—would be amenable to being involved in the research.

The Synagogue

A permanent Jewish community in Nashville dates to about 1850. By the early 1870s three synagogues served that community, and the city's Jewish population was roughly what it is today, if expressed as a percentage of the city's total population.[3] According to West End Synagogue's 1974 centennial history, in 1874 twenty families organized the congregation that would eventually become the synagogue. The name they gave that congregation, Khal Kodesh Adath Israel (Congregation Assembly of Israel), remains part of West End Synagogue's full title.[4]

In 1886 the congregation bought its first house of worship, a former residence. Mamie Stravinsky, a member of the congregation, established the first Sunday school in 1896. Two years later the *American Israelite* announced, "On March 8, the Purim Play was presented to a large audience by members of the KKAI [Khal Kodesh Adath Israel] Sunday school."[5] By 1924 the synagogue's Board of Education had divided into two committees, one for the Sunday school, the other for the weekday Hebrew school, evidence that Sunday school had already been joined by weekday afternoon school. At about the same time classes moved to the YMHA (Young Men's Hebrew Association) building, which had more classrooms. Enrollment was approximately fifty students.

In 1902 the congregation erected a building—the Gay Street Synagogue. By 1947 the congregation decided to move to a larger facility and chose an existing building at 3810 West End Avenue. Four years later the main section of the current West End Synagogue structure opened its doors on that site. A fund-raising drive began in 1959 for the purpose of adding a religious school wing to the synagogue. One rationale for the fund drive was the assertion that "Religious education is the foundation of Judaism." The U-shaped wing was completed in 1961.

Today West End Synagogue is a well-maintained, dark brick building, located on a four-lane artery which traverses an established, upper middle-class neighborhood. The Jewish Community Center and Sherith Israel, the Orthodox synagogue, are within walking distance. That section of West End Avenue is also the site of a number of substantial churches and a Bible college. Rabbi Glazer and his family live in a house, recently built by the congregation, directly behind the synagogue.

The synagogue itself has about five hundred member families. A lay board governs the synagogue, and the rabbi, a cantor, and the education director administer it. At the time of my research the cantor was preparing to leave for a position elsewhere and the synagogue was going through the process of seeking a replacement. Support staff includes secretaries, a kitchen supervisor, and custodians. There are, of course, a number of teachers. The synagogue has a range of facilities, including halls of worship, a large social hall, and offices for the three salaried professionals. In addition, the building contains a school office, kitchen, library, and at least twelve classrooms. Parking areas border the synagogue on both ends and at the rear.

School Administration

A fifteen-member lay Education Committee oversees the school. Composed largely of parents who have children enrolled in religious school, the committee meets regularly. Members serve two-year terms.

Miriam Halachmi is the school's full-time, salaried education director. An Israeli educated in both her native country and the United States, Ms. Halachmi has a background in both education and counseling. She is currently in her third year as director, having previously taught at Akiva, Nashville's Hebrew day school. When Ms. Halachmi began at West End the position was defined as half-time, but that soon changed. She works Mondays, Tuesdays, Thursdays, Fridays (until the Sabbath begins at sundown), and Sunday mornings, typically putting in more than forty hours a week. In addition, she usually attends Shabbat services because the school expects her students to attend. She works eleven months a year.

According to her job description, Ms. Halachmi's responsibilities include hiring and training teachers; developing the curriculum; handling public relations; programming holidays and the Shabbat; supervising the school building and its equipment; solving problems; ordering supplies and audiovisual equipment; carrying out liaison with youth organizations; reporting to the religious school committee; teaching religious school; working with other professionals, which includes weekly meetings with the Rabbi and cantor; setting school policy; handling school administration; participating in adult Jewish education; maintaining school records; and enrolling and placing students. As one of the synagogue's three salaried professionals, she directs virtually every aspect of the religious school.

Rabbi Glazer is also involved in education at the synagogue, although not in the same ways as Ms. Halachmi. In his own words:

You may call me the executive educator. That's really how I see the role of the rabbi. The rabbi's an educator, and I function as such through my own teaching—that is, I have adult education classes, as well as teaching classes in the religious school. I teach a class, the bar and bat mitzvah class.... In addition, I supervise, although not very tightly, our educational director, on the assumption that the goals are shared by both of us and it's her school. And yet we meet together pretty much daily to talk about goals, and programming, and ideas, and problems. So I keep my finger on what's going on in the school, while not interfering in the day-to-day operation. (ES82-BF-R13)

Teachers

About twenty adults teach at the West End Synagogue School in various capacities. Miriam Halachmi, Rabbi Glazer, and the cantor each do some teaching, as does Donna Glazer, the rabbi's wife. In addition, the synagogue employs a staff of salaried, part-time teachers. According to Ms. Halachmi, the school formerly considered its own graduates to be qualified to instruct, but in recent years there has been an attempt to hire teachers who have not only a background in Judaism but also teaching certification. The teachers are all women, except for the rabbi, cantor, and eleventh grade teacher.

The religious school catalog contains brief descriptions of the qualifications of most, but not all, teachers. The range of academic qualifications include: an M.S. in Educational Psychology from Vanderbilt University; a B.A. in French Literature from Columbia and a B.H.L. from the Jewish Theological Seminary; and a degree in Jewish Philosophy from Haifa University in Israel. The emphasis on credentials reflects a national concern in Jewish education.[6] Although Miriam Halachmi, teacher Sharon Beck, and Rabbi Glazer attended a national conference last year sponsored by an organization called the Coalition on Alternatives in Jewish Education, few of the teachers actively participate in educators' organizations.

Most of the teachers do not have other employment. The school pays teachers according to experience and credentials. Not all teachers are Conservative Jews. Sharon Beck, for example, is Orthodox and has had to reconcile her own beliefs with the tenets of the Conservative movement. Art and music teachers, who supplement the primary teachers for the lower grades, need not be Jewish. The school publishes a teachers' manual as well as an annual school catalog.[7]

I was impressed by the caliber of the teaching I observed. Every teacher seemed knowledgeable. They were generally casual and friendly, most showing good rapport with the students.

Classes and Curriculum

Religious school has two components. Hebrew school meets on Tuesday and Thursday afternoons from 4:10 P.M. until 5:40 P.M. Sunday school convenes at 9 A.M. and runs until 12:00 noon. Students can begin religious school at three years of age. For those who continue through the full program, a graduation ceremony marks the conclusion of the eleventh grade. The school had approximately 150 students during the 1981–82 academic year, which ran from September 13 through May 23. There is no summer school.

Age and secular school grade determine the grade level in religious school. Preschool at the synagogue includes separate classes for three-year-olds and four-year-olds. From kindergarten through eleventh grade students are grouped into classes on the basis of their grade level in secular school. Thus a fifth grade student in secular school would be in the fifth grade at religious school. Sixth and seventh grades are combined. As a result, there are thirteen separate class levels, counting the preschool classes.

Preschool through first grade students attend school on Sundays only. Students in the eighth through tenth grades do the same. Second graders attend on Sundays and Tuesdays in preparation for the full Sunday, Tuesday, and Thursday schedule for grades three through seven. Eleventh grade students attend on alternate Sundays only.

Many schools associated with the Conservative movement end after tenth grade with a confirmation ceremony for the students. At West End an efmony at the end of the eleventh grade replaces the more typical tenth grade confirmation.

Once they reach the second grade students begin to change classes and teachers during each day's session. Sundays include three, fifty-five-minute periods with breaks in between. Weekdays include two, forty-minute classes. Each class period features a separate subject taught by a teacher who specializes in the topic.

The synagogue has clearly designed its curriculum to impart to the students a sense of their Jewish identity. The United Synagogues of America, the Conservative movement's national lay organization, sets certain minimal standards for education in schools sponsored by Conservative synagogues, but the individual schools then play a major role in the determination of their curricula. West End, for example, offers six hours of school each week, following the dictates of United Synagogues. The school has set its own curricular priorities, however, and chooses its own textbooks, primarily through the efforts of Miriam Halachmi.

It is significant that, according to Rabbi Glazer, religious school at his institution is more similar than dissimilar to religious schools at other Conservative synagogues. Having served a number of other congregations, and keeping in touch with his rabbinical colleagues through telephone conversations, the rabbi says that he is generally familiar with the various shapes religious schools assume. Miriam Halachmi is newer to Conservative education and, therefore, less familiar with other schools. She attributes the basic similarity between Conservative schools, which persists without substantial central guidance, to the fact that the vast majority of Conservative rabbis, many school administrators, and even quite a few teachers receive their education at the major Conservative seminary, the Jewish Theological Seminary in New York.

About establishing the curriculum for the middle grades, when students are most involved in the school, Ms. Halachmi says:

When you make a curriculum, first of all, you have to make your priorities. We have major areas—prayer, Hebrew, Jewish studies, ethics, and history. So you have to make your priorities because you have six hours a week and you can't teach everything. The parents would have liked us to, but we can't.

So I guess that we took as our priority for the middle grades the prayers. So Hebrew is taught so that the kids will be fluent when they get to the prayerbook—that they won't have problems reading. If we have time, we teach them some spoken Hebrew, but the stress is really Hebrew in translation. Prayer eventually leads to the child being able to conduct a Friday night service. (ES82-BF-R5)

Prayer, then, is the foundation. Here I want to interject the observation that members of the Jewish community in the United States distinguish their ethnicity on the basis of a shared religious heritage and its concomitant cultural history, rather than in terms of national origins. It therefore stands to reason that the core of an educational process which is designed to inculcate a sense of cultural identity would focus on shared ritual and belief systems.

The emphasis on prayer intensifies in the year preceeding the students' bar or bat mitzvahs. Ms. Halachmi believes that after the bar or bat mitzvah the students should study more history. History, in Ms. Halachmi and the school's view, encompasses Biblical history at one end and modern Jewish-American history and Zionism at the other.

While Miriam Halachmi has been faced with the task of establishing a set of curricular priorities, Rabbi Glazer articulates a more general set of goals for the curriculum.

We have to get kids to understand some notion of history, where we've come from; some notion of who we are now, which means Israel; some notion of our religious attitudes, which means prayer services, and liturgy, and holidays, and life-cycle events. We have to talk about Jewish values because there is a Jewish way of looking at the world. And we have to try to get our kids to understand the difference and try to turn them towards looking at the world Jewishly. That's perhaps the most difficult thing of all. (ES82-BF-R13)

How do these priorities and goals translate into specific course offerings? For the preschool through first grade students the curriculum is intended, according to the school catalog, "to provide an initial exposure to Judaism which will be both fun and informative." By the end of first grade students should have rudimentary Hebrew reading abilities. In those early years students also have art and music classes.

From second through seventh grade the curriculum is compartmentalized. Students have separate teachers for each of three classes—prayer, Hebrew, and Jewish studies. The sixth and seventh graders also have a class in preparation for bar or bat mitzvahs. In sum, during the middle years students achieve a degree of competence in religious ritual, including familiarity with the liturgical language. In these years students also become familiar with the cycle of holidays, learning a basic set of values and something about Biblical history.

In eighth, ninth, and tenth grade the emphasis shifts to socio-cultural studies. Required courses differ from grade to grade, with students in the three grades also choosing electives. Eighth grade classes are "The Early Prophets" and "The Jews of America." In the ninth grade the students take "Milestones in the Life of a Jew" (which discusses traditional rites of passage and contemporary issues, such as dating non-Jews and premarital sex) and "Highlights of Jewish History." Tenth grade students enroll in a class in rabbinical civilization. They also take "The Development of the Four Religious Movements" for half the year and "The Zionist Movement and the Palestinian Issue" for the balance of the year. Electives in the 1981–82 school year included a class on how to deal with evangelical Christians and other missionaries, a course in traditional ethics, a course on the role of women in traditional and contemporary Judaism, and "High School Bowl," patterned on the "College Bowl" television competitions. Eleventh grade students have no set curriculum. Their teacher is listed as a "facilitator," and they take a topical, discussion-oriented approach to subjects which they themselves determine.

There is no dearth of textbooks or other curricular materials for Jewish schools. A number of publishers specialize in textbooks for them. Miriam buys textbooks for West End most frequently from Behrman House in New York. She also uses the catalogs of KTAV and Torah Umesorah, both of which are also in New York. The journal *SAFRA* provides her with reviews of new curricular materials, and publishers' catalogs suggest appropriate grade levels for specific titles. The school also has a collection of filmstrips and other audio-visual materials.

I saw a variety of textbook formats. Some are straightforward histories. Others, particularly those for prayer or Hebrew, are workbooks. The "Milestones" class uses a set of short modules, each focusing on a relevant topic. Many of the books have gone into a number of printings. Some provide teachers' editions. Cabinets in each classroom hold the textbooks when students are not using them. Students do not usually take their books home, which is indicative of the trend not to give homework, in recognition of the teachers' realistic expectations. The school has been conservative about changing texts because of the costs involved. The religious school catalog contains a full list of texts used in each course.

Students

Students attend religious school at West End Synagogue on a tuition basis. The annual tuition of sixty dollars covers approximately a quarter of the actual cost, with the balance coming from the synagogue's general funds, derived for the most part from membership dues assessed on a sliding scale pegged to income. Only children of synagogue members can attend. Scholarships, determined on the basis of need, are available.

It is a truism that the smaller the Jewish community the higher the percentage of children who are enrolled in religious school. West End's enrollment reflects that trend. Rabbi Glazer says there are about 200 school-age children in the congregation; at the start of the 1981–82 school year 150 were enrolled. Ninety-two percent of Nashville's Jews are affiliated with one of the three synagogues, according to the rabbi.

Why are the students enrolled? This question is difficult to answer with statistical precision. The answer seems to involve two simple but related facts. First, most of the students I spoke to began religious school because of their parents' desire that they do so. The majority of the students start religious school at the preschool level, at an age in which they could hardly be expected to make the decision to enroll. So, generally speaking, the decision to attend religious school is not the child's. Second, the school teaches cultural identity and instructs students that a sense of ethnicity is of great importance to American Jews. On the basis of my preliminary fieldwork it is clear that parents wish their children to have a sense of Jewish cultural identity, even above and beyond the matter of religiosity. I will add the observation that religious school is often a family tradition. Parents are quite likely to have gone to Hebrew school; most of the current students will probably send their own children, when the time comes.

Do the students enjoy religious school? Interestingly, most of the adults I queried said "No" emphatically. One teacher-parent said, "They hate it. That's how they feel, the same way I felt when I was going. They despise it." Another teacher said, "They're pretty negative about coming to Hebrew school." Rabbi Glazer spoke facetiously about using "guns and whips" to compel the students to attend. Adults, then, tend to feel it imperative that children attend, but they view the children as unwilling participants.

Students vary in their feelings about religious school. I encountered a range of opinions. Some students validated the adults' contentions, while others valued the experience for various reasons. The younger students—prior to their bar or bat mitzvah—often seem to resent the time they must put into religious school, yet many seem to enjoy the social aspects of the experience. At religious school they see friends whom they would not see in secular school. In fact, some very strong friendships are made in religious school, something valued by many adults who believe that their children should have at least some Jewish friends.

If some students dislike religious school, others respect it. Some of the older students—and most students do continue beyond their bar or bat mitzvahs—share their parents' assessment of the importance of participating in the experience of being a Jew. Religious school becomes the vehicle by which they explore and come to appreciate their heritage.

Parents' Visitation Day at West End Synagogue pre-school, Nashville, Tennessee. (ES82-196112-1-27) Photo by Bob Gates

West End Synagogue School and the Jewish Network

Because Jewish communities are usually highly organized, we cannot view the religious school at West End Synagogue in isolation from a broader organizational context. Religious school at West End is part of a complex organizational and institutional network. That the Nashville community includes a number of Jewish youth groups which involve the students is of particular significance. West End sponsors United Synagogue Youth (USY). Other fraternal and sororal organizations draw students from all three religious schools. The Jewish Community Center sponsors a range of youth activities and provides recreational facilities. It also runs a summer day camp. Some Nashville parents send their children to Jewish summer camps in other parts of the country; for example, a number of the West End parents are sending their children to Camp Ramah in Wisconsin. A more complete study would necessarily examine the school in the context of the broader organizational structure of the Jewish community in Nashville and across the nation.

Purposes of school

The single most important observation which emerges from my field research is that school at West End Synagogue exists to impart a strong sense of Jewish identity to its students. Almost without regard to the content of any specific course or even the curricular priorities, the school constitutes a structure for the formal transmission and reinforcement of that sense of identity, that "Jewish-ness." Every person—administrator, teacher, parent, or student—with whom I spoke agreed on the necessity of understanding one's Jewish identity. On that point a number of significant themes became apparent.

Sharon Beck said that school ought "to teach Jews what it is to be Jewish and why they should be Jewish, and to try and keep them to be Jewish." (ES82-BF-R7) It is the school's job, then, to teach the Jewish tradition, the components of which underlie a person's understanding of who he or she is, at least in terms of ethnicity. As we will see, the premium placed on identity supersedes even the emphasis on matters purely religious.

A recurring theme was that Jews are a distinctive group and that, in a largely non-Jewish world, it is necessary to band together, both to perpetuate a culture which is of great value and to offer protection in a world which is at times hostile. During the civil rights era Nashville's Jewish Community Center was bombed. In the words of one interviewee, Judaism is "a heavy burden." Religious school attempts to provide the important historical and theological basis for comprehending the "otherness" of Jews in America and elsewhere. On that point Rabbi Glazer said:

> If you answer the question, "What is Judaism?" then you know what you should be teaching. And, for me, Judaism is a multi-faceted conglomeration—it's an organism. I call it a civilization.... It goes beyond religion because you can be a good Jew without being religious. I would rather say that we Jews have a civilization all of our own. We have our own liturgy, we have our own calendar, we have our own state, we have our own literature, we have our own laws, we have our own holy days, we have our own language.... We're really a civilization, and so, from my standpoint, to be a Jew means to plug in to whatever part of that civilization appeals to you and makes sense to you. (ES82-BF-R13)

English is the first language of virtually all the West End congregants. Hebrew is not a conversational language for American Jews; yet West End Synagogue places considerable emphasis on Hebrew. If prayer is the foundation of the curriculum, Hebrew is the means by which one traditionally prays. The school offers only one course in conversational Hebrew. The assumption seems to be that Hebrew, as a language of worship, is at the core of Jewishness. One should know the prayers and have the ability to translate. The school teaches no Yiddish; the younger generations seem to feel no need for it.

Too much assimilation, it is thought, destroys Jewish-ness. School, therefore, is important for providing a balance to the tendency toward assimilation. It does so in at least two ways. First and most obvious, it transmits ideas and information about the distinctiveness of Judaism. Second and perhaps equally important, it compels Jewish children to socialize with other Jews. Suburbanization has diffused the community in Nashville. Religious school at West End exposes students to significant Jewish role models, and it makes available a pool of Jewish peers and potential friends.

The school sometimes faces the issue of assimilation head-on. For example, this year it sponsored a high school retreat in the synagogue. The focus of the program was a presentation by a Jew who had joined and later renounced a cult. Essentially, she told the students how to deflect cultists' recruiting tactics. Another example is the elective course "How to Answer," which is concerned with how to cope with evangelical Christians.

There is a great emphasis on rationality and a premium on learning for its own sake in Conservative Judaism. A number of informants told me that, even if a person rejects his or her Jewish identity, religious school is crucial because it allows one to make the decision based on knowledge rather than ignorance.

Miriam Halachmi and Rabbi Glazer are convinced that to accomplish the school's goals it is necessary that the students' homelife reflect and reinforce what the school does. If school is intended to teach Jewishness, it is imperative that family life be Jewish as well. At the visitation day for parents of preschool students, both the Rabbi and Ms. Halachmi spoke about that subject to the assembled parents, saying that a partnership is required for the school to be effective. Rabbi Glazer, though, maintains that in many cases the partnership is not realized. At one point he said to me:

We operate in a vacuum, in a sense, because they go home after they leave here. We only see them six hours a week. And the homes that they go back to are, for the most part, Jewishly dry, and unobservant, and nonpious. That's not to say they're not caring—they are caring—but in terms of ritual observance, synagogue attendance, personal study habits there's usually very little. And so we have an additional burden that we have to come up against, and that is what happens to the kids when they go home. We talk about a partnership all the time with the parents, but I know very well that the kid's Jewish education he's going to get here. (ES82-BF-R13)

In the same vein, Miriam Halachmi adds, "We say we can give information. We cannot teach commitment. . . . So if the families are not doing something to keep the kids Jewish, I don't think we can do the job ourself." (ES82-BF-R5)

The dissonance between the school administrators' emphasis on the importance of homelife and their disappointed perception of the reality is even more striking when viewed against the fact that the majority of parents do send their children to religious school. One explanation for the disparity in attitudes is that parents tend to believe it is the school's responsibility to do what the school's staff believes is a shared responsibility. I prefer to view it differently. To me this situation clearly illustrates the contention that Jewish identity and Jewish religious devotion are not one and the same. Families may not practice religious ritual at home. They may not attend services at the synagogue. But they continue to send their children to school at the synagogue, in my estimation, because they value their Jewish identity above and beyond the devotional aspects of their culture. It can be of great importance to identify yourself as a Jew and to move comfortably in the culture, even if you do not practice the religious ritual. School is important, therefore, because it teaches Jewishness, which is not synonymous with religiosity.

Fieldwork Techniques

My fieldwork commenced just as Passover was beginning. An eight-day holiday during which religious school is cancelled, Passover is observed with ritual meals called seders. My first physical contact with the West End congregation was a seder at Rabbi Melvin Glazer's house. After some preliminary telephone conversations with a member of the synagogue I had decided to phone Rabbi Glazer in an attempt to gain official entry to the synagogue. Rabbi Glazer reminded me that Passover was to begin that evening and invited my wife and me to his family's seder the following evening. The seder was a time to meet the young rabbi and his family and to talk briefly about the project.

On Rabbi Glazer's advice I then telephoned Miriam Halachmi. She asked that I send her something in writing about the project which she could present to the lay committee which governs the school. It was not necessary, she said, for me to meet with the committee. Ms. Halachmi requested that I call back a week later, when she would have had a chance to talk with the committee and when school was back in session. Not wanting me to visit the school before she had had the chance to brief her teachers, she asked that I wait until the week following the first session after Passover.

In the meantime, realizing that Passover is not a holiday in which all secular activities are affected, I began to set up interviews with parents of students. Because of the delay caused by the holiday I had visited and interviewed two mothers of students before I set foot in the school. The first mother, Sandy Averbuch, has a daughter preparing for her bat mitzvah at West End's religious school. In addition, all of her children attend Akiva, the Hebrew day school. A life-long Nashvillian and a graduate of the West End school, Ms. Averbuch is involved in the governance of the Hebrew day school held at the Orthodox synagogue. She is very active in the Jewish community and is a self-described "career volunteer." My second interviewee, Hedy Pollack, has a daughter in the third grade at West End Synagogue. Ms. Pollack also teaches on Sundays for the school. She is a former chair of the synagogue's Education Committee.

The following week I made my first visit to the synagogue, where I interviewed Miriam Halachmi and began sitting in on classes. I made a total of six site visits. School was in session on five of those visits; consequently I had the opportunity to observe a range of classes and teachers, along with other aspects of the school. I interviewed teacher Sharon Beck prior to her class, which I tape-recorded. I attended a Sunday visitation day for parents of preschoolers with Bob Gates, a photographer and folklore graduate student. My wife Maxene, a public school teacher, and I devoted a Sunday to observing the older students in class and interviewing a tenth-grade student who many feel is a model of what the school ought to accomplish. I had the opportunity to speak casually with many other students and teachers. I also made an informal evaluation of the synagogue library and used it for some historical research. After school one Sunday I visited and interviewed Robert Workman, father of two students. My final visit to the synagogue was on a Wednesday, when school was not in session. That day I interviewed Rabbi Glazer and spent a final session with Miriam Halachmi.

On a personal note I might add that this was particularly interesting fieldwork because Jewish communities tend to differ in several significant ways from the other communities in which I have worked. I have done field research in various ethnic communities and in a number of regional cultures. American Jews are statistically among the best educated and most affluent groups in the United States. My informants were all well educated and conversant to more than an average extent with the academic world. Some were familiar with the discipline of folklore—one has a brother who is a folklorist, another studied with a prominent folklorist, and yet another has some familiarity with studies in Jewish folklore. The notion of "the field" as an "other" place—a holdover from our disciplinary past—simply is not relevant here. Not only could I gather information from my resource people, but I could also discuss interpretations and their consequences with community members in ways I have not been able to do on previous projects. In fact, American Jews have a well established tradition of studying themselves. Some informants had relevant statistics and demographic data at their fingertips. Needless to say, in my role as fieldworker, I was also asked some challenging questions.

Conclusions

It has barely been possible to scratch the surface during this project. Ideally, research would follow the school through a full academic year. Regular visits spread out over a year would make it possible to see students learn and to get a much better understanding of the educational process. A year's research would include participation in special events, such as holiday programs, bar and bat mitzvah, and USY-sponsored programs. In addition, for the findings to be anything more than preliminary and speculative, it would be necessary to interview a wider sample of the students, teachers, and parents, as well as conduct follow-up interviews with key participants.

I have pointed out, too, that religious school at West End is part of a Jewish network. For a more complete understanding of the school, it would help to have the opportunity to study the network itself. Finally, Nashville is an ideal city for a broader study of the way in which Jewish community schools function. The three most common forms of American Judaism are represented, each by one school. In that respect the city contains a microcosm of American Judaism. Preliminary research is complete in one of the three schools. It would be worthwhile to broaden and complete the study by moving from the focus on one school to a consideration of the Hebrew community and its schools as a whole.

According to the literature, the structure, administration, and curriculum of Jewish education at West End Synagogue is typical of schools associated with Conservative synagogues.[8] As to the school's spirit and other, less tangible aspects, it is difficult to speak of typicality. I came away from my all-to-brief encounter with the school convinced that I had seen high spirits and strong dedication, with an emphasis on professionalism. All of these characteristics manifested themselves in an ambience which is humane and in a school which is, in large measure, quite a success. Robert Workman, a parent whom I interviewed, grew up in larger Jewish communities in the North. He told me that in medical school his Jewish roommate "came from, I think, Omaha, Nebraska, or something. Probably a Jewish community the same size as Nashville. And I thought he had a fantastic Jewish education. And I couldn't understand how a small city could have educated him so well. But I understand it now." I concur.

Acknowledgments

I owe particular thanks to Miriam Halachmi, Rabbi Melvin Glazer, Sharon Beck, Sharon Gal, Chaya Argaman, Rae Levine, Mark Levine, Robert Workman, Hedy Pollack, Sandy Averbuch, and Tammy Peiser. I am also grateful to William Gralnick of the American Jewish Committee's office in Miami, Judy Peiser of the Center for Southern Folklore, Rachelle Saltzman, and Bob Gates for his photography.

Selected Bibliography

Ackerman, Walter I. "Jewish Education—For What?" In *American Jewish Yearbook 1969,* vol. 70. Morris Fine and Milton Himmelfarb, eds. New York: The American Jewish Committee and Philadelphia: The Jewish Publication Society of America, 1969.

Chyet, Stanley F. "Reflections on Southern-Jewish Historiography." In *"Turn to the South": Essays on Southern Jewry.* Nathan M. Kaganoff and Melvin I. Urofsky, eds. Charlottesville: University Press of Virginia, 1979.

Dinnerstein, Leonard and Mary Dale Palsson, eds. *Jews in the South.* Baton Rouge: Louisiana State University Press, 1973.

Evans, Eli N. "Southern-Jewish History: Alive and Unfolding." In *"Turn to the South": Essays on Southern Jewry.* Nathan M. Kaganoff and Melvin I. Urofsky, eds. Charlottesville: University Press of Virginia, 1979.

Fackenheim, Emil L. *Paths to Jewish Belief: A Systematic Introduction.* New York: Behrman House, Inc., 1960.

Frank, Fedora Small. *Beginnings On Market Street: Nashville and her Jewry 1861–1901*. Nashville: n.p., 1976.

_____. *Five Families and Eight Young Men: Nashville and her Jewry, 1850–1861*. Nashville: Tennessee Book Company, 1962.

Golden, Harry. *Our Southern Landsman*. New York: G. P. Putnam's Sons, 1974.

Kaganoff, Nathan M., and Melvin I. Urofsky, eds. *"Turn to the South": Essays on Southern Jewry*. Charlottesville: University Press of Virginia, 1979.

Lavender, Abraham D. "Jewish Values in the Southern Milieu." In *"Turn to the South": Essays on Southern Jewry*. Nathan M. Kaganoff and Melvin I. Urofsky, eds. Charlottesville: University Press of Virginia, 1979.

Reed, John Shelton. "Shalom, Y'All: Jewish Southerners." In *One South: An Ethnic Approach to Regional Culture*. Baton Rouge: Louisiana State University Press, 1982.

Sklare, Marshall. *Conservative Judaism: An American Religious Movement*, rev. ed. New York: Schocken Books, 1972.

West End Synagogue: 1874–1974. n.p., n.d.

Notes

1. Emil L. Fackenheim, *Paths to Jewish Belief: A Systematic Introduction* (New York: Behrman House, Inc. 1960), pp. 141–42. For a good introduction to Conservative Judaism, see Marshall Sklare, *Conservative Judaism: An American Religious Movement*, rev. ed. (New York: Schocken Books, 1972).

2. I dedicate this report to my parents Stanley and Janice Feintuch, who made me go.

3. Fedora S. Frank, *Five Families and Eight Young Men: Nashville and Her Jewry, 1850–1861* (Nashville: Tennessee Book Company, 1962), pp. 15–18.

4. *West End Synagogue: 1874–1974* contains no publication data and is unpaginated. Copies are available in the synagogue library. All historical data, with the exception of note 3 above, is from that source.

5. As quoted in *West End Synagogue: 1874–1974* (unpaginated).

6. Walter I. Ackerman, "Jewish Education—For What?" in *American Jewish Yearbook 1969*, vol. 70, Morris Fine and Milton Himmelfarb, eds. (New York: The American Jewish Committee and Philadelphia: The Jewish Publication Society of America, 1969), pp. 3–36.

7. Copies of school publications and other materials, such as tests, class handouts, diplomas, graduation programs, the synagogue newsletter (which includes coverage of education), and curricular materials are on deposit with other project materials at the American Folklife Center.

8. Ackerman, 1969.

Hupa Indian Language Schools
Hoopa Valley, California

Lee Davis

The lower course of the Trinity River flows northerly through Hoopa Valley in northwest California's Humboldt County. The principal, twelve-mile-square section of the Hoopa Valley Indian Reservation[1] is traversed by canyons and hills surrounding the river valley. The Trinity has been designated a "wild river" by the state of California.[2] Its valley is isolated by mountain ranges on the east and west and by river gorges on the north and south.

The Hoopa Valley Indian Reservation is rich in natural resources. Deer, squirrel, black bear, fox, raccoon, rabbit, and puma are still hunted for food and hides. Among the renowned fish resources in the region are salmon, trout, sturgeon, suckers, and eel. The main food plants utilized by the Indian people are several varieties of acorns, pine nuts, and lily bulbs, as well as other nuts and berries. The Indian people of Northern California also utilize animal by-products, such as skins, antlers, feathers, bone, and shell, in addition to plant materials used in woodworking and basketry.[3]

The Hupa[4] are Athapaskan-speaking Indians who continue to occupy a major portion of their pre-contact territory. Their territory was set aside as a reservation in 1864, only a generation or two after white contact. This geographical and cultural continuity and relative lack of disruption (compared to other California Indian groups) are major factors in the fact that continuous language and cultural traditions exist as part of the present Native American way of life at Hoopa.

Ruth Bennett using puppets at the Hupa Day Care Center to teach the children about Indian legends.
(ES82-198934-1-11A)
Photo by Lee Davis

The 1980 U.S. Census declared that more American Indian people live in California than in any other state. The Hoopa Valley Indian Reservation is California's largest reservation, both in terms of territory and population. Approximately 1,000 Hupa tribal members, 800 other Indian people, and

2,200 non-Indians live on the reservation. The Hoopa Valley Business Council, a tribal council for the Hupa people, maintains a Hupa Tribal Roll which lists 1,640 tribal members, of whom 640 live off the reservation.[5]

History of the Hupa Indian Language School

The educational system at Hoopa began with a reservation school in the 1870s and an Indian boarding school in 1893. The Hoopa Boarding School was located on Agency Field, sometimes referred to as "the Campus," on the Hoopa Indian Reservation. It became a day school in 1932. Presently the Hoopa Elementary School and the Hoopa High School, both public schools in the Klamath-Trinity School District of Humboldt County, serve the educational needs of the valley residents.

It is important to note the early philosophy governing the public education of the Indian people at Hoopa. About 1880 the military agent at Fort Gaston in command of the reservation devoted his attention to the "assimilation" of the Hupa. "If 'persuasion' would not induce the Indians to change, the agents were told to withhold rations, and, if necessary, use 'other means' to 'reach the desired end.'"[6] The boarding school emphasized "practical" skills. Instruction in manual (or menial) labor (farming, laundry, cooking, and sewing) made up 50 percent of the curriculum.

The learning of English was to be the equalizing mechanism for the achievement of the American melting pot ideal. Alice Pratt, now seventy, recalls the punishments for speaking the Indian language at the boarding school.

We used to get punished for talking Indian at school. I know many times I couldn't come home because I got caught talking Indian. My dad used to bring the horse. He'd come by horseback. He'd come up there, and I'd tell him, "I can't go home." "What's the matter?" I said, "I talked Indian." "Oh, pshaw!" Everything would be "Oh, pshaw" with him. (Alice laughs)[7] (ES82-LD-C1)

The memory of the educational system's harsh attitude regarding the Hupa language is alive today in anyone who attended the boarding school—that is, anyone over sixty. Many, if not most, of the elders learned that harsh lesson well and would not teach the language to their children, to spare them criticism and punishment. Forty-one-year-old Elizabeth Marshall says: